Revitalizing Historic Urban Quarters

Revitalizing Historic Urban Quarters

Steven Tiesdell

Taner Oc

Tim Heath

363.69091732
T56r

Architectural Press
An imprint of Butterworth-Heinemann
Linacre House, Jordan Hill, Oxford OX2 8DP
225 Wildwood Avenue, Woburn, MA 01801-2041
A division of Reed Educational and Professional Publishing Ltd

A member of the Reed Elsevier plc group

OXFORD   BOSTON   JOHANNESBURG
MELBOURNE   NEW DELHI   SINGAPORE

First published 1996
Reprinted 1998

British Library Cataloguing in Publication Data
A catalogue record for this book is available from the British Library.

Library of Congress Cataloguing in Publication Data
A catalogue record for this book is available from the Library of Congress

ISBN 0 7506 2890 1

Printed in Great Britain by MPG Books, Bodmin, Cornwall.

CONTENTS

PREFACE

Many cities have quarters that confer on them a sense of place and identity through the historic and cultural associations they provide. They are often an integral part of the city's charm and appeal, and their visual and functional qualities are important elements of the city's image and identity. In addition, as historic quarters are often located in central areas, their revitalization is often part and parcel of the general revitalization of cities. Attracting workers, shoppers, tourists and – perhaps more importantly – people to live and animate these inner areas is symbolic of a contemporary re-enchantment with cities and urbanity.

Nevertheless, the qualities of such quarters have not always been appreciated and valued. Until the 1960s they were often regarded as obsolete and the subject of proposals for clearance and comprehensive redevelopment. In the 1970s, however, there was a change of values and such places became protected and preserved. As all such areas cannot become museums or museum environments, there has been a need for their revitalization as functioning parts of their city. Earlier conservation policies have therefore progressed from a simple and restrictive concern with preservation to an increased concern for revitalization and enhancement. Revitalization has focused on attempts to generate the economic development able to provide the finance necessary to conserve, maintain and enhance the quarter. This has usually meant either the indigenous regeneration of the traditional activities of the locality or a restructuring of the quarter's economic base. Restructuring also makes it necessary to distinguish between *functional* and *physical* conservation.

Revitalization efforts have had to operate within a sensitive context and environment which acts as both a constraint and a benefit. All urban areas undergo change, but historic urban quarters have to cope with change in their economic fortunes while change in their physical landscapes is restricted and controlled in the interests of conservation. This places additional concern on the quality of design of new developments and on the quality of spaces between the buildings. In such quarters, the necessity of reconciling the various exigencies of conservation and revitalization, of balancing economic development while respecting environmental quality is particularly challenging. This interface between urban design and urban regeneration is explored in this book. As contemporary urban design is about creating a sense of place and place making, good urban quarters are also good examples of urban design.

The book therefore attempts to synthesize urban design and urban regeneration through examining the revitalization of a number of historic urban quarters. The case studies from North America and Europe are selected to show a variety of approaches to, and outcomes of, revitalization. The lessons and observations from experience of the revitalization of such historic urban quarters forms the core of this book. Its focus is on quarters or areas where there is a significant number of historic buildings concentrated in a small area; with places and area-based approaches; with urban design and planning rather than with individual buildings and architecture.

ACKNOWLEDGEMENTS

We would like to thank the many students at the Department of Urban Planning, University of Nottingham, whose work has contributed directly and indirectly to some of the case study materials. The following should be acknowledged by name: Caroline Bond, Helen Burley, Carly Gorten, Suzy Harrison, Alex Lewis, Anna Raymond, Graham Stark, Matthew Stock and Richard Wilson. We would also like to thank the many people in the various case study locations who have given their time and/or provided additional information. For their help with the various aspects in the production of this book, we would like to thank Linda Francis, Sarah Shaw and Jenny Chambers. Tim Lloyd and Oliver Morrissey deserve special mention for their instructive and useful comments on Chapter 2. Dave Atherton deserves particular mention for being an accommodating and obliging mail drop in Chicago.

Our thanks go to Steven Thornton-Jones for preparing the illustrations and Glynn Halls for processing and developing all the photographs. All illustrations and photographs are the authors' own or have been redrawn with the following exceptions which we would like to acknowledge: Figure 2.1 was taken by Orhan Tuncay; Figures 3.5 and 3.6 are used by kind permission of Birmingham City Council Planning Department.

THE AUTHORS

Each of the authors is an architect planner. **Steven Tiesdell** was educated at the University of Nottingham. He currently teaches at the Department of Urban Planning, University of Nottingham, has research interests in urban design, urban regeneration and housing and is co-author of *Urban Design: Ornament and Decoration.* **Taner Oc** was educated at the Middle East Technical University, the University of Chicago and the University of Pennsylvania. He is currently Head of the Department of Urban Planning, University of Nottingham, has research interests in urban design, urban regeneration and planning for safer cities, and is co-author of *Urban Design: Ornament and Decoration* and co-editor of *Current Issues in Planning Volumes I & II.* **Tim Heath** was educated at the University of Manchester and the University of Nottingham. He currently teaches at the Department of Urban Planning, University of Nottingham and has research interests in urban design, urban regeneration and computer aided design.

1

REVITALIZING HISTORIC URBAN QUARTERS

INTRODUCTION

Dealing appropriately with the valued legacy of the past is a challenging problem for many cities. Since the 1970s, historic areas and quarters of cities have undergone a re-evaluation of their importance. The first wave of historic preservation policies protected individual buildings, structures and other artefacts. Such preservation was often nationalist and/or religious. Buildings and other artefacts were preserved because of their relation to the great figures from the nation's history or, as in Britain and France, the cathedrals and churches of established religions. These initial preservation policies were significantly limited in effect. A particular concern was the damage caused by inappropriate development close to the protected building. Adam Ferguson (from Appleyard, 1979, p. 16) noted that in Bath although the set piece monuments such as the Royal Crescent, the Circus and the Pump Room had been preserved, their contexts were in danger of destruction 'like mountains without foothills, Old Masters without frames'. An example of this is the Hilton hotel which disrupts the historic setting of Buda (Figure 1.1).

The concern to protect the settings of historic buildings broadened into area-based policies. This second wave of preservation or – more accurately – conservation policies was concerned with groups of historic buildings, townscape, and the spaces between buildings. Preservation – from its original sense of 'pickling' – is concerned with limiting change, conservation is about the inevitability of change and the management of that change. In the UK, this is evident in the legal definition of conservation areas: 'areas of special architectural or historic interest the character of which it is desirable to preserve or enhance' (Civic Amenities Act, 1967).

Area-based conservation also came about as a reaction to the evident social, cultural and physical disruption of lives caused by policies of clearance,

1

Figure 1.1

The design of the Hilton Hotel in Buda competes with and disrupts the setting of the Matyas church.

comprehensive redevelopment and, later, road building schemes. What is also notable is the emergence of area-based conservation which occurred in most European countries around the same time. The 1961 Monument Act in the Netherlands was the first, followed in France by the 'Loi Malraux'. In the UK in 1967 there was the Civic Amenities Act, in Italy, in the same year, the Urban Planning Act, and in Turkey in 1973 the Monument and Historic Buildings Act. In the USA there had been several historic preservation districts prior to the Second World War. In 1926, a private-sector area designation was made in Williamsburg,

Figure 1.2

Created in 1933, the Vieux Carre, New Orleans, was the second public preservation zoning in the USA.

with millions of dollars made available by John D. Rockefeller, effectively turning the town into a museum. In 1931 in Charleston, South Carolina, a protective zoning was created for an area called the Battery. As Murtagh (1992, p. 51) notes: 'The approach marked a major juncture in American preservation thinking, firmly establishing concern for a non-museum environment as a valid preservation premise'. Another protective zoning was created in 1933 in the Vieux Carre, New Orleans (Figure 1.2). However, federal legislation was not put in place until the 1966 National Historic Preservation Act.

Designation of conservation areas or historic preservation districts also entailed more extensive public curatorial commitment. 'The conferring of statutory protection upon buildings or areas, as allowed and implicitly encouraged by the legislation, incurs in itself no direct public costs . . . The problem is that conferring of such status contains an open-ended permanent commitment to the maintenance, renovation and rehabilitation of the area as a whole' (Ashworth and Tunbridge, 1990, p. 16). Nevertheless, the preservation and conservation of such areas could not practically occur solely at the public expense. As the designated areas were assessed as a totality regardless of the merits of individual buildings and structures, the second wave brought many more mundane and everyday historic buildings under conservation control and restrictions. Such protected buildings could not all become museums or contribute directly to the economy of the area deriving from conservation or from conservation-related tourism, creating a need for their occupation for viable economic uses. Burtenshaw *et al.* (1991, pp. 157–158) observe that the failure to find new uses for preserved buildings 'condemns the city to an existence as an open-air museum'. Thus, in addition to the visual, architectural and historical qualities, consideration of the functional characteristics of areas and the active economic use of the protected buildings was introduced as a conservation concern: 'The preservation of form has implications for urban functions, and conservation therefore becomes an instrument of urban management' (Burtenshaw *et al.*, 1991, p. 154).

The second wave of conservation policies and legislation was enacted during a period of steady economic growth in most countries. Thus, as Ashworth and Tunbridge (1990, p. 17) state, 'it was reasonable to assume that the task of conservation planners was to control and channel the various competing demands for space in the city'. In most countries, however, the policies were to be implemented during a period of economic stagnation following the property collapse of the early 1970s. As this halted demolition and redevelopment schemes, it was beneficial for preservation. Furthermore, in the USA and in many European countries, throughout the 1960s and 1970s, the qualities of older housing were recognized in a wave of rehabilitation – and subsequently, gentrification – of those inner urban areas that had escaped the bulldozer. However, this economic stagnation also inhibited attempts to create economic growth to revitalize the conserved areas. In the new conservation legislation very little attention had been given to the problem of encouraging the utilization of the increasing stock of conserved space, especially once the overall demand for space in the city eased off. Using negative powers of control, planners have generally found it easier to prevent undesirable uses for occupying buildings than to attract more desirable uses.

In most countries, the change from the protection of individual buildings to conservation areas rapidly developed from a straightforward and restrictive concern with preservation to a concern with revitalization and enhancement. Simultaneously, the locus of professional concern was largely transferred from architects and art historians to planners and others concerned with economic development (Ashworth and Tunbridge, 1990). The preservation of individual buildings and spaces was regarded as a necessary but not a sufficient condition of conservation. The concept of preservation and conservation also broadened from a special reaction in exceptional cases to an integral part of urban planning. When the townscape and the street pattern as a whole are the objects of concern, this has implications for the functioning of such areas which had not been so obvious when monuments could be treated as isolated islands: 'Current and future land-uses, traffic circulation and, not least, the demographic and social composition in such areas become involved in conservation issues' (Ashworth and Tunbridge, 1990, pp. 14–15).

As a result there has subsequently been a third – more fragmented, *ad hoc* and local – wave of policies. The new policies have been concerned with the revitalization of the protected historic urban areas and quarters through growth management. Efforts have focused on attempts to generate the investment and local economic development able to provide the finance necessary to conserve and enhance the quarter. The initial preservation policies had largely been concerned with the pastness of the past, the later conservation and revitalization policies were about a future for the past. Revitalization attempts within historic urban quarters have to operate within a sensitive context and environment; the areas have to cope with inexorable change in their economic fortunes while change in their physical landscapes is restricted and controlled in the interests of preservation. In such areas, the necessity to reconcile the various exigencies of conservation and regeneration, of balancing economic development with respect for environmental quality, is particularly challenging. This book attempts to synthesize the urban design and urban regeneration dimensions by examining the processes, conflicts and results of the conservation and revitalization of historic quarters in a number of cities.

COVENT GARDEN

In the heart of London's West End, Covent Garden demonstrates how an initial concern for historic preservation rapidly becomes a necessity for revitalization. Covent Garden is also significant due to the extent of the involvement of community groups and other activists. The key building in the area is the market building itself being both a symbolic and an integral functional part of the wider Soho and Covent Garden area (Figure 1.3). Designed by Inigo Jones

Figure 1.3

The Market Buildings, Covent Garden. Originally constructed in 1830, these buildings were renovated in the late 1970s to become a festival market. The Covent Garden piazza forms the centre of the wider Covent Garden area.

in the early seventeenth century as an open square, the right to hold a market in the piazza was granted by Charles II in 1670. The market building itself dates from 1830. In the late 1960s and early 1970s, the Covent Garden market site seemed a prime site for large-scale commercial redevelopment. A major redevelopment scheme was supported and promoted by the Greater London Council (GLC). Nevertheless, as Ravetz (1980, pp. 102–103) describes: 'This was an area where an incredible complex of speciality trades and residents mingled with the wholesale flower and vegetable market and opera house was to be replaced by a grandiose scheme composed of roads, hotels and a conference centre.'

Development schemes, however, were opposed by a coalition of local businesses, residents and preservationists who variously feared displacement and the loss of historic buildings and character. One victory for this coalition was in 1973 when, following a public inquiry, the GLC's controversial Strand relief road – which would have involved a great deal of destruction – was dropped from the *Initial Development Plan for Greater London.* Nevertheless, in 1974, the Covent Garden area was designated as a Comprehensive Development Area and, at the end of that year, the market was relocated to a new site away from London's centre. As Cantacuzino and Brandt (1980, p. 56) describe: 'Within twenty four hours the colour, humour, noise, congestion, debris of the market vanished and Covent Garden lay open to the ravages of the developer and the road engineer.'

During that same year, however, campaigners presented a list of 200 buildings for possible listing to the Secretary of State for the Environment. As Binney (1984, pp. 136–137) recounts, this was significant because the Secretary of State has a statutory duty to list buildings of architectural and historic interest; he cannot simply refuse to list buildings because of other considerations, such as the potential redevelopment value of the site or other political considerations. Equally such points might have to be taken into account when determining any future application for demolition. By subsequently listing over 100 buildings, the Secretary of State, effectively prevented wholesale redevelopment and returned the scheme for reconsideration by the planners (Ravetz, 1980, p. 103).

The danger of Covent Garden becoming an office development was finally averted with the publication of the *Covent Garden Action Area Plan* in 1978. In this document, the GLC's Covent Garden Committee recognized and respected the area's unique character and potential contribution to the life of central London. The area was subsequently replanned with a greater element of historic preservation. Although the preservation of many of the buildings was an initial success, the more problematic and complex process of revitalization has had to occur: new uses and functions needed to be found to utilize the historic buildings and keep them in good repair; the streets of the quarter needed to be animated with people and activities. Covent Garden has been fortunate in that it is a highly desirable area, in one of the busiest tourist cities in the world, and close to the established entertainment districts of the West End. As will be discussed in this book, many quarters do not have these advantages.

HISTORIC URBAN QUARTERS

Contemporary – or postmodern[1] – urban design and planning emphasizes the significance of the local context informing the design through the continuity of local character, historic fabric and street pattern. As Robins (1991, p. 34) states: 'There is a strong sense that Modernist planning was associated with universalizing and abstract tendencies, whilst postmodernism is about drawing upon the sense of place, about revalidating and revitalizing the local and the particular.' One dimension of this – an idea with increasing currency – is the notion of urban quarters or, in a more specifically British context, 'urban villages'. The essence of such quarters is considered to be relatively small size, mixed uses, a pedestrian-friendly environment (catering for but not encouraging car usage), and a mixture of type and sizes of buildings and diverse tenure. The concept draws upon the traditional, mixed use *quartiers* of many continental European cities. The Marais quarter of Paris and the central area of Bologna are examples of this. Arguably, this interest reflects concerns about the loss of local identity and character, and evokes nostalgic yearnings for 'community'. Many cities have a series of neighbourhoods of distinct character. In cities such as Birmingham (see BUDS, 1990) and Glasgow (City of Glasgow District Council (CGDC), 1992), recent local plans have identified areas of character and intrinsic identity with policies to enhance and emphasize this distinct and diverse character.

The revitalization of the Marais quarter and central Bologna both form case studies in this book. On the continent of Europe there is a longer tradition of mixed use quarters; the mixed use of which includes both workplaces and residences. However, due to industrialization occurring along different lines, there are fewer of the larger scale warehouses and industrial buildings that are found in Britain and America. Thus, the building form and townscape found in such continental *quartiers* is different. By contrast, the British and American quarters are not typically residential quarters, most of them are nineteenth-century urban industrial areas or quarters. Such areas were used for either manufacturing and production, or storage and transportation.

The quarters featured in this book also contain significant historic urban fabric of townscape merit. Reflecting the great wealth of nineteenth-century industrial buildings that exist on both sides of the Atlantic, the USA and the UK are especially prominent in the case study examples. They consist largely of sturdy brick and stone buildings or early steel and cast-iron framed structures with usually a brick or masonry envelope or cladding. The solidity of this architecture evokes a powerful sense of character and identity, defining both a meaningful

[1] In this book, the terms 'Modern Movement' and 'Modernism' (with this capitalization) are used. In both architecture and planning there is a *relative consensus* of what these terms represent (Le Corbusier, Charter of Athens, the Bauhaus, the Machine Age and industrial aesthetics). In dealing with the more disparate movements of the period after Modernism, we distinguish between postmodern (without capitalization) as relating to the historical condition or period of being *after* Modernism, and a *Stylistic* Post Modernism (with capitalization) as relating to the Post Modern Style(s) as principally defined by Charles Jencks (1977) in *The Language of Post Modern Architecture.*

time and place. As Ford (1994, p. 113) writes: 'While people tend to grimace at the mention of the words heavy industry and to conjure up images of belching smokestacks and piles of slag, many of the Victorian factories were monumentally picturesque. The exaggerated opulence that characterised offices, hotels, department stores, and apartments during the late 1800s was also applied to many large factories and warehouses.' In the 1960s and early 1970s, in such areas as San Francisco's Ghirardhelli Square and New York's SoHo, the 'industrial chic' dimension of historic preservation had a widespread aesthetic appeal. Furthermore, the conversion of warehouses offers considerably more freedom than the conversion of buildings of outstanding architectural importance that require scholarly restoration and inhibit changes of use.

The focus of this book is with quarters or areas: with urban design and planning rather than with individual buildings and architecture. In particular, the book is concerned with areas where there are a significant number of historic buildings concentrated in a small area. There is also a sense of loss since so many have been lost and cannot be recreated. Some of this loss was in the general destruction of the Second World War but as much came with post-war reconstruction and comprehensive redevelopment. Such areas therefore have a scarcity value: they are irreplaceable and, in recent years, have been protected by a variety of building preservation controls.

Although the buildings cannot be demolished nor the areas comprehensively cleared and redeveloped, their original and existing uses are often in decline or have vanished from the historic townscape. Rather than being simply rundown or derelict space, such areas need to retain a useful function within the city. The particular economic problems of historic urban quarters and the issues of attracting inward investment and encouraging endogenous growth are examined in Chapter Two. Nineteenth-century industrial areas are of particular interest because they have the potential or need for changes of use with consequent implications for their character. If they do not or cannot remain in industrial use (centres of production) what other uses might be appropriate? With the exception of the Marais quarter and central Bologna, most of the quarters featured in this book are changing character, for example, from areas of (essentially) industrial production to office use and various forms of consumption: retail, leisure and tourism. There are also pressures and desires to enable the development or retention of residential development and uses, particularly through the conversion of industrial space and space at the lower end of the office market. Such quarters also tend to have a diffuse pattern of land ownership. Rather than being highly concentrated in a relatively few hands, there are often many smaller land owners. In Europe, the largest land owner is often the public authority which has acquired and assembled land for different purposes – perhaps for a comprehensive redevelopment of the area that is ultimately cancelled.

Revitalization efforts operating within a sensitive context and environment place additional concerns on the quality of design for both rehabilitation and new developments and on the quality of the spaces between the buildings. This interface between urban design and urban revitalization is explored throughout the book, receiving particular attention in Chapters Three and Seven.

DEFINING URBAN QUARTERS

In considering the physical parameters of historic urban quarters, there is an important issue of size. This book focuses on areas which retain their historic integrity and cohesion as quarters – rather than fragmentary remnants of previously much larger entities. Gratz (1989, p. 258) states that: 'The restoration of a historic area often obscures the fact that what is being restored is of only meagre meaning to the larger context of the whole city and is of a scale too small to remain or become again

Figure 1.4

La Clede's Landing, St Louis. Separated by narrow 32-foot streets, nine street blocks are the last remnant of the historic St Louis riverfront. Since the mid-1970s buildings have been rehabilitated and restored to form an important element of architectural and environmental diversity within the modern city. At present, however, they remain isolated and separate from the city centre itself.

a significantly productive patch of the larger urban fabric.' She continues: 'Cities like Louisville, Fort Worth, Atlanta, San Diego, St Louis and countless others show off a few blocks of a restored downtown when the rest of downtown is too much of a bulldozed, rebuilt nightmare' (Gratz, 1989, pp. 258–259).

St Louis is a particularly good example of this phenomenon. In 1939, Giedion (1947, p. 130) was able to view a complete district comprising about 500 buildings in which there were some particularly fine specimens of cast-iron construction. He further noted that: 'The half-deserted river front has survived as a witness to one of the most exciting periods in the development of America. Some of its commercial buildings . . . exhibit an architecture far in advance of the ordinary standards at the time of their erection' (Giedion, 1947, p. 135). However its survival was soon to come to an end. By the 1947 edition of the same book, Giedion (1947, p. 135) is forced to lament in a footnote that forty blocks of the river front had been taken over by the US government for clearance for the erection of the Jefferson National Expansion Memorial. A mere nine blocks of this historic riverfront remain; now known as La Clede's Landing after the founder of the city (Figure 1.4).

There are three ways in which quarters may be typically defined or identified: by physical boundaries; through their particular identity and character; and by functional and economic linkages.

Boundaries

Quarters can be defined by very discrete and obvious boundaries. The boundary might be defined by a distinct rupture of physical character, by a physical obstacle or edge, for example, a river or a busy road, or it might be determined artificially for administrative convenience. Boundaries may have arisen autonomously and have subsequently been codified for administrative purposes. Conversely, an historic delineation might also have contributed to its subsequent character. This may or may not be congruent with the subsequent conservation area or historic preservation district boundary. Clear cut boundaries to a quarter may also enhance the identity of that area and encourage the development of functional, economic and social interaction within the area. It also enables it to be promoted collectively. Nevertheless, in discussing street-neighbourhoods, Jane Jacobs (1961) argues that a great part of their success depends on the overlapping and interweaving of activities. Hence, it is useless to try to define accurately their limits because wherever they work best, they have no beginnings or ends setting them apart as distinct units.

Character and identity

Lynch (1960, p. 47), in his taxonomy of the constituent elements of the image of the city, defines districts as 'the medium-to-large sections of the city, conceived of as having two-dimensional extent, which the observer mentally enters "inside of", and which are recognizable as having some common, identifying character. Always identifiable from the inside, they are also used for exterior reference if visible from the outside.' The common, identifying character of a quarter has both physical and functional dimensions. That identity and character might be embodied in the very bricks and mortar of the place; it might also be the result of the activities that traditionally occurred in the area.

Functional and economic linkages

The character of a quarter can derive from the agglomeration of closely-related activities that depend on one another economically as in the case of the *Jewellery* Quarter and the *Lace* Market. Many of the quarters in this book were centres for the clothing and textiles industries where there is often a functional integration as well as a division of labour between firms within the industries. There is, however, a need to find a balance between the agglomeration of particular uses to give character and to gain the benefits of economic integration and a range of uses to provide vitality.

HISTORIC PRESERVATION

As the example of St Louis indicates, the desire to preserve and conserve material works from the past is relatively recent. Lowenthal (1981a, p. 10) notes: 'Isolated instances of deliberate preservation can be cited from time immemorial . . . But to retain any substantial part of the material works of our predecessors is an idea of quite recent vintage.' The desire to preserve evidence of the past has many justifications. Rypkema (1992, p. 206) notes: 'Preservationists often talk about the "value" of historic properties: the social value, the cultural value, aesthetic value, urban context value, architectural value, historical value, the value of sense of place. In fact one of the strongest arguments for preservation ought to be that a historic building has multiple layers of "value" to its community.' Underpinning the other justifications, however, are arguments based on 'economic value'. The desire to preserve must ultimately be a rational economic and commercial choice; problems will arise where buildings are preserved only as a consequence of legal and land use planning controls. In the absence of commercial justifications, however, most preservation occurs only because there are legal and land use planning controls that restrict physical change and prohibit demolition. Such protection is an example of public intervention in the interests of communal welfare. In the absence of such controls, the market might often fail to protect buildings which society deems worthy of retention. It is important to review the desires whose influence has resulted in the creation of the legal controls.

The principal justifications for historic preservation are given in the following seven subsections.

Aesthetic value

The aesthetics of the past might simply be appreciated and valued for their own sake. Old buildings and towns are valued because they are intrinsically beautiful or

Figure 1.5

In New York's SoHo, the historic preservationists and the artists' community were able to find a common consensus and desire to save the cast-iron fronted buildings but ultimately for different reasons: the preservationists for the buildings' historicity; the artists as homes and studios.

'antique', or – more simply – because they are old and have a scarcity value. Nevertheless, Lynch (1972, p. 56) warns of 'dogma about the intrinsic goodness of old things'. Given the blandness of much contemporary architecture, historic buildings are often more interesting than 'post-industrial' offices, houses and shopping centres. Zukin (1989, p. 59) notes of former industrial buildings: 'Their structure has both a solidity and a gracefulness that suggest a time when form still identified "place" rather than "function". Their façades are often adorned with archaic emblems and sculpture, apparently showing the archaic skills of masons and carvers.' Historic buildings and areas have picturesque qualities; they are redolent of a period of genuine craftsmanship and individuality that has been lost in a period of modern industrialized building products and systems of construction. Arguably, there is an instinctive subliminal identification with natural materials that wear and weather better than machine-made ones. Appleyard (1979, p. 19), for example, observes how physical comfort, cheaper products, and security are bought at the cost of depersonalization: 'The old city exemplifies the human scale, individuality, care and craftsmanship, richness and diversity that are lacking in the modern plastic, machine-made city with its repetitive components and large-scale projects.'

Taken to an extreme, preserving the entire built environment can bring a complete halt to a city's evolution and development, fossilizing its fabric and structure. The closer conservation comes to this, the more important it is that the *capacity for change* is preserved (Ashworth and Tunbridge, 1990). There may also be a conflict between 'purists' and 'populists': those who want to preserve and those who want to use the building; for example, conflicts between the art historian and the general public. In New York's SoHo, the historic preservationists and the artists' community were able to find a common consensus and desire to save the cast-iron fronted buildings but ultimately for different reasons: the preservationists for the buildings' historicity; the artists as homes and studios (Figure 1.5).

In a world of rapid change, visible and tangible evidence of the past may also be valued for the sense of place and continuity it conveys. The presence of historic buildings is a testimony to the passage of time in a particular locality. Ashworth and Tunbridge (1990, p.28) argue: 'place familiarity is valuable in maintaining the individual's psychological stability and an over-abrupt change in the physical environment must be modified by conservational policies, so that the excitement of the future should be anchored in the security of the past' (Lynch, 1960).

Value for architectural diversity

The aesthetic appeal of an historic place may result from the combination or juxtaposition of many buildings rather than the individual merits of any particular building. Most cities are made up of buildings from a range of periods in a variety of styles and idioms. Thus, the past may be valued because of its juxtaposition with the present. In particular, older buildings provide a potent contrast to the interminable sterility and monotony of much Modernist architecture. Such diversity is usually viewed positively. Mumford (1938) in his book *The Culture of Cities* vividly observes how 'by the diversity of its time structures, the city in the past escapes the tyranny of a single present, and the monotony of a future that consists in repeating only a single beat heard in the past'. Hence, even relatively mundane historic buildings will have value through their contribution to the aesthetic diversity of the urban scene.

Value for environmental diversity

At a larger scale, architectural diversity also contributes to an environmental diversity. Particularly in many North American cities, there is often a stimulating contrast between the human scale environment of an historic quarter and the monumental scale of the more modern central business district (CBD). In Boston, there is a vibrant

Figures 1.6 and 1.7

In Boston, there is a vibrant environmental juxtaposition between the sprawling desolation of the Government Centre (Figure 1.6) with its oversized, windswept plaza and the smaller, more intimate and comfortable pedestrian spaces around Faneuil Hall and Quincy Market (Figure 1.7).

environmental juxtaposition between the Government Centre and Quincy Market (Figures 1.6 and 1.7).

Value for functional diversity

The range of renting profiles resulting from a diverse range of different types of space in buildings of varying ages, enables a mix of uses. Thus, there may be a synergy between different functional uses in adjacent areas resulting from the nature of the property in each area. For example, the French Quarter of New Orleans as an entertainment quarter enjoys a beneficial symbiotic and synergistic relationship with the nearby office district with the whole being greater than the sum of the parts (Ford, 1994, p. 74). Similarly, historic areas may offer lower rents that allow economically marginal but socially important activities to have a place in the city. Large scale redevelopment often forces out these small uses which rarely return. In Denver, the preservation of the Lower Downtown area was justified, in part, by virtue of its functional contrast with the nearby CBD.

Resource value

Lichfield (1988, p. 29) gives two definitions for conservation. The first is to check the rate of exhaustion of natural or human resources. The second is to check obsolescence (or diminished utility) in manmade resources, for example, buildings. Whether beautiful, historic or just plain practical, buildings may be better used than replaced. Their value exists as the investment – or committed expenditure – of resources. As rehabilitation is less expensive in terms of absolute energy usage, the reuse of buildings constitutes the conservation of scarce resources, a reduction in the consumption of energy and materials in construction, and good resource management. Nevertheless, at present, the energy value of resources is poorly accounted for through the price mechanism.

Value for continuity of cultural memory/heritage value

It is not merely an aesthetic or visual continuity, but also a continuity of cultural memory that seems important. Since the mid 1960s this justification for preservation has been of increasing significance, broadening the original élitist concern and preoccupation with the aesthetic properties of historic artefacts. Visible evidence of the past can contribute pedagogically and educationally to the cultural identity and memory of a particular people or place, locating a contemporary society in relation to a previous tradition and giving meaning to the present by interpreting the past (Hewison, 1987, p. 85). Morton (1993, p. 21) argues: 'The built environment is one of the elements which when woven with other evidence such as writings, sculpture, music, etc. forms the palimpsest which is our inheritance from the past. It also provides the basis for understanding the times in which we live.' This idea is also made explicit in the preamble to the American National Historic Preservation Act (1966) 'the historical and cultural foundations of the Nation should be preserved as a living part of our community life and development in order to give a sense of orientation to the American People' (from Brown Morton III, 1992, p. 37). Nevertheless, this concern for cultural continuity can be manipulated to add specific – often political – connotations and distortions to preservation. This process of interpretation can turn historic buildings and environments from relatively neutral artefacts into a politically charged 'heritage'; what is preserved depends on who chooses and what they perceive history to be.

An aesthetic preference and concern for a visible cultural continuity can also have more negative justifications: a fear of change and a fear of an unknown future. It is in times of change and danger – either from without or from within – that a national or local consciousness of heritage increases. The heritage is held to represent some form of security and refuge, a point of visible and tangible reference which seems stable and unchanged. In this respect, it is useful to observe that nostalgia actually means 'not merely the recall of pleasant memories but literally the pain experienced through the unattainable longing to return to the past' (Ashworth and Tunbridge, 1990, p. 23). Hewison (1987, p. 46) is careful to warn that nostalgic memory should not be confused with true recall: 'For the individual, nostalgia filters out unpleasant aspects of the past, and of our former selves, creating a self-esteem that helps us rise above the anxieties of the present.'

An increased concern for the continuity of identity in a particular locality has signified the historical change from Modernism to postmodernism in urban design and planning. While Modernist planning tended towards the universal, postmodernism draws more upon the sense of place, the local and the particular. As Robins (1991, p. 34) states: 'This cultural localism reflects . . . deeper feelings about the inscription of human lives in space and time. There is a growing interest in the embeddedness of life histories within the boundaries of place, and with the continuities of identity and community through local memory and heritage.' This interest is related to sociological concerns about the lack of individuality and the anonymity of the modern city and forms a resistance against the homogenization of an increasingly global culture.

Economic and commercial value

The justifications for preservation reviewed so far generally have an aesthetic, social and cultural value rather than a tangible economic or commercial value. Nevertheless, in a context where public funds cannot subsidize all the required or desired preservation, then economic and commercial justifications for preservation and conservation must ultimately underpin all others. In the private sector, unless there is a clear economic rationale for a particular course of action that action is unlikely to occur. However, economic arguments are often ranged against the strictures of conservation or preservation. Conservation policies are regarded as a more extreme version of planning, which – it is argued – inevitably means greater intervention into private land and property markets, more bureaucracy restrictions and delay. More precisely the advocates of such arguments are generally opposed to State planning in general and public intervention into private property markets in particular.

Whether it is an unfettered market or one in which there is a significant public intervention, historic buildings must have effective economic value. Rypkema (1992, p. 206) offers a four-part syllogism: 'Historic preservation primarily involves buildings; historic buildings are real estate, and real estate is a commodity; for a commodity to attract investment capital, it must have economic value. Therefore, to attract private investment to historic preservation, it is necessary first to create and then to enhance economic value.' He argues that for any commodity – including real estate – to have economic value, four characteristics must be in place: *scarcity*, *purchasing power*, *desire* and *utility*. For any economic value to exist, all four must be present.

Historic buildings usually possess *scarcity*: their supply cannot be increased. That scarcity can also present opportunities for direct economic gain, for example, from tourism. However, few buildings, apart from museums and cafés, receive this as a direct benefit. The scarcity might also offer additional commercial value against an otherwise undifferentiated supply. For example, industrial buildings converted to residential use offer dwellings possessing the premium of greater character and individuality. Thus, recently (1995), loft apartments in converted industrial buildings in London have held their value and remained saleable despite a depressed housing market. In a conservationist climate or where there is a widespread fear of change, an element of historic preservation may make a development more acceptable to the local community or to the local planning committee.

While, generally, some level of *purchasing power* will exist, the problem is that it is likely to be invested elsewhere. If the other factors are in position, then purchasing power will be available. Thus, what is most often lacking for historic buildings is utility and desire. The *desire* has to ultimately come from one particular segment of users of real estate. As Rypkema (1992, p. 206) states: 'It is not sufficient that preservationists and other activists "desire" that the building be saved. That desire has to come from a broad segment of users of real estate in the market place. And this cannot be in the metaphysical abstract. It has to be expressed with a chequebook.' For commercial desire to exist there has to be a functional and financial utility for occupiers and investors.

A building's lack – or a diminution – of *utility* is a function of its obsolescence. Obsolescence is the reduction in the useful life of a capital good. From its first day of life a building starts to become obsolete; the state where it is 'completely useless with respect to all the uses they might be called upon to support' (Lichfield, 1988, p. 22). There are several different dimensions to the concept of obsolescence involving both buildings and areas; these are discussed in detail in Chapter Two. The most significant dimension is the relative or economic obsolescence: the obsolescence with regard to the cost of alternate opportunities. The alternate opportunities include both the cost of alternate development on the site and the cost of development on an alternate site. As Rypkema (1992, p. 207) states: 'it is rarely argued that historic buildings have no utility or that there is no desire in the marketplace for their use. Rather, the contention is that the economic value of these structures is less than the alternative'. To attract investment capital, the historic building must have greater economic value than the next best alternative. Or, in other words, the cost of utilization of that historic building has to be lower than the competitive supply.

REVITALIZING HISTORIC URBAN QUARTERS

If, for a myriad of reasons, it is desirable to preserve historic urban quarters, how should they be enhanced and revitalized? Lessons and observations from experiences of the revitalization of historic urban quarters form the core of this book.

The obsolescence of buildings and areas is expressed in a mismatch between 'the services offered by the fabric and the needs seen through contemporary eyes' (Lichfield,1988, p. 25). Revitalization entails reconciling this mismatch; the mismatch might have its source in the physical fabric or in the economic activities within the fabric. The fabric may be adapted to contemporary requirements through various modes of renewal: refurbishment, conversion or by demolition and redevelopment. In terms of economic activity, renewal can also arise from changes in occupation with new uses or activities replacing the former ones – on a large scale this is a 'functional restructuring' or 'functional diversification' – or with the existing uses remaining but operating more efficiently or profitably – on a large scale this is a 'functional regeneration'.[2] A physical revitalization results in an attractive, well-maintained *physical* public realm. However, in the longer term, a deeper economic revitalization is required because ultimately it is the private realm – the activities within the buildings – that pays for the maintenance of the public realm. A merely physical revitalization may be unsustained and short-lived. In the absence of large public subsidies directed at keeping the historic quarter as a public outdoor museum, historic forms must be occupied and utilized by economic uses which provide the sustained investment required to refurbish and maintain the buildings, and indirectly for the spaces between those buildings. Thus, the revitalization of historic urban quarters involves both the renewal of the physical fabric and the active economic use of those buildings and spaces.

In addition, the *social* public realm of the quarter must also be revitalized and animated. Rehabilitated buildings only provide the stage set – the physical receptacle for the public realm; the public realm is also a social construct. The vitality and animation of the historic quarter therefore needs to be 'authentic' rather than contrived or prettified; a 'genuine' working, functioning quarter that is naturally animated rather than a theatrical stageset with actors hired from central casting. This issue is discussed throughout this book and is given particular attention in the eighth and final chapter.

The particular economic problems of historic urban quarters and the issues of attracting inward investment and encouraging growth in particular areas are reviewed in Chapter Two. Chapter Three examines the change from Modernist to postmodern ideas about the appreciation and design of urban space and form. The book then develops these ideas through a number of case study examples which

---

[2] In this book, rather than its more common usage, the term 'regeneration' is only used in this more limited sense.

illustrate the revitalization of a number of historic quarters within the centres of various cities. The case studies are selected for their historic and conservation value, as examples of *quarters* in the case of the European examples and, in the case of the British and American examples, for their relative similarity as nineteenth-century industrial areas. The quarters also exhibit differences in terms of the continuity of their historic fabric, the presence of their original or traditional industries, the diversity of approaches adopted and their wider significance within the city. Chapter Four examines attempts at tourism and culture-led revitalizations of historic quarters which seek to build on the legacy of the area's historic character, associations and sense of place. Chapter Five examines attempts and experiences of revitalizing quarters through residential conversions and mixed use. Chapter Six examines attempts at the revitalization of quarters which are still in predominantly industrial or commercial use. It is important to stress that most of the quarters have broad revitalizations that include – to varying degrees – all aspects of these approaches/ themes. Chapter Seven examines the design issues raised by rehabilitation and new build developments with respect to the urban form and the architectural language and character of the quarter. The final chapter concludes the book and outlines a framework of the key issues involved in the revitalization of historic urban quarters.

2

ECONOMIC CHALLENGES OF HISTORIC URBAN QUARTERS

INTRODUCTION

The revitalization of historic urban quarters involves both the renewal of the physical fabric and the active economic use – or utilization – of buildings and spaces. Accordingly, there is a need for both physical and economic revitalization. One may prefigure the other, for example, a cosmetic or 'physical' revitalization may be a short-term strategy intended to induce a deeper 'economic' revitalization in the longer term. A physical revitalization can result in an attractive, well-maintained public realm. However, in the longer term, economic revitalization is required because ultimately it is the productive utilization of the private realm which pays for the maintenance of the public realm.

This chapter will outline the general themes involved in economic revitalization and the tensions induced by concerns for preservation and conservation. Although, all urban areas undergo economic change, historic urban quarters have to cope with change in their economic fortunes while change in their physical landscapes is restricted and controlled in the interests of conservation. In such quarters, the necessity of reconciling the various exigencies of conservation and revitalization, of balancing economic development while respecting environmental quality is particularly challenging.

ECONOMIC CHANGE

Before discussing the particular economic issues in historic urban quarters, it is useful to review the factors influencing all urban areas. In recent years there have been two key changes. The first key change has been the decline in western countries of traditional manufacturing industries, a consequent deindustrialization and the emergence of an informational economy (see, for example, Castells, 1989). As a consequence, many cities in Western Europe and the USA are changing from being *largely* centres of production to become *largely* centres of consumption. In historic urban quarters the physical landscape designed to suit the exigencies of one historical period has to be adapted for another. For example, nineteenth-century industrial quarters are changing to accommodate a post-industrial informational economy. In doing so, many such quarters are making a virtue of their historic character and sense of place.

The second factor has been the restructuring of international capitalism and the advent of an increasingly global economy, by which, for example, western corporations are more easily able to achieve economies by relocating their manufacturing plants in the developing world where labour costs are lower. Furthermore the declining significance of the nation state and the increasing importance of transnational corporations has increased competition at all levels: between countries, regions, cities and within cities. Nevertheless as Castells and Hall (1994, p. 7) state:

> the most fascinating paradox is the fact that in a world economy whose productive infrastructure is made up of information flows, cities and regions are increasingly becoming critical agents of economic development . . . Precisely because the economy is global, national governments suffer from failing powers to act upon the functional processes that shape their economies and societies. But regions and cities are more flexible in adapting to changing conditions of markets, technology, and culture. True, they have less power than national governments, but they have a greater capacity to generate targeted development projects, negotiate with multinational firms, foster the growth of small and medium endogenous firms, and create conditions that will attract the new sources of wealth, power, and prestige. In this process of generating new growth, they compete with each other; but, more often than not, such competition becomes a source of innovation, of efficiency, of a collective effort to create a better place to live and a more effective place to do business.

Paradoxically perhaps neither of these developments necessarily signals the end of cities as significant economic places. In the midst of this social, economic and political change, the physical infrastructure and fabric of cities represents a relatively fixed point. As Castells (1989, pp. 1–2) notes how various prophecies suggest that with the coming of the informational age, the need for cities as they have been known has been superseded: for example, modern telecommunication allows work at home in 'electronic cottages', while remaining at home, people can be open and interactive with a world of images, sounds and communication flows. Yet, he observes (1989, p. 2) 'none of these prophecies stands up to the most elementary confrontation with actual observation of social trends . . . Intensely urban Paris is the success story for the use of home-based telematic systems'.

In terms of the pattern of economic activities, few cities are static: the fortunes of individual areas fluctuate over time. Haughton and Hunter (1994, p. 39) note how every city tends to have a 'golden era' after which, for many, decline ensues. 'Part of the fascination of the twentieth century has been the attempts of some older cities to "reinvent" themselves after initially being written off following rapid deindustrialization.' In many older cities, to achieve a 'second golden era' and to reposition themselves within the global economy, restructuring policies are pursued that sometimes draw on the legacy of the built environment inherited from the first golden age (Haughton and Hunter, 1994, p. 39). Historic urban quarters are part of this economic dynamism, they are rarely autonomous functional zones and usually have a symbiotic relationship with the rest of the city. They must therefore be considered within the context of the city as a whole. In the UK Department of the Environment (1987b) guidance for conservation areas states the policy imperative is 'to preserve their character, but not at the cost of setting them apart; they must be seen as part of the living and working community'. The changing fortunes of areas of cities and their physical fabric can be usefully analysed by considering them in terms of obsolescence, and in particular the way in which preservation controls check the ability of the market to remedy or address obsolescence.

OBSOLESCENCE

The presence of historic quarters in cities is often a mixed blessing. Such areas establish character and identity, concretizing a meaningful place that has endured over time. However, they also present problems. Many of these problems pertain to the obsolescence of the building stock and/or the area. One of Lichfield's definitions of conservation is to check the obsolescence of manmade resources (Lichfield, 1988, p. 29). Obsolescence, or diminished utility, is the reduction in the useful life of a capital good. In the main, obsolescence is a consequence of change – either expected or unexpected – and the relative fixity of the built fabric and its location.

When commissioned and built, a building is usually 'state of the art' in terms of its functional requirements. It will also be built to the contemporary standards of building construction and be appropriately located for its intended function with regard to such factors as the transportation of raw materials and access to markets. If it were not, then – presumably – there would not have been an economic case for its construction. Nevertheless, as the building ages and the world around it changes, the building becomes obsolescent and therefore approaches the state when it is 'completely useless with respect to all the uses it might be called upon to support' (Lichfield, 1988, p. 22). Attempts to revitalize historic urban quarters must address and/or remedy obsolescence and extend the economic life of the historic building stock. However, various restrictive preservation and conservation controls and other planning measures may constrain, inhibit or – even – deter rehabilitation and new development. Excessive listing and protection of buildings can blight an area as much as the prospect of major road construction. The combination of obsolescence and restrictive planning controls induces economic tensions by preventing the maximum return, a 'reasonable' return or – even – any return on the site to be obtained, constraining the change that all cities must go through.

There are several interrelated dimensions of obsolescence. Some of these are attributes of the buildings and their functions while others relate to the area as a whole. For each dimension, the degree of obsolescence will not be uniform for any one building or area. Furthermore '"obsolescence" is a relative term with regard to the terminal state, "obsolete", which may never be reached' (Lichfield, 1988, p. 22). For example, unless a building was designed for a very specific purpose (for example, a nuclear power station), it is difficult to conceive of it having no residual physical utility and being impossible to convert to another use. Thus, a state of total obsolescence is rarely reached. Equally, obsolescence is rarely absolute, rather a building or area will be merely more or less obsolescent than the competitive supply.

The dimensions of obsolescence[1] are:

Physical/structural obsolescence

Obsolescence can arise through the physical or structural deterioration of the building. This occurs as the building's fabric deteriorates through the effects of time, the weather, earth movement, traffic vibration, or through poor maintenance. The building needs repair and maintenance over and above that offered by regular, ongoing maintenance. Without such refurbishment the physical condition of the building would interfere with occupation of the building. Obsolescence of this nature is likely to be – at least initially – gradual.

Functional obsolescence

Obsolescence can also arise because of the functional qualities of the building or the area. It may be an attribute of the building; the building's fabric may no longer be suited for the function for which it was designed or is currently used, with regard to the contemporary standards or requirements of the occupier or potential occupiers. This inadequacy can relate to the fabric itself, for example, the building does not have central heating, air conditioning or lifts, or the building may be unable to accommodate modern telecommunications facilities. Equally contemporary production methods may require a production line on a single floor rather than in a multistorey building. As a consequence of functional obsolescence, a technological disadvantage may arise; as the premises are less efficient, the firm is correspondingly less competitive.

Functional obsolescence may also arise from the attributes of the area. Inadequacy can result from external factors on which the function of the building depends: for example, there may be inadequate parking on site or in the surrounding streets, or difficulties of access as a result of narrow streets or traffic congestion. Thus, retaining an area's historic street pattern inhibits its ability to cater for contemporary traffic and accessibility requirements.

[1] These dimensions of obsolescence are adapted and developed from Lichfield, 1988, pp. 22–25.

Image obsolescence

Image obsolescence is a product of the perception of the building's or area's image. As over time, the human, social, economic or natural environment changes, the fixed historic fabric becomes less suitable in contemporary eyes for the needs it serves. This perception is a value judgement and may – in reality – lack an underlying substance. The image obsolescence might be generic or specific to a particular use. For example, the image of inner areas of cities and the connotations of air pollution, noise, vibration, etc. makes them unattractive for the occupation of dwellings built in earlier times. Such areas therefore become outmoded in terms of contemporary standards and expectations. Equally, a building may not convey a suitably 'modern' image for the company which occupies it. Perceptions, however, can change over time. In the immediate post-war period, older buildings were demolished to build new ones whose image would be suitably redolent of their modernity. In the contemporary period where values have changed, older buildings might be more desirable because of the values of stability, tradition and discernment that they might communicate. However unsubstantial the underlying reality, perceptions are important in shaping values and attitudes. In many of the case study quarters, an important element of the revitalization strategy has been a deliberate image reconstruction.

'Legal' and 'official' obsolescence

There is also a 'legal' obsolescence. This is related to the functional and physical dimensions and occurs, for example, where a public agency determines certain minimum standards of functionality. Thus, the introduction of new standards in health and safety, fire or building controls can render the building obsolete. Alternatively, a building may be legally obsolete because the zoning ordinance for the area permits a larger building on the site.

Physical, functional and – sometimes – image obsolescence may result in an 'official' obsolescence where, for example, an area is officially declared a clearance area for road building, road widening or comprehensive redevelopment by the local public planning authorities. In the interim between the announcement of the project and its implementation – if, indeed, it ever is – the area becomes blighted and long-term – even medium-term – investment is deterred. This official obsolescence might also be reinforced by institutional unwillingness to provide insurance or funding for the rehabilitation – or maintenance – of properties within the earmarked zone. However, it should also be recognized that the designation may be unjust, inappropriate or the product of an insubstantial image obsolescence. Many of the quarters in this book have been blighted by clearance schemes that were subsequently cancelled.

Locational obsolescence

Locational obsolescence is primarily an attribute of the functional activities within the area. When the building was originally built its location was determined in terms of the accessibility to other uses, markets and suppliers, transport infrastructure, etc., but over time the location may become obsolete for the activities for which the building was constructed. Locational obsolescence occurs due to the fixity of a particular location relative to changes in the wider pattern of accessibility and labour costs. This state of locational obsolescence operates at various scales – internationally between countries or within cities between central and peripheral sites, for example, where firms move from the city centre to more accessible locations on suburban industrial estates. Certain specific changes could introduce locational obsolescence, for example, shops built around a hospital or railway station that becomes defunct (Lichfield, 1988, p. 23).

This form of obsolescence might also arise from the migration of the central business district. The introduction of modern building codes from the early 1900s encouraged the rebuilding of downtown areas. In Europe this rebuilding was largely done *in situ*, however, in America it was often easier for the downtown area to migrate to a new location. In American cities, without the anchor of a major plaza or cathedral square, the peak land value intersection (PLVI) of the office core could often migrate considerable distances (Ford, 1994, p. 64). Thus, Ford argues, the frame around the core can be divided into two distinctive areas: the 'zone of discard' – the area from which the PLVI is moving – and the 'zone of assimilation' – the area the PLVI is moving toward. The zone of discard therefore suffers a relative locational obsolescence. In many waterside cities, such as St Louis and Seattle, over time, the PLVI migrated 'from the semi-industrial chaos of the waterfront, with its possible flood hazards and congestion to an area on higher ground which was once a zone of better residences' (Ford, 1994, p. 65).

Financial obsolescence

The preservation of older buildings may not be helped by accounting and taxation procedures which introduce an 'artificial' or financial obsolescence. In accounting, depreciation is used to take into account expected or anticipated obsolescence.[2] Depreciation is the projected reduction in the value of a fixed asset such as land, buildings, plant, machinery, vehicles and furniture over time. Depreciation is used therefore to ensure that the cost of capital assets is included in the calculation price of the company's goods and in assessing its turnover and profitability. The consumption of such assets is one of the costs of earning the revenue of business.

While the rationale for depreciation procedures is acceptable, it can have some undesirable side effects. For tax purposes, buildings are capital assets which are

[2] Note that obsolescence also includes unseen changes in the value of an asset due to, for example, technological or economic reasons. This unseen change is more difficult to account for through depreciation as the timescale is not known.

assigned a depreciable life – the period when it is assumed they will have economic value and can therefore be used to offset tax. Once this period has expired the building no longer appears on the company's balance sheet as its depreciable life has ended and, although the building still has an intrinsic value, it no longer has any value for tax purposes. As Rypkema (1992, p. 210) states this 'begins to mould one's thinking; it makes the asset disposable. Depreciation is justified on real estate's definition as a "wasting" asset. Thus it becomes a wasted asset, razed generations before its physical life is over. Buildings are torn down not because their physical life is over but because their remaining economic life is deemed to be limited' (Rypkema, 1992, p. 210). Thus, there is an argument for depreciation of buildings to be eliminated altogether, so that real estate becomes a renewable capital asset, not a 'wasting' one.

Relative or economic obsolescence

For most practical purposes, obsolescence is not an absolute concept but is always relative to other buildings and areas. As Rypkema (1992, p. 206) notes: 'purchasing power exists. Capital is available – it is just being invested elsewhere'. The reason for this is that the cost of investment in the historic quarter is higher than the alternatives which are consequently more attractive. This introduces the concept of relative or economic obsolescence: the obsolescence with regard to the cost of alternate opportunities. The alternate opportunities include competition from other buildings and areas and, in addition, the cost of alternative development on that particular site and the cost of development on an alternative site.

PRESERVATION AND CONSERVATION CONTROLS

The following section discusses the justification for and notes the effect of preservation and conservation legislation. In an unfettered market, once a building has become economically obsolete then it would simply be abandoned and left to deteriorate, or – if the site retained some value – it might be demolished and the site redeveloped. Demolition might also be a way of realizing a higher value for the site. For example, a means of obtaining the maximum or highest value use for the site rather than accepting a use which does not maximize the site's potential profit, or a means of redeveloping the site up to the maximum permitted plot ratio. However, problems will arise where the option of demolition and redevelopment is effectively precluded or where the options for refurbishment and/or conversion are limited by preservation and control policies. Harvey (1985, p. 25) notes there is a perpetual struggle under capitalism in which 'capital builds a physical landscape appropriate to its own conditions at a particular moment in time . . . only to have to destroy it . . . at a subsequent point in time'. As functions within buildings change and other areas become better suited for certain functions, tensions and conflicts arise where that desire to destroy the physical landscape is thwarted by other considerations. Preservation and conservation controls therefore check the ability of the market to address the issue of obsolescence.

In the long term, through the interaction of supply and demand, land in the private sector will generally transfer to the highest value use. To maximize their own return, owners will generally lease their land or sell their interest to the highest bidders. The users and potential users who are willing to pay the highest rents or prices, will generally be those capable of realizing the greatest benefit from their use of land. Proponents of a *laisser faire* free market economy argue that the most profitable use of land is the most efficient and, therefore, the most desirable. However, this relationship overlooks the importance of social considerations. As Balchin *et al.* (1988, p. 274) state: 'An uncontrolled market ignores social needs – it only exists to maximise private profit and pecuniary satisfaction.' Social needs include historic buildings and areas: as they have a certain intangible value to society at large, their loss or destruction results in a loss of welfare. As discussed in Chapter One, this social value derives variously from the building or quarter's aesthetic value; the value of its architectural and environmental diversity; and its heritage value, its value for the continuity of cultural memory.

The social value of historic buildings and areas is intangible and difficult to put a monetary value on. Consequently it is poorly accounted for in the price mechanism of an unfettered market: it is therefore effectively an 'externality'. Externalities arise when the action of an individual has a direct effect on another individual that is not transmitted through prices. As this external effect is not transmitted, the decision of the individual creating it does not generally take its effects into account. If an activity gives rise to a positive externality, there might be a case for the offer of a subsidy to encourage that activity. If the activity gives rise to a negative externality, there is often a case for public intervention. There are two approaches to dealing with negative externalities: firstly, to prohibit the action which creates the externality, for example, for the State to prohibit or require permission to be obtained for the demolition of certain protected buildings, or for the State itself to acquire the threatened building. Secondly, by some form of intervention, to increase the effective price paid for that activity, to ameliorate its effects, or to subsidize more preferable alternate courses of action. Nevertheless, as Balchin *et al.* (1988, p. 275) warn, intervening agencies must 'fully appreciate the working of the market mechanism and [be] able to predict most of the direct and indirect consequences of their intervention'. The second approach is generally preferred as it produces an optimal – 'market-based' – resource allocation and is therefore economically more efficient. Most historic preservation ordinances and funding systems have an element of each method. Such protection is therefore an example of public intervention because a market for what has become a 'public good' fails to emerge; the unfettered market fails to protect buildings that society deems worthy of retention.

Police powers

All markets are reflections of demand and supply conditions. Thus, in the land market, any intervention to adjust demand and supply will create new conditions for decision-making which – in turn – will modify land values and land-use patterns. Interventions therefore usually intend to incorporate social factors into this decision-making process thereby altering the relationship between supply and demand, giving what – it is hoped – will be a more desirable pattern of land use (Balchin *et al.*, 1988, p. 274–275). Public intervention into the private property market through conservation and preservation controls is therefore a way of making building owners more aware of the social value.

To exercise any form of intervention or control needs 'police powers'. In general terms, most aspects of statutory planning involve the use of police powers. Under the police power, the State denies property owners certain rights of use because they are regarded as contrary or detrimental to public welfare. However, unlike the instance of 'eminent domain', the State does not 'take' the property from its owner. In addition, police powers may be exercised with or without the payment of compensation; in most countries, the latter is more common. In most societies, the State's police powers – its controls and interventions – have been justified to and legitimized by the democratic process. However, it was not possible to intervene significantly in the private property market until after the Second World War in most European countries. In the USA, in particular, there has always been greater concern given to the protection of individual property rights.

Whatever their justification, conservation and preservation controls can inhibit the ability of the market to address the issue of obsolescence. For example, difficulties are created when buildings are preserved because it is no longer permissable to demolish them. As a consequence, public intervention into the market in the interests of conservation can create a situation where a building stands vacant and derelict because it cannot legally be converted to a new use. Nor can it be demolished and the site redeveloped. It has therefore become a public good, for which a market fails to emerge. Thus, although preservation controls are an intervention to incorporate social values into the property market, they do not necessarily command universal approval and consent, particularly among those property owners who are adversely affected. This raises the issue of the legitimacy of public intervention into private property markets. Conflicts may arise due both to the *principle* and the *practice* of intervention. While not dismissing the issue of the practice, it is the principle that will be discussed here.

In the USA in particular, the public sector's interest in historic preservation and conservation has been opposed by a strongly held principle of the liberal state, that of individual property rights (Ashworth and Tunbridge, 1990, p. 10). Arguments have been advanced that historic landmark designations and controls infringe the property rights supposedly guaranteed in the US constitution. These 'property rights' are based on the 'Just Compensation Clause', or 'Takings Clause', of the Fifth Amendment to the Constitution, which states 'nor shall private property be taken for public use without just compensation'.

In the USA, the Takings Clause has had special significance since the Supreme Court decision in the Penn Central case in 1978. In this landmark decision, 'the high court upheld the constitutionality of municipal landmark ordinance as a proper exercise of the police power. The Court also ruled that the application of the landmarks ordinance, which had the effect of denying a property owner the maximum profit on real estate, was not an unconstitutional taking, provided a property owner retains the reasonable economic use of the property' (Doheny, 1993,

p. 7). Thus, by placing itself on the side of preservation, the Court ruled that while owners were entitled to a *reasonable* financial return on their property, the law does not necessarily guarantee them a *maximum* return. Furthermore, the decision reaffirms the State's police powers standing for 'the proposition that the rights incident to property ownership are not absolute, but are subject to reasonable regulation for the benefit of the community without the necessity of requiring the public to pay monetary compensation' (Doheny, 1993, p. 7). Equally 'just compensation' could be interpreted more broadly: Brown Morton III argues: 'Is money the only "just compensation"? Could . . . the preservation of a sense of place . . . also be called just compensation?' (Brown Morton III, 1992).

Despite the Supreme Court decision in the Penn Central case, a 1991 Pennsylvania Supreme Court decision called the principle into question again. The case concerned the historic preservation of a relatively mundane 1928 Movie Palace, the Boyd Theatre, in Philadelphia. The judge, Justice Rolf Larsen, held that historical designation of the theatre would constitute a taking of property rights without compensation. The decision 'rocked the preservation community by challenging the legality of the city's preservation ordinance' (Mitchell, 1992, p. 68). Sax (from Lee, 1992, p. 243) comments that the court appeared: 'to be reverting to the old view that aesthetic reasons alone are not enough to support an exercise of police power, or

Figure 2.1

The Boyd Theatre, Philadelphia. The subject of a court case which challenged Philadelphia's historic preservation ordinance. Although the building has been preserved, it has now been converted into a discount store.

alternatively holding the more substantial, but equally unconventional, view that a historic preservation ordinance is, in effect, an exaction that compels the owner "to dedicate his property without compensation for public historical, aesthetic, educational and museum purposes, which in reality are public uses'". The decision, however, was overturned on reargument and the building has been preserved.

In most cases it is difficult to argue that the case for preservation is sufficiently compelling to constitute 'eminent domain' and necessitates the taking of private property. Preservation and conservation controls are therefore usually operated through a State's police powers, the justifications for which are always value judgements. Rypkema (1992, p. 210), for instance, argues: 'It is not an issue of property rights; it is a question of equity, fairness, and a return on everybody's investment.' Ultimately, therefore, the issue of preservation and conservation controls is one of communal welfare – social value – versus individual profit and the absolute sovereignty of property rights. Preservation controls are therefore usually legitimized by their attempt to balance collective welfare against private interest and by including consideration of certain negative externalities into the price mechanism.

In terms of historic urban quarters, there is a further economic justification for land use and preservation controls: to create and maintain a context that sustains and reinforces the composite value of the area. Unlike most other investments, buildings are interdependent assets. This is a positive externality; when a property is rehabilitated or kept in good repair there is an external benefit to neighbouring properties. Equally, the reverse is also true: if a property is neglected there is an external cost to its neighbours. Protective and restrictive ordinances ensure that: 'everyone is playing by the same rules and that an investment will not be wiped out later by less scrupulous development' (Uhlman, 1976, p. 6). Thus, although a well-drawn historic district ordinance may diminish the maximum value of any single property, it will enhance the cumulative sum of values within the area: 'The ordinance is not a case of the public versus the private sector; it is the communal economic benefit of all of the owners versus the economic windfall of a single owner' (Rypkema, 1992, p. 210).

THE REVITALIZATION OF HISTORIC URBAN QUARTERS

Efforts to address obsolescence in order to extend the useful lives of buildings are called renewal. To address or ameliorate the various dimensions of obsolescence demands both building and/or area-based renewal. For the purposes of this book, renewal is part of the broader process which has been termed revitalization. Renewal entails reconciling the mismatch created by obsolescence between 'the services offered by the fabric and the needs seen through contemporary eyes' (Lichfield, 1988, p. 25). This mismatch has its source either in the (physical) urban fabric or the change in the (economic) activities in the fabric. To reconcile the mismatch requires a change in the supply or the pattern of demand or both. Historic buildings are a scarce resource; their supply cannot expand. Thus, the only supply-side measures are those which stop the reduction or diminution of the building stock, such as demolition controls and those that limit the magnitude of change to historic buildings, such as listings and preservation controls. All other measures are therefore on the demand side and seek to increase the utilization of the resource by lowering the effective price paid. These measures predominantly relate to the quality of the building stock and the physical environment of the quarter and/or the economic activities occurring within that fabric.

THE PHYSICAL REVITALIZATION OF HISTORIC URBAN QUARTERS

Improving the quality of the stock of property in a given area entails efforts to address or remedy certain dimensions of that property's obsolescence. Owners and occupiers of buildings can address the dimensions of obsolescence that are within their abilities; mainly the structural, functional and image dimensions. There are three possible courses of action to increase the utility of a building and site: demolition and redevelopment; refurbishment for its current use, and conversion for a new use. The economic principles of these changes are discussed in this chapter, the physical and design implications of rehabilitation and redevelopment on the quarter's physical character are discussed in greater detail in Chapter Seven.

Determining the particular course of action to address the obsolescence or diminished utility of buildings and other individual structures is usually a rational economic process which assesses the costs and benefits of the various courses of action. Unless the additional expected returns for any future use of the building exceed the costs of remedying the obsolescence, those actions will generally not occur. In addition the return on the investment must be considered relative to other possible investments. Hence, there must be a commercial rationale to undertake actions to address obsolescence.

The demolition of historic buildings

Within the various dimensions of obsolescence, there are a variety of reasons why there might be desires to demolish historic buildings. When buildings are regarded as obsolete, an important distinction must be drawn between the obsolescence of a building in its *current use* and the building being obsolete for *any use*. In the former instance, the existing uses might be unviable or unable to physically preserve the historic fabric. Then the options of either demolition and redevelopment for a new use or conversion to a new use must be considered. In either case, since building owners will normally seek to secure the highest value use for their building, they will try to trade up to a more viable use. This may result in displacement. In the second instance, when a building is obsolete for any use, demolition might be expected but would be checked by preservation controls. As the terminal obsolescence is frequently a value judgement, it is often the source of conflicts between building owners and public planning authorities.

Rather than being terminally obsolete, it is more likely that the building is economically obsolete. This is the situation where a building is not obsolete in its current use but the potential value of the site for redevelopment is higher than the value of the site as it stands. As Lichfield (1988, p. 131) states 'the building may not be obsolete in the sense of being "completely useless with respect to all uses it might be called upon to support" and may still be maintained to support its current use. But it can be regarded as economically obsolete and on economic grounds . . . it will not be renewed but allowed to deteriorate in anticipation of its next phase in the life cycle'. Thus, if the redevelopment value of the site is sufficiently higher, by at least the developer's profit, the building and the site could be described as being economically obsolete in its current use. This might therefore result in the demolition of buildings – which are not obsolete in an absolute sense – simply for the purposes of replacing them with new stock. Again, due to differing interests, there is often a conflict of interest between building owners and public planning authorities.

Pressure to demolish a building may also result from a building's 'legal' obsolescence. As historic buildings are generally smaller than modern buildings, they are often not developed up to the maximum permissable plot ratio: 'A building with a floor area of three, in a district that permits eighteen, is more valuable dead than alive if there is a strong real estate market, no matter how important its architecture or associations may be' (Barnett, 1982, p. 39). Many cities in the USA have introduced transferable development rights to enable the legal transfer of 'air-rights' from an historic building to another site. This concept was originated in 1968 by John Costanis, a lawyer, concerned with preserving the early high-rise structures concentrated in Chicago's Loop (Murtagh, 1992, p. 53). As a preservation concept it was first implemented in New York. However, where the benefiting site is near to the donor site, the density bonus may have unfortunate consequences on the setting of the historic building.

The viability of redevelopment of the site over rehabilitation of the existing building relates to the relationship between the capital value of the cleared site (for its best use) less the costs of demolishing the existing building and constructing a new building compared to the capital value of the existing building and site (in its best use) less the cost of refurbishment or conversion. In some situations redevelopment will be more economic than rehabilitation, and in other situations rehabilitation will be more economic. Due to the dynamic nature of property markets, this relationship may change over time.

If an urban area is revitalized by, for example, the improvement of infrastructure, the capital value of both buildings and sites will generally rise. However, the value of the existing building may ultimately check the increase in the composite value of the building and site. In such cases there will be pressure for the demolition and replacement of the existing building, provided that the new value of the site (less the costs of demolition and construction of a new building) is greater – by at least the developer's profit – than the value of the existing building and site. Equally the economic value of a cleared site might be greater than the economic value of the site with the building on it. In this instance, the owner has concluded that the net contributory economic value of the building is less than zero, or at least to the extent of the demolition cost. In both instances as a result of the area's improvement, there are pressures for the demolition of buildings. This situation gives rise to an apparent paradox: the revitalization of historic urban quarters – by increasing property values

– also increases pressure for the demolition of some of the historic buildings. However, the significance of the building's historic character and its contribution to the revitalization will temper pressures for demolition and redevelopment.

If the reverse trend occurs, a decaying infrastructure, the capital value of sites and buildings will fall. This is the situation that many historic areas were in prior to any revitalization efforts. If the value of the site falls relative to the value of the building on them, then this will tend to extend the building's economic life *if* it remains in active use. Equally, it might shorten it, *if* as a consequence it falls into vacancy and dereliction.

However, as previously noted, although redevelopment might be more economic, preservation and conservation controls might intervene preventing the 'normal' cycle of demolition and redevelopment. Where demolition and redevelopment is not possible, the displacement of existing uses can still occur as new interest generated in the area increases property prices and rents putting pressure on lower value uses to the extent that they are effectively driven from the area. This may be desirable in terms of the quarter's physical conservation – the buildings will be kept in a better state of repair – but detrimental to its functional and historic character. This is a process of economic or functional restructuring and is discussed again later in the chapter.

The extent and degree of demolition controls in conservation areas is one of the most controversial issues in conservation. Practice varies among countries in Europe and among individual states and cities in the USA. In the USA, the prohibition of demolition is usually part of the ordinance of the local historic preservation district. However, as a result of strong representation or influence from the development industry, some ordinances do not include this provision. For example, in Denver, control over demolition was one of the most important features of the designation of a Historic District in the Lower Downtown (see Chapter Six).

In the UK's more discretionary planning system, the current national planning guidance (DOE, 1994) illustrates the key factors in the decision making process:

> the Secretaries of State would not expect consent to be given for the total or substantial demolition of any listed building without clear and convincing evidence that all reasonable efforts have been made to sustain existing uses or find viable new uses, and these efforts have failed; that preservation in some form of charitable or community ownership is not possible or suitable; or that redevelopment would produce substantial benefits for the community which would decisively outweigh the loss resulting from the demolition (DOE, 1994, PPG15, p. 10).

Furthermore, demolition on purely economic grounds is specifically ruled out: 'The Secretaries of State would not expect consent to any demolition to be given simply because redevelopment is economically more attractive to the developer than repair and re-use of a historic building, or because the developer acquired the building at a price that reflected the potential redevelopment rather than the condition and constraints of the existing historic building.' However, this national policy guideline only refers to buildings that have the benefit of being listed. Demolition of unlisted buildings in conservation areas has required the express grant of planning permission since 1974. In many countries, historic quarters often contain significant numbers of buildings which do not have listed or landmark status.

Where the option of demolition is controlled, owners of obsolete and/or economically obsolete buildings may purposefully permit dereliction, decay and vacancy to hasten a – probably reluctant – permission for demolition and redevelopment of the site in the interests of public safety. Thus, the State is compelled to recognize that the buildings are physically – and therefore legally – obsolete. To stop this form of benign neglect in Seattle's Pioneer Square a 'minimum maintenance ordinance' was introduced in 1974. When any building in the historic district deteriorates to the point where its preservation is in danger or it poses a safety hazard to its occupants or the general public, the city superintendent of buildings can intervene. An order can be issued for the work that needs to be done. If the order is not overturned by an appeal process, the city can undertake the repair work and recover the cost from the owner. In cases of hardship, however, this sanction must be balanced by the incentive of grant aid. This is similar to the repairs notice in the UK.

The rehabilitation of historic buildings

Where demolition is precluded – or undesirable – and the historic building retains some economic value or utility, then renewal measures will have to be devised to retard the obsolescence and extend the building's remaining life. With respect to historic buildings, Fitch (1990, pp. 46–47) suggests a useful classification of 'levels of intervention according to a scale of increasing radicality' (see Figure 7.2). These are: preservation; restoration; refurbishment; reconstitution; conversion; reconstruction; and replication. The term 'rehabilitation' is used here as a generic term to include restoration, refurbishment and conversion. In this chapter, it is only refurbishment and conversion which are of direct concern. The rehabilitation of a building takes place when works are carried out to overcome at least some of the obsolescence, normally structural and functional (Lichfield, 1988, p. 132). The owner's economic calculus is similar to that for demolition and new development but the site cost is already sunk (committed or 'historical'). The utility can be increased by rehabilitation in either of two ways: by adaptation to contemporary requirements through *refurbishment* for its existing use or by *conversion* and reuse for a different purpose or function.

Refurbishment addresses the obsolescence of a building in its existing use. Area-based refurbishment schemes might be part and parcel of a functional regeneration of the existing uses within the quarter. Conversion or the adaptive reuse of historic buildings restores the utility by changing the building's function. Rypkema (1992, p. 206) observes that 'a major benefit of the amount of historic preservation activity over the past 25 years has been the demonstration that there is, in fact, an alternate use for virtually every kind of structure. Furthermore, good architects around the country have devised innovative ways to mitigate or overcome what might otherwise be defined as utility-diminishing design deficiencies of old buildings'. If this process occurs on a large scale throughout the quarter, it becomes an integral part of a functional restructuring of the area. For example, the conversion of industrial loft spaces to residential use in the SoHo quarter of New York was a functional restructuring of the quarter.

The demands of preservation and rehabilitation inexorably involve a conflict which those involved in the conservation of buildings and areas must recognize (Yeomans, 1994, p. 159). By introducing necessary changes, rehabilitation seeks to extend the useful life of an existing building; conversely historic building legislation seeks to protect and preserve an historic building's character. Further conflicts occur when the retention of historic character makes rehabilitation more difficult or more expensive. The physical task of refurbishment or conversion is rarely a major problem. In many historic buildings, particularly nineteenth-century industrial buildings, the physical fabric is relatively robust and the structure sturdy. What might be a more important problem is the lack of available investment capital to carry out rehabilitation. It is therefore important to consider the funding of building rehabilitation.

For investment to occur to improve the physical fabric and therefore the stock of property within an historic urban quarter, there must be a commercial rationale. For a commercial rationale to exist, the buildings must have an economic value or the potential for economic value to be created. The most significant dimension in the commercial calculus to invest is the cost of alternate opportunities, such as the cost of alternate development on the site and the cost of development on an alternative site. That is, so that the historic building has greater economic value than the next best alternative.

To make such buildings commercially competitive often requires some form of public subsidy ('gap-funding', direct grants, low interest loans, etc.) to aid their refurbishment or conversion, thereby effectively lowering the price of utilization. Incentives and other public actions and funding may frequently be an important factor or component of the commercial calculus and decision to invest. Such public subsidies are used to offset additional costs resulting from the legal protection of the building or area or to encourage the market to pursue a particular course of action it would otherwise not undertake. Nevertheless, public subsidies have to be justified on the basis that the resulting project produces a social or community benefit which in the absence of the subsidy would not have occurred. The economic case for a subsidy is usually where the social benefit of a course of action outweighs the private benefit: for example, the general public's pleasure and well-being created by the retention of a landmark building is greater than the value of the subsidy to the building owner. The value of the subsidy should be commensurate with the public benefit gained, although, as stated previously, the social value of historic buildings is intangible.

In the UK, there are various conservation-related grant schemes to encourage the rehabilitation of historic buildings. However, the indirect tax system, value added tax (VAT), actually works against conservation. Construction on green field sites is not liable for VAT, neither are major works of alteration and reconstruction of listed buildings, but repairs and maintenance of listed buildings are liable. As Cantacuzino (1989, p. 10) notes: 'There is therefore a positive incentive substantially to alter, renew and, inevitably, damage listed buildings. This is one reason why listed buildings are often totally reconstructed within the existing outer shell, making a travesty of conservation.'

Except where they are required by a local ordinance, changes to historic buildings in the USA do not normally require permits. Control over rehabilitation is, however, exerted through a system of financial and tax incentives to encourage owners to rehabilitate historic buildings to acceptable standards, originally introduced in the 1976 Federal Tax Reform Act.[3] Prior to this, as tax deductions were allowable for the costs of demolition, tax laws actually discouraged the preservation and rehabilitation of historic properties. Any work to an 'historic' building for which a tax credit is sought has to be reviewed by the National Park Service for compliance with the Secretary of the Interior's Standards for Rehabilitation (see Figure 7.2) to assure consistency with the building's historic character.

The local taxation system in the USA also permits some local incentives. In 1985, the State of Washington introduced a special valuation for rehabilitated historic properties (City of Seattle, 1990, p. 25). Prior to the passage of this new law, owners restoring historic buildings were subject to increased property taxes once improvements were made. This had the effect of discouraging the rehabilitation of some historically significant buildings. The new law provided for a ten-year special valuation for property tax purposes provided there had been substantial and approved rehabilitation. By 1990, twenty buildings in Seattle's Pioneer Square quarter had qualified for this special status.

Another form of funding is through a 'revolving fund' where a sum of money is dedicated for the particular purpose of historic preservation, conservation and revitalization. These revolving funds also offer the possibility of cross-subsidy from profitable to less profitable projects. In the USA, the first public revolving fund was created in 1972 in Seattle as part of the Historic Seattle Preservation and Development Authority for the revitalization of Pioneer Square. The fund was modelled after the private funds of Charleston and Savannah. Rather than using the fund for active involvement in rehabilitation, the fund was designed to acquire endangered or stagnating buildings temporarily. Many of the buildings did not even require purchase but could be obtained with an option. Buyers prepared to undertake sensitive restoration were then sought and their purchase money was put back into the fund to enable further acquisitions. Some funds are used to help fund rehabilitation. For example, the Lower Downtown Revolving Loan Fund (RLF) was established by the City of Denver in 1988 to stimulate the revitalization of its Lower Downtown. Its funds are used to provide gap funding to renovate and preserve buildings which are designated as 'contributing' to the Lower Downtown District. The RLF makes

---

[3] The system was revised in the 1981 Economic Recovery Act and again in the 1986 Tax Reform Act because of abuse in the system by large investors and developers (Murtagh, 1988, p. 212). The latest revision reduced the generosity of the tax credits. The immediate effect was that in 1987 the number of rehabilitation projects declined by 35 per cent (Cantacuzino, 1989, p. 10). The highest rate of tax credit is 20 per cent for 'historic' buildings which are listed on the National Register of Historic Places or are in a National Register district, provided that there is 'substantial' rehabilitation. There is also a 10 per cent credit for 'old but not historic' buildings more than forty years old.

low interest loans not grants and loan applicants must present evidence of repayment ability.

Area-based renewal

Economic value must be created at two scales: at the level of the individual building and collectively as buildings within an area. The rehabilitation and/or conversion of individual buildings in isolation may not make a significant difference to an area's economy. As previously noted, buildings are interdependent assets; the quality, condition, maintenance and management of neighbouring properties and the immediate environment has a direct effect on the value of any given building: 'The value of real estate comes primarily from the investments others have made: taxpayers, other property owners, employers. Take away a community's sidewalks, streets, sewage disposal system, waterplant, police protection, jobs, and people, and what is the value of any building? Virtually zero. The generation of economic value in real estate is largely external to the lot lines' (Rypkema, 1992, p. 210). This factor reinforces the need for a more comprehensive area-based approach to revitalization. As buildings are interdependent assets and although key initial and demonstration projects are important, historic quarters of cities should be considered collectively as areas. Thus, measures to improve the stock of property or the physical environment of a locality ought to be planned to occur on a comprehensive rather than a piecemeal basis.

Many area-based revitalization strategies inevitably have an approach which is based on property measures. These attempt to revive the economic fortunes of areas through enhancing the physical fabric and/or changing the stock of space in a particular location. They focus on unblocking supply-side constraints on land and property development in order to aid revitalization. The rationale is that growth can be stimulated by improvements in the supply of land, labour, capital and entrepreneurship (Solesbury, 1990): for example, by removing difficulties with respect to ownership, ground and site conditions, planning policy and infrastructure provision, and speeding up the process of land acquisition and assembly (Healey, 1991). In terms of the property itself, and in addition to procedural and institutional change, where the existing property offered in a location is not being fully utilized, a more suitable stock may need to be created as improvements to a given stock of property can reduce the effective price of utilization and therefore stimulate user demand. Thus, actions to remedy the property's image obsolescence or other – more substantial – dimensions of its obsolescence must be undertaken.

Property measures offer the potential to achieve visible results and symbolize a commitment to action, changing the appearance and/or enhancing the image of an area if nothing else. Since property plays an important part in bestowing a 'sense of place' upon cities and urban areas, mainly surface or external rehabilitations can be employed to improve or change the 'image' of the area. While poor physical environments may be authentic symptoms of deeper problems of low income and underinvestment, negative perceptions undermine and further weaken the area's economy and competitiveness, entraining a spiral of decline which may substantiate the negative image. Thus, it is argued, investment in the physical fabric will help break this vicious circle. By virtue of these physical actions, the intention is therefore to attract – indirectly – inward investment that will support existing businesses and residents (Figure 2.2). Conscious confidence building and the active promotion of positive external images are established techniques of this approach. However, unless supported by other more tangible economic impacts able to reinforce and substantiate the positive image, the 'boostered' image has a short 'half-life' after which even the initial physical improvements may not be sustained. This might result in a short-term physical revitalization that ultimately has little impact on the utilization of property in the locality. Alternatively, property measures might address the functional obsolescence of existing buildings, for example, a supply of buildings

Figure 2.2

Cast-iron-fronted building in TriBeCa, New York. Buildings that are derelict or in poor repair adversely affect the image of a location. Thus, many revitalization programmes initiate physical improvements to buildings to improve their image and restore confidence in the area.

able to accommodate the new demands of highly serviced computer-based offices would create demand by virtue of the incapacity of existing office buildings (see Duffy and Henney, 1989).

Property-led revitalization strategies are therefore intended either to *restore* confidence or *create* new confidence in an area's economy (see Solesbury, 1990). In each approach, demonstration and flagship projects are important, but the intention is to encourage comprehensive change in the area. The first approach is short term and concentrates on restoring confidence to stabilize or revitalize the competitive position of an urban area with a sound economy or one with the potential for endogenous/indigenous functional regeneration.

At the outset of a revitalization strategy, area-wide improvements can be the first step towards building confidence in an area. As its outlay can often be recouped through higher tax revenues, the public sector may often finance improvements to an historic quarter's public realm to demonstrate 'confidence' in the area. As Uhlman (1975, p. 6) states: 'Investment in the external environment is a reassuring symbol of confidence in the area by the public sector.' This has been the approach recently adopted in the LoDo quarter of Denver (see Chapter Six). In many cities in America, funds can be raised through the designation – by popular vote – of special assessment districts (SAAs) or business improvement districts (BIDs). All businesses in such districts pay a special levy which is used to fund environmental improvements within the area. For example, in Seattle, the City and the Pioneer Square community established a Parking and Business Improvement Area (PBIA) to provide funds for increased maintenance, amenities and promotional activities for Pioneer Square (City of Seattle, 1990, p. 1).

A policy in the UK that was extensively used in historic urban quarters was the designation of Industrial and Commercial Improvement Areas (IIAs and CIAs) introduced under the 1978 Inner Urban Areas Act. The effect of the designation enabled property owners in the area to receive a 50 per cent subsidy towards the cost of internal and external rehabilitation. However, the impact of the grant was diluted by the piecemeal – rather than comprehensive – nature of the grant giving mechanism. A similar project has been Nottingham's 'Operation Clean-Up ' which provided public sector money to help encourage private sector funds to improve the external appearance of buildings. This scheme was used extensively in the city's Lace Market quarter.

The second approach is longer term. Where the existing economy is in decline, this approach seeks to build new confidence through a deliberate functional diversification and/or restructuring. This involves conversions and adaptive reuse on a large scale. Areas of vacant land or structures that are obsolete for their original use often provide a convenient physical focus for action to bring about this functional diversification and restructuring by enabling different kinds of spaces to be provided to accommodate new economic activities and functions. This restructuring might be plan-led; by conversion or redevelopment a better stock of space is created which can be occupied by different activities: 'effectively creating demand by offering supply' (Solesbury, 1990, p. 193). There is an implicit assumption in this approach that property markets have an internal dynamic: the provision of new and refurbished property is not just a passive response to demand, but could stimulate demand by offering a better quality of supply or by meeting a previously unmet or latent demand for property.

Once a higher quality or more appropriate stock of space has been created following investment in either an area's buildings and/or its public realm, confidence in the quarter may be further demonstrated by the public sector. For example, various public sector agencies who have a choice might rent space in that particular area. This occurred in Seattle's Pioneer Square where, to encourage private-sector interest in renovated buildings, the city located governmental agencies in newly renovated buildings in Pioneer Square (Ford, 1994, p. 78). By occupying them for a three-year period, the city guaranteed some immediate return on the developer's investment and – at the same time – convinced them of the city's commitment to the area.

The limitations of property measures

The limitations of property development and property measures in revitalization must also be recognized. Property measures to improve the building stock might have a limited impact due to weaknesses in terms of user demand. Turok (1992, p. 376) notes that appropriate property development could and should provide the physical platform for a comprehensive programme intended to achieve all-round revitalization. However, a strong role for property measures will only be important in particular and limited circumstances. For example, areas where there are extensive problems due to land conditions and the fabric of buildings; where constraints to redevelopment are physical, institutional, and/or economic; where shortages of land and/or floorspace restrict inward investment and indigenous growth; and where the response of the private sector is either insufficient or inappropriate to users' needs (Turok, 1992, p. 377).

Turok (1992, p. 370) further suggests that the basic requirements for property measures to make a significant difference to the level of local economic activity are: that other conditions in the target area are opportune such as transport links and other infrastructure, for example, the area does not also have a terminal locational obsolescence; that property constraints exist in established locations; and that the economy itself is expanding. The competitive advantage of a locality can be enhanced by restrictive planning controls which reduce the competitive supply of land and property. Thus, the management of development pressures at city and regional level can support or hinder the success of local conservation pressures, particularly through the management of competing supplies of development land. To achieve this requires a strong and robust planning system and a buoyant local property market, otherwise investors may be deterred from investing in the city at all. In Glasgow, the housing-led revitalization of the Merchant City was aided by the city's planning authority's related policies which prohibited residential development on the city's periphery (CGDC, 1992).

The property-led revitalization of an historic quarter might also be limited by factors that do not relate to the stock of land and buildings. These relate to the area's locational obsolescence, such as: human resource issues, such as, education and training; the underlying competitiveness of local industries (including its technology, productivity, and innovative capacity); and investment in essential basic infra-structure, such as, transport and communication (Turok, 1992, p. 376). Hence physical renewal might be a necessary condition of revitalization but it is not a sufficient condition.

THE ECONOMIC REVITALIZATION OF HISTORIC URBAN QUARTERS

While it is important to increase the physical quality of the historic fabric, the concomitant necessity of purposeful utilization must also be recognized. Most (property-based) revitalization actions address the physical side of the mismatch between fabric and users but the utilization of that improved stock must also be considered. The physical revitalization of the properties in an area will help to increase confidence in an area, but the maintenance of that confidence requires an economic revitalization. Without economic improvements, physical improvements are unlikely to be maintained. Historic forms must be occupied by uses which will provide the sustained investment required to refurbish and maintain the buildings. Thus, a more sustainable revitalization demands a purposeful occupation of the properties. However, as the British experience of Enterprise Zones illustrates, attracting economic development to a particular location, even in relatively unfettered circumstances, is problematic. Hence it is doubly so where economic activity and development are required not only to create and retain employment but also to maintain and respect a valued environment.

While the stock of suitable property in a certain location can be improved, how can user demand for such property also be stimulated? Rypkema (1992, p. 210), in criticizing American preservation policies, notes that nearly every preservation incentive is directed at 'maintaining the supply of space in historic structures. Almost nothing is available to increase the demand for space within those buildings. Yet it is the increase in demand (or the reduction of competitive supply) that will ultimately increase the economic value of properties'. Arguably, however, as discussed previously, improving the quality of a given stock of property, thereby reducing the effective cost of utilization, can stimulate demand.

Historic areas of cities often suffer from a relative locational obsolescence that results in a low utilization because other areas have a greater competitive advantage. The competitive advantage may be the result of various factors, for example: lower labour costs; better access to skills in the labour force; better access to markets or raw materials; superior organization and production methods; better access to concentra-tions of related firms; the assets and abilities of embedded institutions; natural and manmade resources, including townscape and historic associations; etc. To remedy locational obsolescence and to restore the economic fortunes of an area requires the development of a competitive advantage for that location relative to other areas. In terms of the human activities within the building fabric, economic growth can arise from changes in occupation: for example, new uses or activities replacing the former ones; this results in a *functional restructuring*. Alternatively the existing uses may remain but operate more efficiently or profitably; this is a *functional regeneration*.

Functional regeneration entails maintaining and improving the competitiveness of the area's existing industrial/employment concentrations and agglomerations. There might also be a *functional diversification* – a more limited restructuring – which brings in new uses able to synchronize and support the quarter's existing economic base. In each case, the aim is to increase the effective demand for and utilization of space.

The distinction between the functional regeneration of the traditional activities of a locality and the functional restructuring of the area's economic base has important consequences for the character of the quarter. Restructuring entails changing the economic functions within the historic quarter. Thus, unless the buildings are empty, restructuring also entails the displacement of existing functions and users. This is the process known as gentrification. In all instances the mechanism is similar: building owners and other landlords seek to increase or maximize their profits by trying to attract higher value uses and/or tenants able to pay higher rents. The physical upgrading of areas inevitably – and perhaps purposefully – sets in motion a process of rising land values and rents. However, displacement is sometimes regarded as undesirable because part of an historic quarter's sense of place derives from its functional character. Although, it is most widely known in the residential sector where higher income residents displace lower income residents, it can happen in all sectors. As Ford (1994, p. 82) observes that the Vieux Carre in New Orleans 'has lost most of its local businesses and is now filling up with chain restaurants such as Benihana of Tokyo that have nothing to do with the traditional sense of place'.

Given the premium that is attached to employment uses many authorities try to resist gentrification and displacement that results in a loss of industrial and commercial floorspace by resisting the conversion of 'employment floorspace' to other uses. Zukin (1989, p. 3) notes how the conversion of industrial buildings to residential uses 'annihilates light manufacturing activity. Lofts that are converted to residential use can no longer be used as machine shops, printing plants, dress factories, or die-cutting operations. The residential conversion of manufacturing lofts confirms and symbolizes the death of an urban manufacturing centre'. However, if the original inhabitants and businesses are property owners rather than tenants, displacement is not necessarily wholly negative. Such owners can forego their allegiance or commitment to the area by realizing the value of their appreciating assets. These issues are discussed with reference to particular historic urban quarters in Chapters Five and Six.

Creating growth

Positive revitalization measures require the creation of growth either from 'within' or from 'without'. In either case, there are two distinct paths to increased competitiveness: 'the most important distinction being between raising the rate of exploitation of labour power (absolute surplus value) or seeking out superior technologies and organization (relative surplus value)' (Harvey, 1989b, p. 45). For example, during the 1980s, the clothing and textile firms in the Lace Market quarter of Nottingham underwent an internal restructuring. In the early 1980s they competed principally on price, by the late 1980s, through superior technology and organization, they competed principally on quality (see Crewe and Forster, 1993a; 1993b).

Growth from within involves local economic development focusing on increasing the (economic) advantages of the locality: addressing the area's locational obsolescence and the loss of competitiveness of local firms and businesses; encouraging an internal demand for space by making local firms more profitable and therefore able to invest in the physical fabric of the locality. Growth from within usually involves development of the area's existing economic base and the retention of existing employment. A key issue is the companies' and firms' locational inertia, commitment and allegiance to a locality. Some have extensive investment – whether capital or symbolic – within a locality which mitigates against relocation, while others actively seek the synergy of a milieu of innovation and the benefits from the agglomeration of nearby firms engaged in related operations.

If growth from within is not possible, the other source of growth is to attract external investment and demand for space – persuading, encouraging or allowing new activities to locate in the quarter. In some instances, subsidies and other incentives are offered to initial tenants until a critical mass of activities and a market is created in the area. After which it is hoped that the quarter will become an attractive place to invest in for particular activities and be sustainable without further subsidy. The effect of a number of individual (commercial or market) decisions to locate in the area can in aggregate result in the area's functional restructuring, for example, the change of New York's SoHo from an industrial area to a mixed-use area. In a plan-led restructuring, the appropriate type of space is created in order to attract users, as, for example in Glasgow's Merchant City; the supply stimulates demand rather than demand creating a supply. This entails addressing the physical deficiencies of the area's property stock but might also involve exploiting the (physical) advantages of the locality, for example, its scarcity or its historic fabric, associations and character for the purpose of tourism. Equally, the restructuring might be market- or demand-led; space is appropriated by the prospective user and converted to the required use. Such changes of use may or may not require a formal planning permission or consent, or – while technically illegal and despite code violations – the new uses might be 'tolerated', for example, artists' occupation of industrial buildings in SoHo.

The apparent imperative of attracting investment induces competition between cities and between areas within cities. Cities and areas within cities succeed or fail on their ability to compete. Harvey (1989b, pp. 45–50) states that this competition between cities occurs in any or all of four principal economic areas; an historic urban quarter needs to develop a competitive advantage in at least one of these ways. Although generally sceptical of competition, Harvey (1989b, p. 45) notes its short-term benefits: 'Heightened competition between urban regions, like heightened competition between firms, does not necessarily lead capitalism back to some comfortable equilibrium but can spark movements that push the system further away from it. Nevertheless, those urban regions that achieve a superior competitive position survive, at least in the short run, better than those who do not.' In this general competition for inward investment, there is usually extensive image building – both physical and perceptual – and marketing. As a result of flexibility of information systems and the speed and density of the transport network, firms and businesses are becoming entirely footloose in their choice of location. Suitable locations are increasingly being selected on the basis of access to either cheap or high quality labour. In the latter case of attracting high quality employees, the quality of the working and residential environment is very important; a major contributor to this quality is conservation. As historic areas have scarcity value, they make a unique contribution to the image and identity of the city. For general image promotion, the historic urban quarter may form a part of the attractive image, while for more specific tourist attraction, the historic urban quarter may provide a part of the attraction itself.

Harvey's four areas of competition are, first, that areas might compete for position as centres of production: for example, industries in particular areas may compete on the basis of superior technology and organization or on unit cost. The area's industrial structure will have a crucial effect on its ability to enhance its position in the international division of labour. Historic urban quarters which have principally competed in this way are discussed in Chapters Four and Six. Secondly, areas might compete for position as centres of consumption: for example, areas may compete for – largely individualized – mobile capital. The particular infrastructure of the quarter, including its built and natural environment, historic and cultural associations and sense of place will have a crucial impact on its success as a centre of consumption. Historic urban quarters which have principally competed in this way are discussed in Chapters Four and Five. Thirdly, areas might compete or bid for governmental redistributions. Thus, areas might compete for allocations of government funding related to certain designations, for example, as regional development zones. In Lowell, Massachusetts, the city authorities sought and received funding for the designation of a National Urban Heritage Park. At a smaller scale, virtually all of the quarters have received some form of public subsidies whether to the quarter as a whole or to individual buildings within the quarter. Fourthly, areas might compete for control and command functions: for example, those key functions which exert economic and political influence. However, competition in this realm is very difficult as it is 'an arena characterised by monopoly power that is hard to break' (Harvey, 1989b, p. 49). Edinburgh is attempting to gain a place as a financial centre and is enabling the conversion of houses in its New Town quarter.

CONCLUSION

Property development and rehabilitation is a necessary – but not a sufficient condition – of revitalization. Revitalization is more than just bricks and mortar; more than just real estate. As well as property measures, concern and efforts need to be directed towards the quarter's economic infrastructure and development, stimulating growth and encouraging greater utilization of the historic building stock. For investment to occur within a particular area or historic urban quarter, there must be a commercial rationale for that investment. Incentives and other public actions may frequently be an important factor or component of that desire to invest. In the absence of large-scale public subsidies, historic urban quarters need to establish and maintain their positions as centres of production and/or consumption; in particular they need to utilize and exploit their key resources: their historical fabric, associations and sense of place. Chapters Four, Five and Six of this book discuss these ideas through a number of case study examples.

3

RE-EVALUATION OF THE QUALITIES OF HISTORIC URBAN QUARTERS

INTRODUCTION

Many of the historic quarters featured in this book were rescued from comprehensive redevelopment and various road building schemes by designation as conservation or historic preservation areas. It is only since the 1960s that historic areas and quarters of cities have had a significant re-evaluation of their positive qualities. Similarly it is only relatively recently that there has been a widespread public consensus in favour of conservation. This consensus was initially reactionary; the public had had enough of the brutal change that was an intrinsic part of post-war policies of comprehensive redevelopment and inner-area road building. They desired familiar environments to be improved but kept intact. What is equally important was an official and professional 'desire' in favour of the conservation of historic buildings and areas, and the emergence of publicly sponsored, systematic attempts to preserve historic environments. The rise of the lobby for conservation and policies for preservation and conservation are related to the change from an orthodox Modernism to the various strands and types of postmodernism. Thus, the rise of conservation and the fall of the Modern Movement are inextricably linked. As Barnett (1982, p. 37) states: 'The historic preservation movement is the most important change to have occurred to architecture and urban design since the so-called Modern Movement, which can be considered its antithesis.'

This chapter will discuss the change from notions of comprehensive redevelopment and the total physical transformation of sites to conservation and urban designs that display greater concern and sympathy for the site's existing physical character, its sense of place, and historical and cultural associations. Two instances of preservation and conservation projects are discussed to illustrate different approaches: Seattle's Pioneer Square and The Pastures in Albany.

MODERNISM – A NEW AGE

Modernism[1] heralded and drew stimulus from the perception of the start of a new age – the Machine Age – the age of industrial production. Modernist ideals can be subsumed under the key idea of living up to the challenge of that new age. Their enthusiasm for the zeitgeist – the spirit of the age – was in part a reaction to nineteenth-century historicism. According to its key proponents 'modern architecture liberated us by freeing us from the dead weight of traditional styles. This freedom came at the price of new restrictions: historical references were forbidden and decoration was a crime' (Kolb, 1990, p. 87).

A sense of a radical break with the past was evident from the early Modern Movement. This represented much more than a mere aesthetic break: 'It constituted a moral crusade which required that all art should reflect the "spirit" of the industrial age' (Richards, 1994, p. 33). Thus, it sought to emphasize the differences with the past, rather than to acknowledge the continuities. Accordingly, the Modernists had a strong belief in progress and in the technological potential of the new age. Walter Gropius (from Kolb, 1990, p. 88) wrote: 'A breach has been made with the past, which allows us to envisage a new aspect of architecture corresponding to the technical civilization of the age we live in; the morphology of dead style has been destroyed; and we are returning to honesty of thought and feeling.' The imperative of technological progress required the bridging of what Giedion (1947, p. 146) would later term a 'schism' between nineteenth-century architecture and changing building technology. There was also a sincere and genuine belief that the social and human problems of the period were to a large extent the product of a false and deficient environment. Thus, one of the driving forces of Modernist culture was the idea of social transformation through architecture and technology.

For this book, perhaps the most critical strand of Modernist architectural thought was their attitude to the legacy of the past. 'Modernism was especially well defined in architecture and especially hostile to tradition and history' (Kolb, 1990, p. 3). The new architecture was expected to create new forms to meet the functional demands and challenges of the twentieth century. As Middleton (1983, p. 730) explains: 'Henry Ford is usually credited with the slogan "History is bunk" but the same sentiment was voiced by Walter Gropius at the Bauhaus . . . But this crude dismissal of the past was, equally, a matter of rhetoric rather than reality; polemics rather than practice.' Nevertheless that polemic was important in shaping attitudes and values.

MODERNIST URBAN SPACE AND FORM

Kolb (1990, p. 176) argues that: 'The Moderns oscillated between the total plan that rigidly controlled every aspect of the city, and the practice of making each building

[1] In presenting a critique of Modernist ideas in architecture, urban design and planning, we must concur with Charles Jencks. What we must inexorably write is 'a caricature, a polemic. The virtue of this genre (as well as its vice) is its license to cut through the large generalities with a certain abandon and enjoyment, overlooking all the exceptions and subtleties of the argument. Caricature is not the whole truth' (Jencks, 1977, p. 10).

an isolated monument with no regard for its neighbours.' It is useful therefore to discuss Modernist urban form and Modernist architecture separately. In terms of urban design and town planning, a number of contemporary problems and challenges characterized Modernist concepts of urban space design. Early Modernist planning was a reaction to the effect of the Industrial Revolution and the physical conditions of the nineteenth-century industrial cities with their squalor, congestion and overcrowding. The solution was generally agreed to be more light and air, through a prescription of decongestion, lower residential densities and the segregation of housing from industry and its pollution.

At the time, the concept of functional zoning had a strong appeal given the necessity to separate dirty, noxious heavy industries from residential development. The concept of zoning has its roots in nineteenth-century German thought and practice. It was also a fundamental part of the International Congress of Modern Architecture's (CIAM) *Charter of Athens*. CIAM was an architectural forum established in the 1920s by, among others, Le Corbusier, and *The Charter of Athens* – the report of its 1933 Congress – its best known treatise; although, inexplicably, it was not published until a decade later. The Congress theme was 'The Functional City'; this prescribed a rigid functional zoning of city plans with green belts between areas reserved for different functional uses. Functional zoning was viable because new forms of transport, including the motor car and the prospect of mass car ownership, would be able to tie the separated areas together. The car was a potent symbol of the potential drama and excitement of the new age: *The Charter of Athens* advocated the primacy of the motor car, while Le Corbusier's drawings of his Contemporary City show lovingly rendered images of roads full of cars. Special arrangements were also deemed necessary to segregate the vehicle from the pedestrian.

Modernists felt that contemporary cities were not responding radically enough to the challenges of the Modern Age; the magnitude of the problems suggested that 'great transformations are necessary' (*Charter of Athens*, from Conrads, 1964, p. 140). Furthermore, Modernist planners and architects argued that existing cities were ill-equipped to accommodate the motor car and other forms of mechanized transport; providing a further justification for the total physical transformation of the city. Little thought was given to making localized interventions to existing cities, instead there was to be comprehensive redevelopment. The past was seen as a hindrance to the future. The historic legacy of most cities was simply obsolete; an obstruction to attempts to build in a rational and functional manner to relieve the problems of the city. Le Corbusier's Plan Voisin for Paris, his attempt to adapt his ideal city plans to an existing city, involved the demolition of two square miles of central Paris (Figure 3.1).

Just as Modernists strove to create environments that provided healthier conditions than the slums of the industrial cities, they also strove to design buildings that would provide healthier internal conditions. *The Charter of Athens* called for: 'The key functions, housing, work and recreation develop inside built volumes subject to three imperious necessities: sufficient space, sun, ventilation' (from Conrads, 1964, p. 141). The best way to get more light and air was to build upwards where it was plentiful. The building form that readily exploited the new construction techniques and

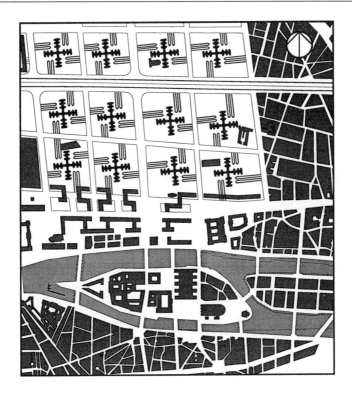

Figure 3.1

Figure–ground study redrawn from Le Corbusier's Plan Voisin for Paris. The dramatic disruption to the historic grain of the city is clearly evident.

materials was the skyscraper. The use of the skyscraper offered a totally new image to the city and the potential future of urban areas. As Summerson (1949, p. 191) said of Le Corbusier's Contemporary City: 'The park is not in the city, the city is in the park.' Architects became closely involved in research to determine the optimum design and distribution of building blocks on a site to maximize the egress of sun and daylight, and minimize overshadowing. As a result higher rise slabs and point blocks were favoured over low rise streets and terraces.

In combination with the concern for healthier internal conditions, was a concern for the functional requirements of the building. In terms of individual building design, there was an apparent misinterpretation of Louis Sullivan's maxim 'Form follows Function'. This had been intended as a reaction to the excesses of formalism, Sullivan arguing instead for a rational exploration of the problem at hand before devising a solution in built form using appropriate technology. However, it was interpreted in a too literal sense as the advocation of a mechanistic relationship between function and its formal expression. As interpreted it suggested the hegemony of the programme in determining a building's form. Furthermore, Le Corbusier (1927, p. 167) also prioritized the role of the internal functions in determining a building's external form: 'A building is like a soap bubble. This bubble is perfect and harmonious as if the breath has been evenly distributed from the inside. The exterior is the result of the interior.'

As a consequence many Modernist buildings appeared to have been designed responding only to their own programme and functional requirements and to the logical and defensible presuppositions of Modernist architecture: the importance of light, air, hygiene, aspect, prospect, recreation, movement, openness. Thus, buildings became sculptures or 'objects in space' following *primarily* their own internal logic rather than responding *primarily* to their urban context. This approach is notably less successful in established urban contexts than it is in greenfield sites, in parks or on large, cleared urban sites. This self-referential notion was in distinct contrast to the façade's traditional role of enclosing and defining urban space. The result of the interplay of these various factors was a new concept of urban space and urban form. Traditional, relatively low rise streets and squares were eschewed in favour of a rational – usually orthogonal – distribution of slab and point blocks, set in parkland and other open space. This was to be a free flowing urban space, with space flowing around buildings rather than being enclosed and contained by them.

MODERNIST PRACTICE

Although Modernist ideas of urban space design were largely formed prior to the Second World War, there was neither the opportunity nor the political will to develop them in practice on an appropriately large scale. That situation was to change after 1945, with the opportunity to build Modernist schemes on a large scale coming initially in the post-war reconstruction of blitzed cities in Britain, Germany, France and much of central and eastern Europe. The challenges of post-war reconstruction were evident and called for a large-scale public sector response. Post-war governments had to address public demands for full employment and the provision of decent housing, social facilities and welfare services, and generally to meet the challenge of building a better future. While approaches and conditions differed from country to country, the general tendency was to look to the wartime experience of mass production and planning as a means to undertake a major programme of reconstruction and reorganization. An important part of this was the reconstruction, re-shaping, and renewal of the urban fabric. The context for this was provided by the ideas of CIAM, Le Corbusier and others. However, as Harvey (1989a, p. 69) notes, it was less 'a controlling force of ideas over production than a theoretical framework and justification for what practical-minded engineers, politicians, builders, and developers were in many cases engaged upon out of sheer social, economic, and political necessity'. Reconstruction was soon followed by slum clearance programmes. Inevitably this necessitated the scaling down of the Utopian concept of the complete city to more localized interventions responding in part to the existing city. Nevertheless, although the existing town could not be demolished in its entirety, comprehensive redevelopment of large sites was the preferred mode rather than rehabilitation and refurbishment.

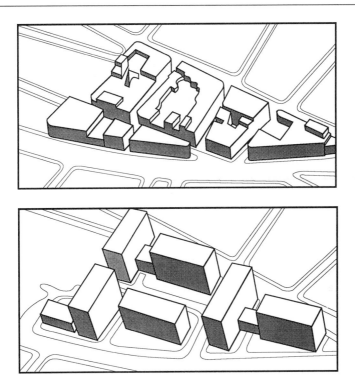

Figures 3.2 and 3.3

Diagrams illustrating the change in physical form as a result of redevelopment. Redevelopment offered significant physical improvements over the earlier urban form. Redevelopments of slab and tower blocks in large units with open planning permitted comprehensive and flexible planning; clear and efficient access and circulation; adequate parking; good daylighting and ventilation in all rooms; improved sound insulation; and open space on all sides (redrawn from original).

Reconstruction also yielded the opportunity to rebuild cities with better physical conditions. Such redevelopments ostensibly offered significant physical improvements over the earlier urban form. Many of the areas had become physically and functionally obsolete. Redevelopments of slab and tower blocks in large units with open planning permitted comprehensive and flexible planning; clear and efficient access and circulation; adequate parking; good daylighting and ventilation in all rooms; improved sound insulation; and open space on all sides (Figures 3.2 and 3.3). That many similar such improvements could be achieved through rehabilitation, refurbishment, selective clearance and infill development – with the additional bonus of greater public acceptance – had yet to be fully appreciated and explored.

The post-war attitudes to planning and physical intervention gained momentum in the 1950s and 1960s. The typical urban policy was for slum clearance and comprehensive redevelopment. Such policies were augmented by road building schemes. The major cause of change in the urban environment in the post-war period was increasing car ownership. Thus, a significant challenge of the age was the accommodation of the car within the city. Grand plans were made to fundamentally restructure cities to accommodate the demands of modern business which included making efficient access for cars.

With the introduction of sufficiently powerful planning legislation, after the Second World War, accommodating the car led to urban motorway schemes and other transport improvements through existing towns. In the 1950s and 1960s, as an increasingly affluent population moved further into the suburbs, inner-area road building schemes were proposed to meet the increasing need for access from the suburbs to the city centres. Ravetz (1985, p. 82) argues that, in essence, much of planning of the 1960s was planning for roads. Many authorities planned and built massive schemes, many of which were uncoordinated and/or left unfinished, or more piecemeal improvements which created more congestion (Ravetz, 1985, p. 83). It was these inner-area road building schemes rather than slum clearance which threatened the future of many of the historic quarters in this book. When planning new roads, it appeared logical to take them through the areas of the city which were obsolete and outmoded rather than through more modern areas. In Nottingham, for example, Maid Marian Way cut across the historic fabric of the city separating the castle from the historic market place (Figure 3.4). There was also a proposal to bring a trunk road through the centre of the city's historic Lace Market quarter.

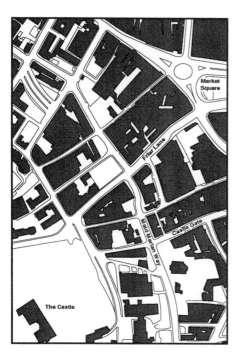 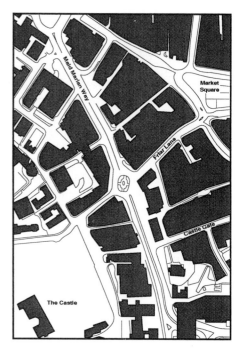

Figure 3.4

Figure–ground diagrams showing the urban grain before and after the construction of Maid Marian Way, Nottingham. The road cut across the historic fabric of the city separating the castle from the city's historic market place.

Comprehensive redevelopment and large road building schemes could be presented either as urban renewal of the worst kind or as a city's economic salvation: as the anonymous American infantry officer in Vietnam stated: 'we had to destroy that village to save it'. Although urban change on this scale was often a painful process, throughout most of the initial post-war period, the destruction of much of the social and cultural fabric of inner city areas and poorer, working-class residential areas was accepted without serious question. By the mid-1960s, however, the social effects of the destruction of urban neighbourhoods and cherished environments was becoming evident. Eventually there was frequent and increasingly widespread public protest.

Nevertheless, Harvey (1989a, p. 70) notes it would 'be both erroneous and unjust to depict these "Modernist" solutions to the dilemmas of postwar urban development and redevelopment as unalloyed failures'. In Europe, the war-torn cities had been rapidly reconstructed, and populations housed under much better conditions than had been the case in the inter-war years. In laying blame, however, Harvey is more critical of capitalism than of Modernism: 'It is completely wrong . . . to lay all the blame for the urban ills of postwar development at the Modern Movement's door, without regard to the political-economic tune to which postwar urbanization was dancing' (Harvey, 1989a, p. 71).

THE CONSERVATIONIST REACTION

From the early 1960s in both Europe and America, a reaction to large-scale comprehensive redevelopment and social disruption was under way. Books such as Jane Jacobs' *The Death and Life of Great American Cities* and Herbert Gans' *The Urban Villagers* 'cautioned practitioners to be more aware of the diverse, smaller-scale building blocks of planning and more appreciative of the beauty and functionalism of existing neighbourhood organization' (Birch and Roby, 1984, p. 200). Especially in America, Martin Anderson's *The Federal Bulldozer* (1964), provided planners with evidence of the failure of the clearance strategy: 'Documenting the high cost and slow progress of massive demolition, he called for scrapping the whole programme' (Birch and Roby, 1984, p. 200). Brown Morton III (1992, p. 40) graphically relates: 'The death rattle of so much of our cultural heritage, as bulldozers swept unchecked across the urban and rural landscapes, renewed public interest in American history and the sights, sounds, tastes, and activities of the past.'

Why had Modern Movement ideas of urban space and form gone so wrong? Comprehensive redevelopment and large-scale clearance and road building schemes were the visible problems, but there was also a loss of urban vitality caused to a large part by a deliberate and planned functional zoning of cities and urban areas. While the process of redevelopment was highly disruptive to small firms and businesses, the product was also fatally flawed. Large, relatively simple blocks inevitably simplified the land use pattern removing the 'nooks and crannies' that could house the economically marginal but socially desirable uses and activities that gave life and variety to an area. Such developments also disrupted historical patterns of settlement and communication. The subtitle of

Jacobs' (1961) seminal book, *The Death and Life of Great American Cities: The Failure of Town Planning*, was particularly apt. Jacobs argued that a range of different building types and ages, with their variety of renting profiles, was vital to the life of urban areas.

There were – and have been – many critics of a rigid zoning approach. Jacobs (1961) argued that a great part of the success of neighbourhoods depended on the overlapping and interweaving of activities and areas. Alexander (1965) in his seminal essay 'A City is Not A Tree' argued the merits of a 'semi-lattice' over a 'tree' structure for a city: tree-like structures led to rigid separations but semi-lattices contained complex overlappings, mergings and fusings together. More recently, Leon Krier (1984) criticized the 'over-concentration' of single uses. 'The principal modern building types and planning models such as the Skyscraper, the Groundscraper, the Central Business District, the Commercial Strip, the Office Park, the Residential Suburb, etc. are invariably horizontal or vertical over-concentrations of single uses in one urban zone, in one building programme, or under one roof' (Krier, 1984). Krier contrasts this with the 'good city' in which 'the totality of urban functions' is provided for within 'compatible and pleasant walking distance'.

The contemporary or 'post-industrial' cities of the West have been shedding certain functions and acquiring others. The pre-industrial city was the centre for services for the agrarian society – the primary sector. The industrial city was dominated and structured by the secondary sector and the services for it. The post-industrial city is mainly the centre for the tertiary sector providing services for itself and for other areas of the world where industry has relocated. It is also inventing new tertiary activities. Thus, as the tertiary sector lends itself to mixed use; the city form advocated by Modernists to isolate undesirable industry has become redundant.

A mixture of uses also reduces the need for transportation between the various zones. Nevertheless, while inner ring roads were stopped, the amount of traffic has continued to increase and now saturates the old street systems of European cities. Within city centres, it has taken a long time to realize that combined with the appropriate integration of transport and land use policies, policies such as pedestrianization and traffic-calming techniques can more satisfactorily accommodate the motor car in urban areas. The contemporary attitude is to accommodate the car, while giving priority to the comfort and convenience of the pedestrian. Increasingly cities are also examining ways of reintroducing public transport.

With the advent of an increasingly global economy and the restructuring of international capitalism, the period from the early 1970s saw further deindustrialization in many western cities. Furthermore, the 1973 oil crisis changed perceptions about the use of scarce resources ushering in a greater concern for resource management, including the resource of the manmade environment. The pace and rate of the suburban expansion of cities was checked. Ultimately, the more-conservationist attitude led to the demise of comprehensive redevelopment as official planning policy, heralding an historic break and the transition to postmodern ideas of planning and urban form.

POSTMODERN REACTIONS

Until the Industrial Revolution, and except when natural forces or war wreacked wholesale destruction, change in the urban fabric was slow. This enabled successive generations to derive a sense of continuity and stability from their physical surroundings. Nevertheless, there have been highly disruptive events in the gradual evolution of cities. One of these was the Industrial Revolution, occurring in European cities in the nineteenth and early twentieth centuries. Another was the Modernist reaction to the Industrial Revolution, occurring in European and American cities after the Second World War. In each case there was a dramatic acceleration in the pace and physical scale of the cycle of demolition and renewal. As Ashworth and Tunbridge (1990, p. 1) describe: 'A generation's concentration on the almost overwhelming needs for new housing, new industry and new infrastructure had led to an abrupt break in the centuries-long evolution of the physical fabric of cities. The past and its values had been rejected in favour of a "brave new world" whose creation threatened to destroy all trace of preceding architectural achievement.'

There were two principal and related reactions to this situation: firstly, a new awareness of the qualities and scale of the 'traditional city'. Secondly, there was a desire to keep existing and familiar environments intact. Jane Jacobs (1961) was among the first to highlight the social virtues of streets and other traditional urban forms over environments designed in accordance with Modernist principles.

The design of postmodern urban space

Most postmodern urban space design is strongly informed by a reaction to Modernism's stance on history and tradition and by a greater appreciation of traditional urban processes and precedents. The reaction is generally informed by a new consideration of the qualities and scale of the 'traditional' city. For influence, many urban design theorists and practitioners returned to images of the period of urban evolution prior to the Industrial Revolution, usually the eighteenth century – a period known in Europe as the Urban Renaissance, when streets and squares first began to be paved. The influence can be to varying degrees 'ironic' or 'earnest'. Irony, according to Charles Jencks (1986) is 'the most prevalent aspect of Post-Modernism.'

Among the first to produce a coherent critique of Modernist theories of urban space were Colin Rowe and Fred Koetter, first in the *Architectural Review* (1975) and then subsequently in book form, *The Collage City* (1978). Rowe and Koetter (1978, pp. 50–85) described the spatial predicament of the Modernist city as being one of 'objects' and 'texture'. Their object is the sculptural building standing freely in space, while the texture is the background, continuous matrix of built form that provides the definition of that space by establishing the street corridor or the wall to a square. Rowe and Koetter did not advocate a preference either for buildings in space or spaces enclosed by buildings but for the two together; a dialectic of mass and space where 'buildings *and* spaces exist in an equality of

Figures 3.5

Artist's impression of a 1943 proposal for the reconstruction of the Jewellery Quarter in Birmingham as a series of flatted factories within formal gardens.

sustained debate' (Rowe and Koetter, 1978, p. 83). Such debate gives 'the apparent virtues of the traditional city: the solid and continuous matrix or texture giving energy to its reciprocal condition, the specific space; the ensuing squares and streets . . . [provide] . . . some condition of legible structure' (Rowe and Koetter, 1978, pp. 62–63).

What many individual Modernist buildings and developments lacked was a positive response to the external – and often historic – context. Where all buildings are all objects in space, there is no texture to define that space. With an increasing aggregation of individual self-referential developments, a city gradually loses its spatial coherence; becoming a 'jumble' of competing or isolated monuments and small complexes of buildings surrounded by roads.

The contemporary challenge has therefore been to restore the spatial discipline of the street and square. Thus, within the criticism of Modernism starting from Rowe and Koetter's work, there has been a resurgence of interest in the traditional city: the city of the street, square and urban block, the qualities and scale of which made the distinction between object and texture very clear. This has resulted in a change in the preferred physical form of urban space. Higher rise slab and point blocks have been rejected as models of desirable urban form in favour of low rise urban blocks defining streets and squares. This change from a Modernist to a postmodernist conception of desirable urban form is vividly illustrated by comparing a plan for the redevelopment of Birmingham's Jewellery Quarter made in 1943 with one made in 1990 (Figures 3.5 and 3.6).

As previously stated, the predominant influence on many current urban theorists is – to a greater or lesser degree – historicism. Cross (from Gosling and Maitland, 1984), for example, states: 'In contrast to the prevailing circumstances in which armies of specialists might surround themselves with data and labour for years to organise the typical chaos of a modern city, it seemed there should be a

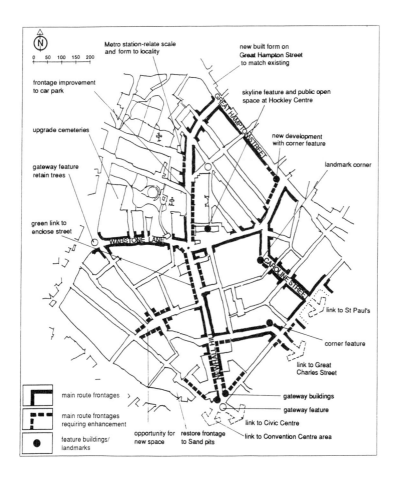

Figure 3.6

In contrast to Figure 3.5, a proposed urban design framework for the same area from the 1990 *Birmingham City Centre Design Strategy*. The 1990 proposal illustrates an 'urban healing' approach.

return to the use of traditional systems and paradigms. With a rediscovered understanding of these systems it might be quickly possible to propose new cities, or more believably, interventions within old cities.' This view parallels that of the New Rationalists, a movement initiated by the publication of Aldo Rossi's *The Architecture of the City* (1982). As a movement, it drew inspiration from the city as a historical fact – the city as an artefact. It saw no radical break with the past which the Modern Movement sought to prove, but rather postulated the continual transformation of tradition and an autonomous architecture responding to its own 'typological' laws of streets, squares and city blocks. Thus, according to Maitland (1984, p. 5): 'The city in history . . . provides the themes and inspiration for contemporary action, but in novel and unpredictable ways.'

The most straightforward source of such durable forms is the city itself. Rather than regarding it as a blank site for the construction of solutions to urban problems, it can be seen as a species of viable organisms which have already defined the generic type-solutions available to use and which need not be re-invented but only reapplied. In the case of the city, the type-solutions include the quarter, the block and a variety of urban-space types such as streets, avenues, squares, arcades and colonnades. An example of these is Rob Krier's collection of squares as illustrated in his book *Urban Space* (1979). This is a formal approach to city design – based on images and ideas of urban form rather than economic and social arguments. Appleyard (1979, p. 21) criticizes this approach which inspires urban designs that look like eighteenth- and nineteenth-century cities, but 'does not involve much analysis beyond classification'. He suggests that what is lacking 'seems to be any great concern with the relationship between the physical form of the city, everyday life, and the actual inhabitants' (Appleyard, 1979, p. 22). Similarly MacCormac (1984, p. 46) comments on this interest: 'in the formal structures of urbanism, rather than the way in which those structures can be brought alive by activities, and make places'.

Many, however, are sceptical of an overly historicist approach: Read (1982), for example, warns: 'We are now far enough removed from the ideal concepts [of the Modern Movement] to recognise their limitations, and also to recognise that the problems which the reformers did address, however limited, were real problems. While it may be reasonable now to reject the forms which they evolved in their response to the problems of the industrial city, those problems will not be removed simply by looking further back to the pre-industrial city.' In this respect, it is appropriate to question how far the traditional city is an appropriate precedent since it did not have to contend with contemporary developments such as widespread car ownership and modern construction techniques which – for all its other apparent failings – the Modernist's Functional City took on. The Modernists had tried to derive efficient and rational urban form *de novo* from first principles of function and according to a particular vision of society. Ultimately, that social vision and the form was too simplistic and reductionist. Postmodernists have accepted traditional urban forms as the result of an historical evolution. However, by largely stopping prior to the Industrial Revolution and by ignoring the two hundred years of subsequent technological developments, their remedial and romantic images of the traditional city are often also reductionist, over-simplifications of contemporary urban living.

Equally, although much of the current urban design polemic is concerned with the physical significance of traditional urban spatial arrangements and urban forms, it is more than the spatial definition of the public realm which is important. Contemporary urban design is about place making, enhancing the public realm of cities and making urban environments people-friendly. However, it is important to appreciate that the public realm is both a physical *and* a social construct. Not only is a spatially defined physical public realm required, but that public realm needs to be animated by people: spaces become places through their use by people. This issue will be discussed further in Chapter Eight.

Conservation and rehabilitation

Arguably more important than the design of new urban spaces that drew lessons from traditional urban spaces, was a concern for the preservation and conservation of existing environments. The first wave of preservation policies was intended to protect individual buildings and structures. In many countries, policies to protect monuments, individual buildings and other structures had their origins in the nineteenth century. Such protection was largely piecemeal and *ad hoc*. The first comprehensive attempt to record and protect occupied historic buildings came in the UK during the Second World War. The 1944 Town and Country Planning Act introduced the concept of lists of historic buildings. The 1947 Town and Country Planning Act altered the Ministry's power to compile lists into a statutory duty; owners were given no right of appeal against listing and no compensation was payable for listing. The act of listing gave statutory protection to buildings of historic or architectural interest.[2] Although it was soon evident that the protection of individual buildings was not sufficient, it is a curiosity in the UK that it took more than twenty years to progress to the protection of areas.

By the 1960s, the value of traditional environments was increasingly being recognized in contrast to – and as a reaction against – Modernist environments. In particular, there was a recognition of the qualities of the built environment, its cultural and historic attributes. This led to a strong conservationist lobby, initially – by force of circumstance – defensive, reactionary and obstructive to change. In parallel, within housing areas there was a growing interest in rehabilitation rather than demolition. There were also economic arguments put forward in favour of rehabilitation and repair in housing instead of demolition and new build. This was expressed in planning policy in the UK by the introduction of General Improvement Areas in 1968 and Housing Action Areas in 1974. The housing in such areas was protected even if it did not have intrinsic aesthetic qualities, because it made economic and social sense. In the private sector, throughout the 1960s and 1970s, the qualities of older housing were recognized in a wave of rehabilitation and gentrification of inner urban areas that had escaped the bulldozer. This interest soon began to spread to more commercial areas.

As stated in Chapter One, the emergence of area-based conservation policies occurred in most developed countries during the 1960s. In terms of area-based conservation in the UK, the 1963 Buchanan report *Traffic in Towns* was of early significance. Although the author saw the report as an invitation to debate the issue of traffic and the environment, it was widely seen as a recipe for urban destruction in favour of the motor car (Tarn, 1985, p. 256). Following the report, there was increased awareness of the threat to the historic cores of towns and cities. In 1966, a further government report *Historic Towns and the Planning Process* prepared the ground for what were to become conservation areas, while, in 1967, a report by the Ministry of Housing and Local Government, *Preservation and Change* advocated

---

[2] By the completion of the first survey in 1969, there were almost 120 000 buildings which had been given statutory protection (Ross, 1991, p. 24). Currently nearly 500 000 buildings are listed.

concern for 'the whole physical composition of areas'. It also emphasized that the preservation of an area of architectural or historic interest should be compatible with change. In the same year, a Private Member's Bill, supported by the government, eventually became the Civic Amenities Act. This Act formally introduced the conservation area concept. As control over demolition is a prerequisite of effective preservation, one of the main advantages of conservation area status, was that from the early 1970s planning consent was required for the demolition of all buildings within the area.[3]

In the USA, area-based preservation policies had existed prior to the Second World War. In 1931, the city of Charleston, South Carolina, had created a protective zoning for a quarter of the city called The Battery. The designation of The Battery as an 'Old and Historic District' restricted – to an unprecedented level – the changes that private owners could make to their own properties. As Murtagh (1992, p. 51) has observed this established 'non-museum environments' as legitimate preservation concerns. At the federal level, however, the most significant event in the move toward historic preservation areas was the publication in 1966 of a powerfully eloquent manifesto *With Heritage So Rich* by the US Conference of Mayors and the National Trust for Historic Preservation: Cullingworth (1992, p. 67) describes it as 'cogently argued, dramatically illustrated and persuasive'. In the same year, the National Historic Preservation Act was enacted, simultaneously creating the National Advisory Council on Historic Preservation and the National Register of Historic Places.

Among the earliest successful preservation schemes were large building complexes where ownership was concentrated into a relatively few hands. These were building complexes rather than areas, for example, Ghirardhelli Square, San Francisco. The first phase of this project was opened to the public in 1964, with the nearby Cannery – a complex of renovated red-brick cannery buildings – opening in 1968. Ghirardhelli Square was significantly different from suburban shopping centres in terms of both design and location. The complex was a set of industrial buildings – a chocolate factory, a mustard factory, a woollen mill, and a rebuilt box factory – linked by a number of courtyards. As Ford (1994, p. 114) states 'the spaces in the complex were more like a mysterious medieval city than a standard shopping centre'. Festival shopping centres of this nature based on an element of historic preservation followed at, for example, Quincy Market, Boston in the late 1970s (Figures 1.7; 7.3). Slightly later was London's Covent Garden market buildings, completed in 1980 (Figure 1.3).

CASE STUDIES

Despite both the popular and professional consensus in favour of preservation and conservation, the implementation of enhancement and revitalization schemes for areas has rarely been unqualified successes. The following section describes the

[3] Prior to the early 1990s, only listed buildings had this protection; demolition was not regarded as development and therefore did not need planning permission. It was not until 1991 that all demolition in the UK – whether in a conservation area or not – required planning permission.

contrasting experiences of revitalization programmes which focused on areas rather than building complexes in two American cities: Seattle and Albany. These case studies illustrate the greater complexity of problems caused by the change from the Modernist approach of clearance and redevelopment.

PIONEER SQUARE, SEATTLE, WASHINGTON

According to the then Mayor of Seattle, Wes Uhlman (1976, p. 5), in the historic quarter around Pioneer Square there was a conscious choice made between demolition and renovation: 'Seattle chose the second alternative, not only because it was economically smarter, but because there was a psychological and spiritual benefit to it as well. The resurrection of Pioneer Square reminded residents of the proud heritage of the city and proved that the same kind of spirit and commitment could live today in Seattle.' The subsequent preservation and conservation of the Pioneer Square quarter in Seattle has been relatively successful. Pioneer Square, a twenty-five block area on the southern edge of Seattle's CBD, was largely rebuilt in a five-year period following the disastrous fire of 1889 which destroyed the core of the downtown area (Figure 3.7). This concentrated period of rebuilding gave the quarter a distinctive architectural homogeneity.

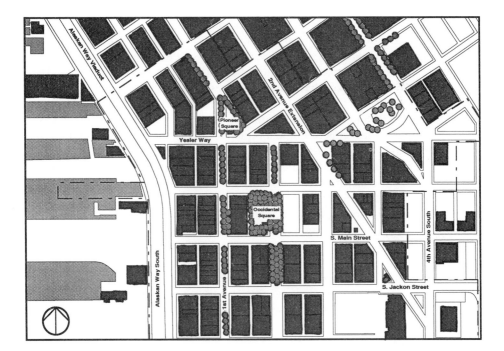

Figure 3.7

Plan of Pioneer Square. This illustrates the core of the quarter. The historic district designation extends along 1st Avenue and to the Kingdome to the south.

Pioneer Square enjoyed its heyday during the Klondike Gold Rush, but throughout the twentieth century, the CBD of Seattle has gradually migrated inland away from Pioneer Square. By the early 1960s, the Pioneer Square quarter had declined, becoming a classic example of Ford's 'zone of discard' (Ford, 1994). Plans were afoot to demolish much of the area to clear the way for speculative development which would have eliminated 75 per cent of the historic structure (Skolnik, 1976, p. 15). The classic problems created by blight – official obsolescence – and the subsequent redlining and avoidance became evident. The number of businesses and residents was plummeting as offices moved to the nearby CBD and hotels were closed for safety violations. The lack of availability of loans for maintenance and mortgages effectively deterred any interest in renovation. In addition, the twenty-five block area accounted for over 15 per cent of the city's crime, further contributing to its poor image as a business location.

Nevertheless as a direct consequence of this blight, the price of unrenovated office buildings in Pioneer Square dropped so low that by the mid-1960s private investors were able to acquire whole buildings very cheaply. Inspired by increasing interest and accounts of successful historic preservation projects, a few architects began to express interest in the Pioneer Square area and to acquire and renovate buildings. The low acquisition costs meant that, even after rehabilitation, space could be made available cheaply (see Black, 1976, for a fuller account). These architects were motivated not only by preservation but also by the opportunity to demonstrate their renovation skills with a showcase office (Ford, 1994, p. 76).

Public awareness of the historic character of Pioneer Square was also stimulated by the 'Seattle Underground Tours' through the quarter's 'areaways'. When the area was rebuilt in the late nineteenth century, its street levels were raised. The areaways are the useable areas constructed beneath the new pavements. Approximately half the pavements in Pioneer Square have these features.

As noted earlier, in the late 1960s, enthusiasm for urban renewal through comprehensive redevelopment waned and interest in historic preservation increased. As a consequence, the status of Pioneer Square changed. In 1971, the City of Seattle removed the threat of possible clearance schemes by declaring the area an historic district; the first legislation of its type in the state of Washington (Black, 1976, p. 21). This ordinance was vital in preserving what was left of the area's historic fabric and preventing the area from being turned into a massive parking lot; buildings of significance could no longer be torn down by slum landlords faced by the need for repairs. The ordinance also established an architectural review board. Any actions that would result in a change in the exterior appearance of the district's building had to be approved in advance by the board. During consideration of the ordinance 'the usual cries were made by the business community that the law would preserve blight and restrict property development and the growth of the downtown area' (Skolnik, 1976, p. 15). However, the protective ordinance protects the composite value of property in an area. Chapman (1976, p. 10) observed how such ordinances helped 'the business community by assuring investors that a tasteful restoration at one site will not be exploited and degraded by a fast-buck development next door . . . control puts a premium on early redevelopment, making sound restrained restoration an inevitability and rewarding the owners who pioneer in a historic district by letting them accrue the greatest proportional increases in the appreciated property values'.

By the early 1970s, as a consequence of the security of the historic district ordinance, banks were more willing to lend money within the area. In 1973, the preservation district was enlarged – almost doubling the size of the area – and additional controls over land use in the quarter were created. In 1974, to stop demolition by neglect, a 'minimum maintenance ordinance' was passed. This allowed the building department to issue a work order when a building deteriorated to the point that safety or preservation was endangered. This was the second such ordinance in the USA; the first affected the Vieux Carre in New Orleans.

The initial actions in the quarter had for the greater part been led by the private sector and focused on single buildings. To ensure that Pioneer Square's infrastructure was upgraded and adequately maintained and to coordinate various city depart-ments, such as water, lighting and engineering, a district manager was appointed. As Arthur Skolnik (1976), the first district manager, states: 'It was city policy not to compete with the private sector in Pioneer Square but to look after its own concerns: streets, sidewalks, the areas that needed public improvement' (Skolnik, 1976, p. 15). The public sector actions were therefore area-based and the city authorities undertook various improvements to the physical public realm of the quarter. Streets were repaved and two new federally funded city parks were created in the quarter:

Figure 3.8

Pioneer Square, Seattle. Part of the initial physical improvements to the quarter, this small cobblestoned urban park adds significantly to the amenities of the district.

Occidental Square and Pioneer Square (Figure 3.8). Both were small cobblestoned urban parks that added significantly to the amenities of the district. Another federal grant made it possible to create a tree-lined pedestrian mall complete with outdoor restaurants and cafés along Occidental Street. The Mall has become the setting for activities that had not initially been expected, for example, artists displaying and selling their works. A median strip of sycamore trees was also planted down the centre of the quarter's main street and architectural corridor, First Avenue. This decision was implemented despite the objections of the city's highway engineers 'who were aghast at the idea of downgrading an arterial road to a non-arterial road' (Ford, 1994, pp. 7–8).

Once sufficiently convinced that Pioneer Square was worth rehabilitating, the City's Building Department began to interpret codes more flexibly (Ford, 1994, p. 79). Old buildings did not have to be brought fully up to code standard; they only needed to be safe. This policy helped reduce the effect of the legal obsolescence of buildings, giving them a new lease of life. A policy of gradual improvement was deemed to be more effective in making buildings safer than inflexible code requirements that led to a total lack of investment and sometimes abandonment. They also sought to work with – instead of against – owners interested in renovation. For example, owners were encouraged to work together by renovating several buildings at once in order to share structural support and fire stairs and exits. By the late 1970s, eighty buildings had been renovated, and rents were rising (Ford, 1994, p. 79).

There was also a deliberate policy of linking the various downtown zones by careful planning. To increase the accessibility of Pioneer Square, a 'Magic Carpet Ride' – a free bus service – was provided throughout the downtown to encourage CBD workers to go to Pioneer Square for lunch or for bookstore browsing during the day. A further boost to the revitalization of Pioneer Square in the mid-1970s was the development of the Kingdome – a huge sports stadium used for professional football, baseball and basketball. The Kingdome was built in a former railroad and industrial area immediately to the south of the historic district. As Ford (1994, p. 92) describes: 'Fans could easily have lunch in Pioneer Square, see a game, and then return to Pioneer Square for dinner and music. A symbiotic relationship was developed between sports and skid row which, by encouraging people to come early and stay after the game, helped alleviate traffic snarls.'

By the mid-1970s, the economic fortunes of the area were also improving. Employment in the district increased from 1 000 in 1970 to over 6 000 in 1976, with more than a 1 000 created by the rehabilitation process itself, many of them low-skilled jobs going to existing residents of the district: 'Tax assessments had increased by 450 percent in three years as buildings became fully occupied, while the overall tax base of the district (including sales tax) increased by 1 000 percent. More than 150 new businesses located in Pioneer Square, 75 percent of them from out-of-town, thus aiding the sluggish economy of Seattle in the early 1970s' (Ford, 1994, p. 79).

The area suffered from a wavering economy in the 1980s and, until the early 1990s, there had been few further public improvements. Since the early 1990s, the City of Seattle has set about picking up the revitalization momentum through repairs to the existing public realm and a series of new physical and environmental improvements to enhance the area's image and identity (City of Seattle, 1990). In a new package of measures, there is a set of 'Image Building Guidelines' to standardize the elements that reinforce the special character of the district, for example, street furniture, bollards, lighting standards, paving schemes including the treatment of particular road intersections, and the redesign of signage within the district. There is also a series of 'Gateway Guidelines' focusing on six important gateways to celebrate the sense of entry into the Historic District. There are also policies to increase and diversify the quarter's housing opportunities.

THE PASTURES, ALBANY, NEW YORK

Despite the experience of Seattle, many well-intentioned revitalizations have floundered. The Pastures, in Albany, New York, provides an example of where area-based preservation and revitalization was misconceived and disastrously implemented (account from Gratz, 1989, pp. 255–256). In the early 1970s, the city of Albany sought to conserve and 'revitalize' the area. One of the city's oldest neighbourhoods, The Pastures is located at the southern end of the downtown, not far from the Hudson River; the waterway that helped create Albany's nineteenth-century commercial prosperity. The Pastures is a thirteen-square-block historic district of mixed residential and commercial character.

In the 1950s and 1960s, though in decline and by 'urban-renewal' standards a 'slum', the quarter remained socially and racially integrated. By the 1970s, however, the quarter was in great need of improvement. Given the new interest in preservation and the recognition of its architectural value and historic character, the Albany urban-renewal agency set out to preserve and revitalize the area. The city's intention was to interest a single developer in rehabilitating the entire neighbourhood, and its first action was to acquire all the land and buildings. To facilitate a comprehensive revitalization of the area, it relocated every family and business out of the area. When the neighbourhood was empty, selective demolition of the shopping strip began. Nearly half of the buildings in the district, deemed by the city to be 'insignificant', were bulldozed. The surviving buildings were mothballed without heating and with their windows boarded up. To fill in the now-empty lots where older-style historic houses once stood, the City made plans to build copies of the remaining houses. As Gratz (1989, p. 255) concludes: 'Physically, the neighbourhood was only partially bulldozed, but economically and socially it was killed completely just as surely as if it had been fully demolished.'

The Pastures area was effectively further blighted by the approach to revitalization adopted. By seeking a more comprehensive approach, rather than a more piecemeal approach of renting or selling properties to individuals who might rehabilitate and reuse them, the City's urban renewal agency effectively let The Pastures sit in desolation. By 1980, the only change was further deterioration of the quarter's vacant buildings. Their lack of use virtually guaranteed decay, while some buildings were destroyed by arson. By then the urban renewal agency was no longer looking for one developer for the entire neighbourhood, but it was still rejecting individuals. Instead developers were being sought who were willing to do one block or a few blocks at a time.

According to Gratz (1989, p. 256), it is difficult to discern the difference between those buildings which have been restored and those newly built to look old. 'The area looks more like a sanitized suburban enclave – plenty of parking opportunities included – than an urban neighbourhood. Pedestrians are few. Whatever character of place had evolved over time out of the indigenous social and economic mix had been 'preserved' out of existence.' This kind of 'preservation' is as destructive as comprehensive redevelopment. Even if the city had succeeded in finding a developer and salvaging the project before the weather irretrievably damaged the surviving buildings, the 'new' Pastures would bear little resemblance to the older organic neighbourhood. As Gratz (1989, pp. 255–256) laments: 'The real place ceased to exist when its last resident was trundled off to a distant housing project. The best that could be hoped for was the survival of shells of a few historic buildings dotted around in a landscape of parking lots and infill houses.'

CONCLUSION

Whereas the internationalism of Modernism sought to make everywhere the same, postmodernism has sought inspiration from the local and the particular. As Maitland (1984, p. 5) states: 'Where the context provides some very clear historical morphology, the new project may derive its authority from its respect of that fact.' Accordingly an emphasis on the local and historic context has been paramount, with a greater respect for the uniqueness of the place and its history, and greater concerns for the continuity of its traditions. For historic areas, the first step must be to recognize its value and a desire to preserve it. Increasingly, urban renewal and redevelopment takes the form of a mixture of old and new, for economic, cultural and aesthetic reasons. Alexander *et al.* (1987) argue that every increment of development should be an attempt to 'heal' or make 'whole' the city. This is an organic approach which stresses continuities rather than ruptures: the way in which most traditional cities grew. Kolb (1990, p. 179) describes it as a 'process of planning by incremental rereading'. The healing approach includes the restoration of the traditional urban forms in terms of identifiable urban spaces and the reconstitution of fragments and lost spaces to form a coherent whole. By utilizing a policy of incremental and infill development, rather than comprehensive redevelopment, existing communities, their environments and social fabric can be kept intact.

However, in many countries, in particular the UK, there is criticism that the conservationist reaction has gone too far. As Tarn describes:

> the development of a vigorous conservation lobby has not only led to articulate criticisms of previous policies but to policies of retrenchment that are stultifying. In a sense the wheel has come full circle and the vigour of renewal has been replaced by the abject reticence of an age no longer capable of believing in itself. There are obvious merits in a more sensitive appraisal of our inheritance, but there are many concerns about using this evaluation of our past heritage as a means of dictating all aspects of the future well-being of towns and cities (Tarn, 1985, p. 249).

Similarly Barnett (1982, p. 53) observes: 'a preservation neurosis, which constructs a rationale for preserving everything'. Some of this is a resistance to the increased emphasis on market forces, whereby the additional strictures of preservation and conservation policies are used to bolster normal planning controls and reasserting 'some local control over redevelopment, challenging the power held by the initiators of development' (Barrett, 1993, p. 436).[4] In the USA, the situation is somewhat different: 'the newly perceived heritage resource is generally in short supply and the planning problem typically becomes that of restraining over-commercialization' (Ashworth and Tunbridge, 1990, p. 17). If the architectural heritage existed in a fixed quantity that could be identified using obvious and intrinsic norms, then little judgement would be required. However, no such immutable stock exists. What is and should be preserved is always a value judgement and an expression of the values of a given period in time. During periods of insecurity and faltering confidence, values take refuge in the security of the past. Most of the early twentieth century was confident and bold, but – unfortunately – mistaken in its confidence.

What is evident in the examples of Pioneer Square and The Pastures is the importance of the management – or even the lack of management – of the conservation and revitalization of historic urban quarters. Initially simple preservation was a 'success'. However, increasingly, as discussed in Chapter Two, it is the economic revitalization of the historic quarter that becomes the important yardstick. The guiding principle, it will be argued, should be the exploitation of opportunities within an overall framework of principles. The next three chapters will describe and discuss the varying experiences of revitalization processes in a number of historic urban quarters.

[4] For example, in the UK, prior to the 1967 Civic Amenities Act, it was estimated that there would be about 1 250 conservation areas. By 1970, there were 1 200. By 1992, there were over 8 000 with 400 new ones being declared each year.

4

TOURISM AND CULTURE-LED REVITALIZATION

INTRODUCTION

To revitalize historic urban quarters, many cities are attempting to attract new activities; a key new activity has been tourism and associated cultural activities. Strategies for tourism or culture-led revitalization have encouraged the exploitation of the area's historic legacy for tourist development. Such development has usually meant a partial or extensive diversification or restructuring of the area's economic base. Tourism is used to combat a quarter's image obsolescence by introducing new uses that take advantage of its historic character, ambience and sense of place. A commonly cited precedent for tourism-led revitalization in urban industrial areas is Lowell, Massachusetts. This rundown textile industrial town was successfully revitalized via tourism development becoming – in the process – the first National Historic Urban Park in the USA. As Falk (1986, p. 148) states: 'The key to its transformation was seeing its heritage as an asset and not just as a liability.' Lewis Mumford in *The Culture of Cities* (1938) noted that one of the functions of a city was to act as a museum of itself, however, many cities are seeking to avoid replicating the example of places such as Williamsburg, Virginia. Williamsburg offers a pastiche history with replicated houses and peopled with 'actors' in period costume. As Greiff (1971, p. 7) states: 'The clock has stopped and the past has been enshrined behind glass . . . having put history in its niche, one can admire and forget it. There is no spillof of history or art as a living presence able to enrich our lives.' Thus, in the process of revitalizing historic quarters it is necessary to integrate the historic legacy, inheritance and sense of place with the demands of contemporary economic, political and social situations.

This chapter will examine the development of tourism and the use of culture as a means of revitalizing historic urban quarters by providing new economic activity to replace or compliment indigenous uses which are in decline or have disappeared from the area. The concept of tourism as an appropriate activity for inner city areas is relatively recent, the prime motivation being the generation of new forms of economic activity and employment. However, the development of tourist and cultural activity is more than simply a component of local economic policy.

TOURISM IN HISTORIC URBAN QUARTERS

The objectives and motivations behind tourism projects vary widely, however, many tourism development projects are often opportunistic. Projects rarely come from a strategic appraisal of opportunities or from an overall strategy but are generated by the characteristics of a site or from a local interest group or private sector entrepreneur. Concern for the conservation and preservation of particular buildings is often an important initial motivator with conservation areas providing the broader physical focus. Nevertheless, a city's determination to develop its tourist industry appears to be a critical element in initiating a programme of tourism development, while planning is required to give coherence to a series of often opportunistic developments by the private sector. Thus, the public sector often has a key role to play in developing a tourist strategy, in providing and managing public open space, in constructing and maintaining some of the principal attractions and in making grant assistance available to the private sector.

The promotion of tourism in many industrial cities in the 1980s was a consequence of two major factors. First, many of these cities had suffered from de-industrialization with a significant loss of jobs in manufacturing, warehousing and transport resulting in high unemployment and many derelict inner-city sites. Cities naturally sought replacement industries which would create employment and re-use derelict areas and buildings. Secondly, tourism was perceived as a growth industry due partly to increased leisure time and travel mobility. Thus, the process has often been encouraged and stimulated by local authorities who have sought to build a degree of tourism and cultural activity into the heart of their city's revitalization. A key issue is that generally the quarters have usually had to change to become tourist attractions. Unlike cities such as Bath, they are not attractions purely on account of their physical landscape alone. Indeed, Law (1994, p. 1) describes how 'Old industrial cities with a poor image and scarred landscapes also sought to develop the industry. The aim of tourism promotion was, then, partly to boost the city, partly to revitalise the city, and partly to physically regenerate areas. From old industrial cities like Baltimore, Cleveland, Detroit and Pittsburgh in the USA and Bradford, Birmingham, Liverpool and Manchester in the UK, to cities like Duisburg and Lyon in continental Europe, the movement for urban tourism was very widespread.'

Destination, image and place marketing

Since the 1980s, in the competition to attract visitors and investment, former industrial cities have attempted to reconstruct their image and replace negative perceptions

(Bianchini *et al.*, in Healey *et al.*, 1992, p. 249). To gain advantage in the increasingly competitive market, towns and cities are exploiting their culture and heritage to emphasize their distinctive qualities and place-specific differences (Robins, 1991, p. 38). The process – known as place marketing – was developed in the USA. Paddison (1993, p. 340) describes how the practice 'has been linked primarily to local economic development, the promotion of place and the encouragement of public–private partnerships to achieve regeneration'.

Place promotion is often aimed at reconstructing a place's image rather than simple advertising and is usually targeted at specific types of activity such as tourism and culture that will both reflect and bolster the image. The primary goal of place marketing is to construct a new image for investors, visitors and residents to replace the existing image which is either too vague or has negative connotations (Kearns and Philo, 1993, p. 133). Furthermore, place marketing is seen as not just promoting and advertising the place, but also adapting the 'product' so that it is more desirable to the 'market'. Thus, place marketing raises questions regarding 'authenticity' as the supply is capable of being tailored to suit the demand. Robins (1991, p. 38) argues: 'In a world where differences are being erased, the commodification of place is about creating distinct place-identities in the eyes of global tourists. Even in the most disadvantaged places, heritage, or the simulacrum of heritage, can be mobilized to gain competitive advantage in the race between places.'

Tourism projects can help to counter image obsolescence by having a positive impact on the perception of a quarter, thereby leading to increased confidence and likelihood of investment. Place marketing involves exploiting attractions and characteristics of a place, its historical legacy or heritage and cultural attractions, and its ambience, combined with explicit image-advertising. In this approach, the place may create new – or exploit existing – tourist magnets supported by a tourist infrastructure. Place promotion can also be for internal consumption; improving the environmental quality of the area encourages residents and the business community to take pride in the area and at the same time boosts local morale.

However, it is not enough merely to improve the image of a place through marketing; any visitor destination also needs special attractions to satisfy both the local community and visitors. Although it is the image and attractions of an area which usually induce the tourist to visit a particular place it is the transport services that enable the trip, the supporting facilities which cater for the comfort of the visit and the infrastructure that enables these to function and to substantiate the new image (Pearce, 1981; Kotler *et al.*, 1993). These 'support' services are invariably the principal forms of spending by visitors and can therefore have a greater economic impact than the attractions themselves. Thus, the provision of successful tourist attractions can be seen to have a positive multiplier effect on the local economy. Spending by the visitors to a destination quarter not only consolidates existing facilities but encourages new entrepreneurial developments that – in turn – attract further visitors. However, the fundamental issues of the totality of the visitor experience must also be considered: 'People must be able to walk the streets safely . . . good hotels and restaurants must be available' (Kotler *et al.*, 1993, p. 39). This experience may affect whether a visitor returns or, indeed, recommends the place to others. It must therefore be considered when promoting urban industrial tourism (see Law, 1994, p. 126).

Management, investment and tourism strategies

The process of introducing tourism into an area is a complicated one. Often attractions will already exist but these may be at a basic level with few ancillary facilities and poor infrastructure. Usually the development of tourism or heritage quarters will result from the recognition and opportunistic exploitation of an area's potential. As Pearce (1981, p. 10) states: 'For tourism to develop, the various components must be exploited or supplied by someone or some organisation. A wide range of development agents exists. The exact composition of these will vary from situation to situation, depending on the historical, political, economic, cultural and geographical context of the development.'

In the development of any local tourist industry a public agency is often the key player in coordinating and creating any tourism strategy. However, both the public and private sectors are usually inextricably linked in the creation of a successful tourist destination. Many factors may induce the public sector to enable tourist development within its historic urban areas including economic, social and environmental reasons. An authority may seize this opportunity to diversify the local economy and create new employment opportunities or to stimulate the private sector in an attempt to encourage economic growth. Social reasons could include both improving or providing new facilities, and increasing local pride and the feeling of well-being. On environmental grounds, the public sector is usually charged with the responsibility of protecting and conserving the physical and cultural environment; tourism is often seen as one means of achieving this objective.

In contrast, the private sector's main objective is to make a profit from its ventures. Nevertheless, many different motives influence private entrepreneurs; as Pearce (1981, p. 11) notes 'there appear to be many ventures not characterised by a sound economic rationale but influenced more by the whims of a managing director or an individual'. Private companies are involved in a highly competitive market, are managed in terms of self-interest and can be reluctant to cooperate with each other in terms of combined strategies and promotion. However, success may well depend upon the general promotion of the whole area and visitor experience, the local authority may often therefore take the role of coordinating and pulling together the various actors in the industry (Law, 1994, p. 146).

The success of any tourism strategy whether this be explicit policies and official strategies, or implicitly expressed through actions and developments, is often due to the various players sharing a common goal and working together to achieve this aim. Bramwell (1993, p. 19) argues that: 'Planning is essential to give coherence to tourist products gained from a legacy of opportunistic development.' Throughout the 1980s, there were an increasing number of government initiatives – both in Europe and the USA – to promote local economic revitalization. This usually included the promotion of tourism and heritage resources with urban planners in effect taking on 'the role not only of market managers through land-use planning regulation but more directly also that of the makers of market places for their town's heritage products' (Prentice, 1993, p. 222). However, whether or not any official tourism strategy does exist within an historic urban quarter, the initial development of tourism in such areas has been the result of entrepreneurial opportunism and determination whether private or public sector led.

CASE STUDIES

In this chapter, three case study areas will be examined and their attempts to exploit the tourism potential inherent in historic urban quarters compared; the Castlefield area of Manchester, Temple Bar in Dublin, and Lowell, Massachusetts. These nineteenth-century urban quarters all lie within close proximity of their respective city centres and have undergone an economic restructuring, changing from areas of primarily industrial production to become mixed function quarters with an emphasis on tourism. Rather than a distinct spatial quarter, the area of Lowell discussed forms a ring around the central core. Nevertheless, it forms a tourist destination within the context of the city as a whole and has served as a precedent for many subsequent historic urban tourist quarters. The character of Temple Bar differs from the other case studies; it relates more to the European conception of an urban *quartier* with a traditional mix of activity and building types. Temple Bar also differs in that it has become more of a cultural – rather than a tourist – quarter and it relies more on its place-ambience than individual visitor attractions.

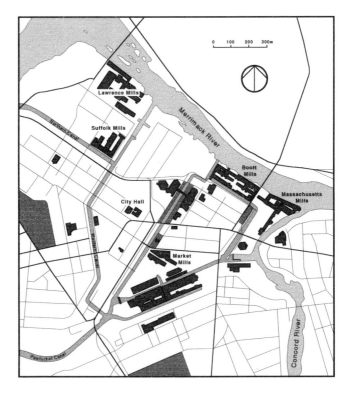

Figure 4.1

Plan of Lowell. Rather than forming a distinct spatial quarter, the area of Lowell discussed forms a ring around the central core.

LOWELL, MASSACHUSETTS

Lowell is a former mill town located twenty-five miles north-west of Boston at the confluence of the Concord and Merrimack rivers and bordering the Eastern Canal (Figure 4.1). Described as the first great manufacturing town of nineteenth-century America (Ryan, 1991, p. 377), Lowell was established as a planned industrial 'city' from 1821, becoming incorporated as a city in 1836. The city expanded rapidly in the second quarter of the nineteenth century and by 1850 there were ten mill complexes and a machine building factory; all were powered by nearly six miles of canals which exploited the 32 feet fall in the Merrimack at Pawtucket Falls. In 1855 there were over 13 000 employees producing cotton cloth. By 1900, it had been transformed into a dense urban concentration of nearly 100 000 people.

The town owes its origins to Francis Cabot Lowell who in the early 1800s toured England and Scotland visiting many of the modern cloth-producing industrial complexes. He is reputed to have memorized the workings of these textile mills in order to replicate them upon his return to America (Freeman, 1990). Unfortunately, he died in 1817 before his espionage could be tested on a large scale. One of his collaborators, Kirk Boott, realized Lowell's vision of a manufacturing community as a model town by designing the first mills, canals and worker housing in Lowell. Boott and the other early mill developers had a paternalistic attitude towards their employees and up to 15 per cent of capital was spent on worker housing and facilities. However, this was a short-lived measure and fierce competition soon led to decreasing wages and standards of living.

The decline and conservation of Lowell

Gall (1991, p. 397) describes the collapse of Lowell's cotton textile industry in the early twentieth century as one of the worst examples of decline in New England's mill towns. The problems actually began with the harnessing of steam-power in the late nineteenth century which superseded Lowell's natural advantage of water-power. In addition, the town suffered from a locational obsolescence as its inland situation soon became a hindrance in terms of transportation. These disadvantages led to many manufacturers moving to the coast for more efficient import/export or to more southerly regions in search of cheaper resources such as labour and raw materials.

The outbreak of the First World War gave a short-lived boost to Lowell's textile and munitions industries with the award of military contracts. After the War, however, the situation soon began to deteriorate further with a severely depressed local economy by 1930. In 1936 there were only 8 000 people employed in the textile industry (the same as in 1736) compared to nearly 21 000 in 175 mills at the turn of the century (LaBreque, 1980). This plight was highlighted by the demolition of entire mills or sections being removed to reduce the tax burden of these massive buildings. The Second World War boosted the economy with the remaining textile mills dramatically increasing employment, but again this boom was only temporary and in the early 1950s the Boott and Merrimack Mills closed. In the late 1950s, Lowell consisted of millions of square feet of empty five- and six-storey brick-built mill complexes, a decaying central business district and high unemployment. The depressed state of the town was epitomized in the early 1960s when the owners of the Merrimack Mill – described by architectural historian Randolph Langenbach as 'the original architectural symbol of the town' – offered the mill to Lowell City Council for $1. The authority declined this offer and the mill was demolished thereby reducing the tax burden on the owners (LaBreque, 1980).

Due to its stagnant economy and decaying physical environment, Lowell attracted little investment for urban renewal and slum clearance in the late 1950s and early 1960s. Nevertheless, this was subsequently to be an advantage. As Senator Paul Tsongas stated: 'Lowell's paralysis in the 1950s and 1960s, which left its original buildings untouched by urban renewal, gave it a better chance to emerge from decay than any amount of new roads or shopping centres would have done' (from Fleming, 1981, p. 166).

The 1960s witnessed the demolition of the mills in Lowell's sister town of Manchester, New Hampshire as part of a government-financed urban renewal project. As Hareven and Langenbach (1981, p. 111) note: 'Ironically, Manchester's complex of mills and workers' housing had been better preserved than had any complex in Lowell.' However, in the USA in the mid- to late 1960s attitudes towards the nation's heritage were changing. Following the demolition of the Merrimack Mill in Lowell, the emerging movement for historic preservation was further sparked by the controversy over the demolition of the Dutton Street Row Houses in August 1966. According to Ryan (1991, p. 380), Lowell's daily newspaper argued that the houses were 'a part of our history that should be forgotten' stirring up feelings of 'working class revenge' in defence of the Dutton Row demolition and highway expansion plans for the town centre. The controversy over the demolition laid the foundations of future conservation efforts and gradually more prominent members of the community joined the fight for the preservation of the remaining physical fabric after these few row houses had been demolished. However, there were few cases to be fought as pressure for demolition and redevelopment was non-existent. As Ryan (1991, p. 384) notes: 'The early 1970's was a time of recession, high unemployment, plant closings, and empty industrial parks, and considerable tension between downtown businesses and neighbourhood groups, between industry and labour, between the city government and the Locks and Canals Company, and between landlords and tenants. It was also a time of financial trouble for the city's leading bank.'

The revitalization of Lowell

The original concept for the tourism-led revitalization in Lowell is credited to educator Patrick Mogan. In 1970, initial funding was acquired from the Great Society Model Cities Programme to create a National Historic Park (Ryan, 1991; Gall, 1991). The idea and precedent for the National Historic Park came from the American National Park concept of an area publicly managed and conserved for the nation's benefit. The National Historic Park idea was an attempt to transfer this concept to an urban setting held to be of national significance. Mogan started the transformation process by educational reforms and attracting finance as early as 1966 with Federal Environmental Education money.

There was sufficient support for preservation in 1973 to form the Lowell Historic Commission and for the city council to designate two historic districts which were entered on the National Register of Historic Places in 1975/1976 (Ryan, 1991). These districts therefore became eligible for federal grants under the National Historic Places Trust and also various tax benefits and incentives. This led to the first small-scale physical improvements to the façades on Main Street under the Model Cities Programme utilizing Commercial Development Block Grants and financing from the Lowell Development and Financial Corporation (LDFC – a consortium of local banks and financial institutions). Also in 1976, the Lowell Historical Society published *Cotton was King: A History of Lowell* which helped to demonstrate a reawakening of the Lowell community's historical appreciation and awareness during the 1970s.

One of the key happenings in the town's revitalization was the election of Lowell resident Paul Tsongas to Congress in 1974. In 1975, Tsongas succeeded in convincing Lowell's bankers to create the Lowell Development and Financial Corporation and to lend 0.05 per cent of all deposits to a fund which would be invested in improvements to the town (Falk, 1986). This provided a revolving fund of $350 000 which helped to provide gap-financing through low cost loans to private sector property developers in the downtown area. Senator Tsongas and Lowell City Manager, Joseph Tully, were the figureheads of these early developments 'whose relentless drive and political skills created the formidable Lowell "delivery system", which captured millions of dollars in federal and state direct appropriations, grants, and loans' (Gall, 1991, p. 403). They were also responsible for creating 'a supportive public-sector climate for private investment during the park's critical early years. Private developers came to know that they could count on the city to deliver promised incentives and cut red tape to the minimum' (Gall, 1991, p. 403)

As well as Tsongas, another important political factor was Massachusetts Governor Michael Dukakis's strong commitment to the state's depressed mill towns. Furthermore, he had close personal ties with Lowell's Greek community and therefore a strong interest in the town (Gall, 1991). Significantly, also in 1975, the State of Massachusetts decided to create the University of Lowell in a rehabilitated mill complex in the town.

Proposed legislation for the National Park was first presented to Congress in 1972, and then resubmitted annually until the Bill was eventually passed in 1974. While this Bill did not create the Park, it did establish a 'politically feasible federal-state-local commission to plan a historic preservation programme' (Ryan, 1991, p. 384). Thus, the Lowell Historic Preservation Commission was established as a multi-agency cooperative effort which resulted in the establishment of the Lowell Heritage State Park in 1976. The Commission together with its partners, the University of Lowell and the Lowell Chamber of Commerce, created the Park with the mission of using history to generate tourism and economic development (Figure 4.2). The initial remit of the Commission was to continue until 1987. Congress extended its lifespan for a further seven years but changed the emphasis away from the physical fabric to an increased tourism approach with particular focus on the 'Canalway', a network of canals, walkways and recreational nodes.

Figure 4.2

Lowell is characterized by large-scale brick-built warehouse and mill complexes. Many of these complexes have been converted into tourist attractions, facilities or residences.

Prior to passage of the legislation creating the Lowell National Historic Park in 1978, various members of Congress questioned whether the bill was really an 'urban renewal' proposal in disguise (Ryan, 1991, p. 387). Despite the general truth in this claim, it was strongly countered by both Lowell residents and their representatives in Congress who successfully argued that the educational, cultural and historical aspects of the park did not constitute urban renewal. Upon designation of the park, Lowell was awarded a $5 million federal grant which helped Tsongas and Tully with one of the most significant achievements persuading the microcomputer firm of Wang to locate its international headquarters in the town (Gall, 1991; Ryan, 1991; Falk, 1986). This Urban Development Grant, like all those made to the LDFC, involves repayments at 4 per cent over 25 years and goes into a revolving fund (Cantacuzino, 1989, p. 132). By 1986, Wang were employing 15 000 people in Lowell, largely located – somewhat controversially – in new-build schemes (Falk, 1986). As Ryan (1991, p. 388) states, this 'buoyed the spirits of those who backed industrial development rather than preservation and downtown revitalization as a development strategy'. Wang's rapid growth in the early 1980s had a multiplier effect on the local economy with many smaller companies supplying and 'feeding-off' this computer giant. By 1980, Lowell had again become an industrial city with manufacturing jobs accounting for 39 per cent of total employment compared to the

US average of 21 per cent (Castells and Hall, 1994, p. 31). As Gall (1991, p. 398) notes: 'The impact of high tech in the community's resurgence has been so powerful that one local politician was said to have remarked, somewhat cynically, that Wang is worth a hundred national parks.'

The 'Wang factor' in Lowell's resurgence is well documented (Gall, 1991; Falk, 1986) and often overstated. Nevertheless, alongside persuading the developer of a Hilton Hotel to locate next to restored locks in the downtown, Wang's relocation and growth created increased activity and spending power in the Park area. The disposable income spending of Wang's employees also contributed to the ambience and character of Lowell, which increased the effect of its visitor attractions. Between 1975 and 1980 state and federal aid through pump-priming funds and 'seed grants' of $170 million resulted in $1 billion of outside investment (Fleming,1981). Due to this investment new construction continued to increase dramatically in the early 1980s Gall (1991) quotes a Dunn and Bradstreet survey which indicated a rise of 1 600 per cent in 1983, larger than any other city of its size in America.

In an effort to continue stimulating new projects Tsongas and Tully conceived 'The Lowell Plan' in 1979. This consisted of a group of business people which would operate parallel but independently from the Lowell Development and Finance Corporation. The Park also had a firm strategy of soliciting local business support and 'a non-confrontational approach to the leading investors in the city' (Ryan, 1991). The National Historic Park helped to create a common sense of purpose and direction for the Lowell community and to develop a local pride that had been missing for most of the twentieth century (Freeman, 1990; LaBreque, 1980).

The National Park service also helped to provide technical assistance to property owners in the renovation of their historic buildings. This resulted in over one hundred old properties being rehabilitated and many new uses being found. This environmental impact in historic urban quarters is important since it usually provides the initial rationale for revitalization; the built environment being the primary resource for tourism in historic quarters. However, the growth of tourism will inevitably lead to modifications in this environment. Thus, as Pearce (1981, p. 44) states 'attention must be directed at the nature, scale, form and location of existing buildings and street patterns as well as existing land uses'.

Tourist attractions

By 1986, there were over 800 000 visitors to the National and State Park organized activities (Gall, 1991) which included canal tours, historic walks, trolley rides and programmes of cultural and recreational entertainment. The two major visitor information attractions are the Park Visitor Centre at Market Mills and the Boott Cotton Mills Museum. Market Mills is the gateway to the Park. This renovated mill complex dates from the 1880s and early 1900s and was part of the Lowell Manufacturing Company, one of the city's original textile corporations. The Centre features visitor shows, concerts and exhibits which explore the park themes – Labour, Machines, Capital, Power and the Industrial City – and is the point of orientation for most tourists in the town (Official National Park Handbook, 1992).

The Boott Cotton Mills with its bell tower is a distinctive landmark in Lowell and its best example of mill architecture. The first four mills in this complex were built between 1835 and 1838 with five more added over the next century. This 260 000 square foot complex closed in 1954, signalling the end of large-scale cotton textile manufacturing in the town. Significantly, the Interpretation Centre and Museum trace the history of industrialization. The mill buildings were renovated by a private developer at a cost of $63 million with grant assistance from the Lowell Historic Preservation Commission to provide mixed use accommodation for a variety of tenants. In addition to the visitor attractions, there are residential apartments, a food hall, artists galleries, the Tsongas Industrial Centre, a Cultural Resource and Folklife Centre, teacher training facilities and other exhibition areas. From here the visitors can take the informative and picturesque tours of the canals and mills with the Park Rangers whose numbers are supplemented in summer by students (Falk,1986). Alongside Boott Mills is Boarding House Park which features an outdoor theatre (Figure 4.3).

Figure 4.3

Boott Mills Boarding House Park, Lowell. This features an outdoor theatre and numerous concerts take place during the summer months to maintain vitality throughout the day for visitors to the town. There are also numerous art and craft exhibitions, concerts and city festivals arranged throughout the year at various locations in the town to maintain visitor interest and variety. Boott Mill Boarding House itself was the subject of a major rehabilitation and restoration project. Over time, the substitution of flat roofs for pitched roofs and the blocking up of many windows had changed the building significantly. In converting the building to a library and museum, what remained of the interior was gutted and a new interior constructed.

The historic core of the town is now highly permeable to the visitor whether by the 'turn-of-the-century' streetcars, the Merrimack River Waterpower Trail and the riverfront Vandenberg Esplanade Park, the 'Canalway' – a system of self-guiding trails along the canal system – or by one of the ranger-led canal cruises or walks. Each of these trails has been designed to have an interpretive theme focusing on the founding and industrialization of the city. The idea for the Lowell National Historic Park Rangers was inherited with the concept for the park as a whole from the American National Park system. The Rangers provide a visible presence, are an invaluable information source for visitors and also help to monitor the environmental quality of the Park.

Lowell has had to carefully avoid creating or manufacturing a false façade to its history. There was a strong desire amongst the local community that the true picture – including the exploitation of workers, poor working conditions, and the role of the immigrant minorities – should be portrayed. Indeed, as Lynch (1972, p. 53) states: 'One problem in the preservation of the environment lies in its very power to encapsulate some image of the past, an image that may in time prove to be mythical or irrelevant.' A disreputable past has often been hidden in the promotion of tourism. As Brown Morton III (1992, p. 38) illustrates: 'American preservation has, far too often, rushed to create a flattering past. Many historic sites and museums routinely misinform the public because the truth is inconvenient. In most places, slavery and economic exploitation are ignored or rendered trivial. Interpretative programmes rarely challenge established American myth. Although the preservation movement is becoming more respectful of our multi-cultural heritage, there is still a marked reluctance to identify and preserve sites that trouble the conscience of the nation.' In Lowell, there was a strong effort to make sure that the museums and exhibitions were factually accurate and did not attempt to deceive visitors (see Ryan, 1991).

Conclusion

By the late 1980s, the boom in Lowell was over again as the region's economy contracted, Wang Industries cut employment and restructured their operations within the town. However, the new mix of technology, improved education and cultural vitality and steady influx of tourist visitors has helped Lowell to ride the current downturn in the economy. The development of the tourism industry and the growth of the high technology related companies have resulted in a varied mix of supporting economic activity.

The catalyst for the revitalization in Lowell has been its ability to build upon its heritage assets and recreate the community's sense of pride. As Gall (1991, p. 404) states: 'If there is a lesson other aging industrial cities can learn from Lowell, it is that revitalization begins with the kinds of changes in a community's self-image which project a palpable sense of confidence and direction.' Gall also notes that: 'Without rejecting its past or clinging mindlessly to it, Lowell translated its heritage into a source of local pride and a touchstone for future development.'

CASTLEFIELD, MANCHESTER

The Castlefield area is located on the western edge of Manchester city centre and is dominated by the railway and canal networks that shaped the history of arguably the world's first industrial city (Figure 4.4). It is in Castlefield that the city of Manchester has its origins, starting in AD 79 with the formation of the first Roman settlement in the area and the village that grew up around the fort until its abandonment in AD 411. In the eighteenth century, the fields around the Roman fort began to increase in importance once more as the city spread along Deansgate with Castlefield becoming the setting for Manchester's industrial revolution.

In 1765, the Duke of Bridgewater's first man-made canal was opened to transport coal from his mines into Manchester. This was later joined to the extended Rochdale Canal (1805) creating a thriving north–south and west–east inland waterways link with the Castlefield basin as its hub. The area around the basin was dominated by the many warehouses which developed to store the various cargoes with names such as Coal Wharf, Potato Wharf, Grocer's Warehouse and Merchant's Warehouse. By 1830, the Liverpool to Manchester Railway – the first railway in the world – had opened

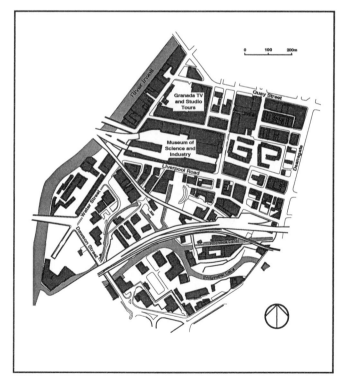

Figure 4.4

Plan of Castlefield, Manchester. The area is dominated by the railway and canal networks.

with the first passenger railway station on Liverpool Road, Castlefield. The subsequent expansion of the rail routes coming into the area resulted in a series of brick and cast-iron bridges and viaducts that are still dominant features of the Castlefield townscape.

The decline and conservation of Castlefield

By the 1960s, with the decline of the textile industries combined with the changes in transportation and storage methods, the quarter had declined into an abandoned industrial wasteland in the heart of the city. There were few positive developments during the 1950s and 1960s. The one notable exception being the decision of Granada Television to establish its headquarters on Quay Street in 1956. In 1975, the quarter's economic plight worsened when the goods depot that had taken over the former railway station also closed and became unused.

In 1972, attention and interest was focused on the Castlefield district when, after the closure of some factories, its Roman remains were excavated. This also served to highlight many of the area's other industrial relics. By 1974, the area's potential was recognized by Manchester City Council through policies in its *Structure Plan*. These policies related mainly to the development of tourism and leisure with emphasis

Figure 4.5

Castlefield is characterized by large-scale brick-built warehouse and mill buildings that are the legacy of the textile industry. Many of these structures have been rehabilitated and new uses found to revitalize the area as a tourism quarter.

placed upon retaining important buildings and excavating the canals. In 1979, the city council designated Castlefield as a conservation area. This was extended in 1985, creating the largest conservation area in the city centre. Following its designation, the DOE accepted the area as 'outstanding' in 1980. Although this superior status has subsequently been abolished nationally, it is nevertheless indicative of the importance attached to the quarter.

The city council recognized that there was a need to combine heritage and renewal. In Castlefield the indigenous economic functions had disappeared from the area leaving a legacy of historic but decaying vacant buildings and infrastructure. Thus, Manchester City Council had few alternatives but to attempt to attract appropriate new economic activities and uses such as tourism in its pursuit of the economic restructuring in the quarter (Figure 4.5).

The revitalization of Castlefield

The 1982 Manchester *City Centre Local Plan* noted the potential impact of tourism in the city, stating that 'visitors attracted by the city's finer architectural and historical features create demands for further facilities and attractions. These demands may then be housed in the more important but presently underused buildings thereby giving them a new lease of life so vital to maintaining their character'. It also noted that museums would complement the planning approach adopted for Castlefield which stressed the importance of maintaining both the character of the area and links with the past whilst also encouraging other economic activity and residential development. The *Local Plan* led to the relocation of a small science museum into the historic 1830 terminus of the Manchester to Liverpool railway. The museum has subsequently expanded to become the Museum of Science and Industry on a seven-acre site, attracting over 300 000 visitors in 1994 (Figure 4.6). This flagship project was intended to act as a catalyst and a symbol of the quarter's revitalization. However, as Bianchini, Dawson and Evans (1992, p. 246) argue 'such projects will only justify their flagship status if they succeed in attracting a flotilla of other developments in their wake'. This 'flotilla' includes not just other front-line attractions but any developments or services which either attract investment or visitors to the area or indeed add to their overall experience.

In 1983, Castlefield adopted the self-proclaimed title of Britain's first Urban Heritage Park – a version of the concept pioneered in Lowell – which was intended to lead to the 'revitalization of older historical areas and the provision of recreational areas and spaces . . . to act as a catalyst for development by means of both public and private investment' (Report of The Officers Working Party, 1982). The Castlefield Working Party proposed a tourism development plan which included the following *essential* elements: the creation of an Urban Heritage Park; the conservation and adaptation of buildings and sites for tourism and leisure; a comprehensive programme of environmental improvements; the provision of an adequate mix of attractions and ancillary facilities; links with the rest of the city by public and private transport and for the pedestrian; and the marketing and promotion of the area. Problems of combining conservation and economic

Figure 4.6

The Museum of Science and Industry, Castlefield. Relocated into the historic 1830 terminus of the Manchester to Liverpool railways, this museum has since expanded over a seven-acre site and attracted 300 000 visitors in 1994.

revitalization through restructuring were also identified in this report: 'the demands of tourism necessitate the need to carefully plan, manage and promote Castlefield as an economic resource so as not to be in conflict with the concern to protect and conserve the very attractions of Castlefield' (Report of The Officers Working Party, 1982). This realization was important in the formulation of tourism policies for the revitalization of Castlefield.

National urban policy in the UK had been relatively slow to appreciate the potential of tourism as a tool for urban regeneration. The *Urban Programme* (1985), for example, stated that 'tourism is never likely to be a dominant component of the Urban Programme.' However, by 1988 the increasing significance of urban tourism was recognized in the *Action for Cities* programme: 'tourism is already making important contributions to inner city development'. It also goes on to state that 'the government believes that tourism potential in inner cities remains underdeveloped' (DOE, 1988c).

The focus on industrial tourism during the 1980s led directly to the English Tourist Board (ETB) – as part of a five-year programme to develop tourism – sponsoring this area of Manchester, Salford and Trafford as a Strategic Development Initiative (SDI). This initiative was aimed at directly encouraging economic revitalization and employment growth through the development of the Manchester Regional Centre as a tourist destination. The ETB and LDR International (a design-planning consultancy) developed concept plans which designated seven districts within the zone (English Tourist Board, 1989). The coordination of the project was the joint responsibility of the ETB Area Development Group in partnership with Manchester City Council, Salford City Council, Trafford Borough Council, Trafford Park Development Corporation, Central Manchester Development Corporation and the North West Tourist Board.

The aims of the project in relation to the Castlefield Quarter were to encourage economic revitalization through the creation of a tourist destination of international status, and to enhance the quality of life for the local community. The SDI was intended to preserve and build upon the industrial heritage; to enhance the physical environment around the museums and visitor attractions; to provide new business and job opportunities; and to increase and strengthen the residential sector (ETB, 1989, p. 8). Two of the seven districts identified by the ETB were in Castlefield. In the Liverpool Road District – as a result of the SDI – new pedestrian linkages were created between the city centre and the river, while the historic Deansgate area was also rehabilitated and infilled with small shops, pubs and other services. The Bridgewater Basin District on the south side of the canal is currently undergoing mixed-use redevelopment with office, residential, commercial and retail developments. Environmental improvements have also been undertaken to the canal towpath, and pedestrian bridges have improved permeability and access.

Central Manchester Development Corporation

Tourism in Castlefield received another major boost in 1988 when the Central Manchester Development Corporation (CMDC) was established as part of the government's Urban Development Corporation programme. The CMDC recognized that tourism would continue to have a major role to play in the revitalization of the quarter by creating jobs and giving the area an image which was more attractive to inward investment (CMDC, 1990). Since 1988, the revitalization process in Castlefield has been accelerated by the CMDC through its role in land assembly and implementing environmental improvements.

In May 1994, CMDC published a *Draft Area Framework* for the quarter. *The Framework* (CMDC, 1994, p. 20) proposed a mixed-use approach to the quarter's revitalization. *The Framework* included the following key aims: strengthening the tourism base; consolidation and support of business activity; establishment of a vibrant residential community; conservation and enhancement of buildings, spaces and transport related structures; imaginative and sensitive use of the physical assets – canals, viaducts and listed buildings; and high standards of urban design and quality buildings. The policy context for this framework was provided by the CMDC Development Strategy; the Castlefield Conservation Area; the Manchester *Unitary Development Plan*; and the city centre *Local Plan*. In Castlefield, the CMDC has established 'General Framework Policies' for: Tourism and Leisure; the Environment; Retail; Housing; Business and Offices; Car and Coach Parking; and Movement (CMDC, 1994). It has also sought to direct tourism related uses to those parts of the

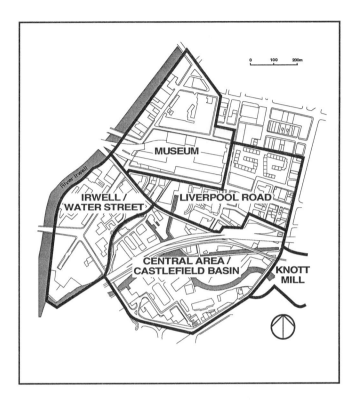

Figure 4.7

Castlefield Zoning Plan

(i) The Irwell/Water Street zone which forms the boundary with Salford at the River Irwell was blighted for many years by the Inner Relief Route road proposal. The long-term strategy for this gateway to the quarter is to enhance and add to the large-scale leisure and retail uses that exist and to improve the provision of car and coach parking.

(ii) The Castlefield Basin includes the historic wharves and is characterized by the canal network. This has once again become a lively thoroughfare with boats present throughout the year. The CMDC is encouraging the development of tourism to bring life and vitality to the canalside and has identified key site strategies within this zone to encourage the rehabilitation of the old industrial sites such as: Potato Wharf, Slate Wharf, Castle Quay, Coal Wharf and Pioneer Quay.

(iii) The Liverpool Road corridor operates as the main artery for the quarter and is bounded by the Museums zone, Granada Studio Tours, the main events arena, the Roman fort and the Visitor Centre.

(iv) The Museums zone provides the main focus for visitors to the quarter's prime attractions – the Granada Studio Tours and the Manchester Museum of Science and Industry – as well as the new V&A Hotel. In this part of the quarter the CMDC has concentrated its efforts on unifying the visitor experience through environmental improvements and parking provision.

(v) Knott Mill is located between Deansgate and Albion Street and has traditionally housed small businesses serving the city centre. This part of the quarter has undergone community-based revitalization. This has been led by the Knott Mill Association which has helped to establish a 'Creative Industrial Quarter' and rehabilitated many redundant buildings.

quarter where they were perceived to be most appropriate; the Castlefield Basin; the Core Visitor Area; and the Water Street/Dawson Street area. To implement these policies, the CMDC divided the quarter into five different zones (Figure 4.7).

Many of the key projects outlined by the CMDC such as hotel, housing and leisure developments, an interpretation and information centre, environmental works and improved parking facilities have now been undertaken, largely with grant assistance. The establishment of the CMDC coincided with Granada Television opening its Granada Studio Tours in 1988. This attraction has expanded on a regular basis and is now a national attraction with approximately 600 000 visitors a year and has resulted in spin-off developments including an associated hotel.

The Castlefield Management Company

To assist in maintaining the high quality environment, the Castlefield Management Company (CMC) was set up in April 1992 – by the CMDC, Manchester City Council, Salford City Council, and the main private sector land-owners – as an independent, non-profit public/private partnership housed in the Castlefield Visitor Centre. The CMC's brief is 'to maintain and actively develop Castlefield Urban Heritage Park as a major visitor destination' (CMC, 1994a). The organization has two major roles: to provide visitor information services and a varied events programme through the Castlefield Centre and Outdoor Arena (Figure 4.8); and to provide an Urban Ranger

Figure 4.8

Castlefield Centre and Outdoor Arena, Castlefield.

Service (CMC,1994a). With the main tourist projects now implemented, the company's main aims are to ensure that an increasing number of people visit the area and that the environmental quality of the area is maintained. Successful urban management is related to the totality of the visitor experience with the need to avoid the eyesores of litter, broken pavements, illegal parking and other anti-social activities. In Castlefield, the Urban Ranger service – the first in the UK – fulfils a similar function to the Urban Park Rangers in Lowell. Their role is to maintain the environment of the Urban Heritage Park, to conduct guided tours and to be a source of visitor information. The presence of the Urban Rangers also helps to demonstrate visibly CMC's commitment to the care, management and promotion of the quarter.

The impact of tourism in Castlefield

Most of the proposed tourism projects planned for Castlefield are now complete and 'the whole area has undergone rapid transformation with the renovation of original warehouses, building of new hotels and residential developments and significant environmental improvements taking place both on and beside the canals' (CMC, 1994a). Investment in tourist facilities, activities and the physical environment and infrastructure in the quarter has inevitably resulted in spin-off benefits for the local residential and business community. However, the costs accrued are not always apparent and it is therefore important to assess the environmental, social/image, and economic impacts.

Tourism development in Castlefield has prompted an increased range of accommodation, refreshment, sport and entertainment facilities. This has not only benefited the local communities but also the city as a whole, by encouraging visitors and their spending power. This influx of visitors into the quarter has led to increased spending at facilities, thereby making these activities more financially viable and of greater benefit to the local community. However, as Bianchini and Schwengel (1991) state: 'the provision of better facilities in these [quarters] should not be acceptable as a substitute for enabling everybody to participate in the life of the city'. Indeed, many arguments against the expansion of tourist facilities in historic quarters have centred around the ethics of spending money on visitors instead of on the residents of an area (Law, 1994, p. 30). However, contact between the local business community and residents in Castlefield – instigated by the Management Company – has positively reduced negative impacts such as crime, vandalism and waste management and 'even parties such as the regular canal users, have noticed a marked improvement in the area' (CMC, 1994b).

The economic impacts of developing the tourism potential of redundant historic urban quarters such as Castlefield are usually seen as being positive. In Western Europe and the USA, many authorities have seen the growth of tourism as an opportunity for absorbing unemployment created by the deindustrialization of their cities. However, a considerable amount of tourist generated employment is part-time, temporary, casual, unskilled and often exhibits a high turnover of staff. Nevertheless, during the 1980s, it has become accepted that tourism employment – despite its negative aspects – has resulted in one of the few labour intensive, low skilled and growth opportunities in the deindustrialized city and town centres (ETB, 1991).

Conclusion

The Castlefield quarter possesses a strong historical and cultural background. The industrial buildings with the river and canal system provide the major physical assets that the city has exploited in attracting investment and changing the image of this quarter of the city. This legacy has provided the special character within the quarter that the tourism developments have built upon. The most significant factors in the revitalization process so far, have been the decision of Manchester City Council to relocate and extend the Museum of Science and Industry into the quarter in 1982 and Granada Television's opening of the highly successful Studio Tours in 1988. The establishment of the Central Manchester Development Corporation in 1988 and the Castlefield Management Company in 1992 resulted in a strategy being developed for the quarter as a whole and helped to consolidate the opportunities in Castlefield created by the opening of these two major attractions. These events have transformed Castlefield from its decaying industrial past into a conventional tourism quarter. The attractions are to a large degree only indirectly related to the history of the quarter and would attract large numbers of visitors to most locations.

Since the revitalization process began, Castlefield has been transformed from an apparently obsolete industrial area into a national visitor destination. The visitor figures which have grown from virtually zero to approximately two million a year provide the evidence. The large numbers of tourists visiting the quarter have helped to contribute towards the first stage of Castlefield's revitalization. The city council and the Development Corporation are still actively trying to encourage the provision of more residential accommodation that will help to add a vibrant quality to the quarter during those times when visitors are not present.

Overall, the quarter has benefited through the impact of tourism which has turned inner city disadvantages into opportunities for local residents and the business community. Castlefield has experienced a dramatic restructuring with over 700 people now employed in the quarter. These are mainly service sector jobs – hotel, catering and visitor service industries – that have been created during the past decade to accommodate the increased visitor demand (CMC, 1994b). There is also an increased public perception of Castlefield and a renewed commercial investment interest in the quarter. Within the area, tourism has created employment, wealth and image enhancement, making Castlefield a growth area that benefits other local attractions. The Global Forum '94 was attracted to the quarter. Together with Manchester's bid for the 1996 Olympic Games, this has helped draw international attention to the area.

TEMPLE BAR, DUBLIN

The Temple Bar quarter, occupying an area of just over 200 acres in the heart of Dublin, is located between the city's two major retail and commercial centres. Dublin Castle and Christchurch Cathedral are also located just to the west of the area, while Trinity College is located on the eastern boundary (Figure 4.9). Formerly part of the tidal land alongside the River Liffey, the area was first developed in the seventeenth

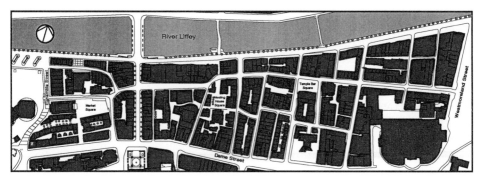

Figure 4.9

Plan of Temple Bar, Dublin. The quarter is bounded by the River Liffey to the north, O'Connell Bridge and Westmoreland Street to the east, and Dame Street and Fishamble Street to the south and west.

and eighteenth centuries and much of the original street pattern and urban grain remain intact.

The first history of the area dates back to an Augustinian Monastery in 1259 but it was not until the seventeenth century when William Temple, Provost of Trinity College built his house here, that the area began to develop. In the eighteenth century, the area was dominated by traders on the south quayside to the Liffey, the transport hub of Dublin, and a network of streets soon developed down to the river. In the mid- to late eighteenth century the area was dominated by printers, bookbinders and publishers. By the nineteenth century, Temple Bar had become a centre for the clothing and woollen trade in the city (Liddy, 1992). This ever-changing vitality of trading and uses in the quarter has led Montgomery (1995a) to describe the recent revival in terms of this history: 'In this way, Temple Bar had always been a centre of craft and creativity, culture and exchange. Its revival since the mid-1980s has marked a return to this energising role.'

The decline and re-emergence of Temple Bar

This varied historical and cultural heritage has left a rich urban fabric and streetscape of short, narrow winding streets with few alterations to the physical fabric since the nineteenth century. Despite this apparent fossilization of the built form, there are some derelict sites and many of the buildings were in a poor state of repair in the early 1990s in marked contrast to the significant office use nearby, including the Stock Exchange and the Central Bank.

In the 1950s, Temple Bar began to experience problems with companies closing and buildings falling into disrepair as improvements in technology began to undermine the viability of the small manufacturing firms. This led to many of the retail and distribution firms that had been prevalent in the area relocating to better locations. The downward spiral continued and in 1981 the Irish state bus company

(CIE) announced plans to redevelop the area as a transportation centre. These plans would have destroyed the historic physical fabric and street pattern that still existed. The Dublin Corporation supported this future for the quarter as the proposal was complementary to their policy of improving Dublin's public transport network. Thus, from 1981, as property prices began to fall CIE began to acquire land and properties in readiness for the demolition and reconstruction.

This planning blight actually breathed new life into the quarter. As Montgomery (1995a, p. 138) notes: 'Paradoxically, the fall in property and rental values which resulted triggered off a process of revitalization. Activities which could afford only low rents on short licenses – or no rent at all – moved into the area.' Another key period was in the early 1980s when as a temporary measure CIE began to lease these buildings – generally in a poor state of repair – to various small traders. These temporary leases and very low rents attracted fringe and alternative activities and businesses – often owned by young people – that would probably not have been able to exist elsewhere in the city. The low-rent was a key factor in the revival of interest in the area.

By the mid-1980s the numerous small businesses began to feed off one another and the existing cultural facilities in the area, such as the Project Arts Centre and the Olympia Theatre. Temple Bar began to emerge during the 1980s as not just a derelict part of the inner city but as a thriving quarter for 'alternative culture' bustling with activity, atmosphere, life and the inter-relationships of small entrepreneurs trading at the margins of profitability, and the quarter began to attract a certain cultural group. As Montgomery (1995a, p. 135) identifies: 'These people and those they attract often follow a particular lifestyle where work and ideas and friendships are pursued in bars, restaurants, clubs, venues, galleries and other semi-public meeting places . . . they are also a terrain or environment in which new ideas, new products and new opportunities can be explored, discussed, tried and tested.'

New initiatives for the 'Cultural Quarter'

In 1985 and 1986 two important studies were commissioned for the quarter: *The Temple Bar Area – A Policy for its Future* and the *Temple Bar Study*. Rejecting the proposal for a transport interchange, each stressed the important qualities of this historic cultural quarter. Emphasizing the area's rich architectural, cultural and community activities, both reports proposed that these could enhance the image of the city and could be exploited to attract both tourists and residents. In 1988, the area's traders, entrepreneurs, community groups, conservationists and historians established the Temple Bar Development Council (TBDC) (Montgomery, 1995a). Early in 1989, the TBDC proposed in their prospectus that a Cultural Enterprise Centre should be created and that a Temple Bar Development Trust should be formed to spearhead the cultural revitalization of the area. Their aim was to project Temple Bar as the flagship of Dublin's role as the European Capital of Culture in 1991 and to exploit this opportunity to acquire funding and support for improvements. The TBDC proposed the purchase of all CIE-owned properties, suggesting three main areas for action: environmental improvements, the physical fabric, and investment in cultural activities. The proposal of creating the Trust was not pursued but many of the ideas were later to be taken on board by Temple Bar Properties Ltd. The potential for tourism in the quarter was also recognized and highlighted by the *Bord Failte* in the 1989 *Tourism Plan for Ireland* (Lim, 1994). The character of Temple Bar against which the policy framework was set is described by Montgomery (1995a, p. 141): 'By 1990, Temple Bar had a reputation as a place of discovery, vitality and a wide range of social and economic exchange. It was frequently called "Dublin's Left Bank".' Surprisingly, in spite of this popular and highly developed cultural economy, it was not until 1990 that the Dublin Corporation finally rejected the idea of a transport interchange. This change of intention resulted in the 1990 *Temple Bar Action Plan*, in which the authority produced a detailed survey of land-use, traffic, building conditions, design, environmental quality and ownership before proposing a planning framework for the future of the quarter. Many of the proposals of this plan, including tax incentives, physical improvements and a new east–west pedestrian route, were to be later implemented in the *Temple Bar Development Plan*.

European interest and awareness of Dublin had increased as a result of its designation as City of Culture for 1991. In 1990, the Dublin Corporation was successful in its application for European Union funds. A £3.6 million ERDF grant was awarded towards a pilot project to determine the feasibility of creating a cultural quarter at Temple Bar. The increased interest in the qualities of Temple Bar signified the growing impetus for revitalization in the area. Prime Minister Charles Haughey's 1991 statement in the *Dail* typified the new vision for this cultural quarter 'The objective in Temple Bar is to create Dublin's Cultural Quarter, building on what has already taken place spontaneously in the area. The project has a five year construction period. The result will be a bustling cultural, residential and small business precinct that will attract visitors in numbers' (from Hooke and MacDonald, from Lim, 1994).

Apart from the honour of being City of Culture, 1991 also signified two important government acts: the 1991 Finance Act and the 1991 Temple Bar Area Renewal and Development Act. The former put the mechanisms in place for the creation of two companies: Temple Bar Properties Ltd. (TBPL) and Temple Bar Renewal Ltd. (TBRL). Both companies were in place by the end of 1991, with the remit of implementing the policy proposals for the quarter's revitalization. The Temple Bar Area Renewal and Development Act created a number of financial incentives to encourage businesses to relocate to or remain in the area and to renovate and build new properties. These inducements included rent allowances, rate remissions and capital allowances against income tax and capital refurbishment expenditure (see Montgomery, 1995a, p. 156). TBRL was formed as the policy making unit with members drawn from the Temple Bar Development Council, government, tourist board and local cultural organizations. The company was formed with £4 million of EU funds and up to £25 million of State-secured private borrowing to acquire and renovate properties in the quarter. It was also responsible for ensuring that proposals accorded with the area's development programme and for administering the various financial incentives that were available.

The TBPL – a state owned trading company – was established as the implementation vehicle for the revitalization of Temple Bar and is, in many respects, similar to an Urban Development Corporation in the UK. The company had the power of compulsory purchase of land and properties where appropriate and it also acquired all CIE and Dublin Corporation property within the quarter. TBPL was formed with an initial stage loan of £5 million from the European Investment Bank and was intended to have a five-year lifespan and to build on what has already taken place spontaneously in the area. To implement its aims and objectives, TBPL is structured into three separate divisions: the Property Division, Cultural Division, and the Marketing Division. The Marketing Division of TBPL was responsible for several place-making surveys and initiatives as part of the process of promoting the distinctiveness of Temple Bar. The Property Division both manages the property portfolio and assists in site assembly and scheme preparation. The role of the Cultural Division is to secure the implementation of cultural developments, and to organize the 'programme of cultural animation' (Montgomery, 1995a, p. 158).

In 1991, an Architectural Framework Competition was the first major initiative undertaken by TBPL. This was published in November 1991, as *Temple Bar Lives!* (TBPL, 1991). The brief for the competition emphasized the importance of the design of the public realm into an overall framework. The major features of the successful plan were: the creation of a new east–west pedestrian priority route through the quarter; the creation of three new public spaces; and the upgrading of the Liffey Quays. The proposals concentrated on the physical urban realm and were designed to improve the permeability and legibility of the quarter.

In 1992, the *Temple Bar Development Programme* introduced a detailed mixed-use plan that included the vertical zoning of land-uses (Figure 4.10). This policy concentrated on the social urban realm and encouraged active ground floor uses such as retail, bars, clubs, galleries and other cultural facilities to help animate the streets and provide a boost to the evening economy and, therefore, the safety of the quarter. The control over the upper floors was more relaxed and allowed for a variety of more 'passive' uses such as residential and office accommodation. TBPL (1992, p. 31) recognized the importance of the Temple Bar's heritage in projecting the quarter's character and image in its Development Programme overview: 'Temple Bar has a highly distinctive historical, architectural and archaeological heritage. It is the policy of Temple Bar Properties to integrate a recognition of the unique qualities of the area's heritage, both historic and contemporary, into all aspects of its development programmes.' Montgomery (1995a, p. 162) recognizes that: 'In this way, culture is not viewed simply as an add-on, or simply as a marketing device, but rather as an integral and key part of Temple Bar's economy and sense of place.'

The Cultural Development Programme

TBPL exploited the opportunity of Temple Bar to promote the Irish cultural scene both nationally and internationally and, therefore, to enhance its appeal as a cultural tourism destination. Of TBPL's total projected investment of £100 million over five years, £35 million is to be spent on the cultural programme. This cultural programme is aimed at expressing the quarter's character and uniqueness, using cultural venues to attract people and generate activity with its associated spending and investment.

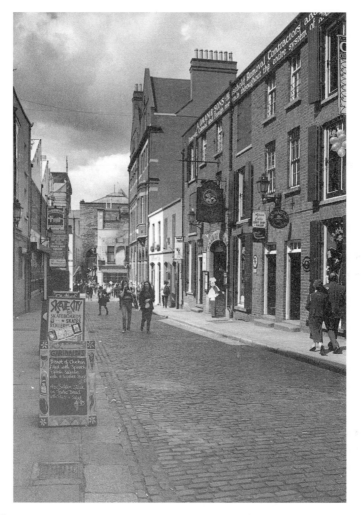

Figure 4.10

The 1992 *Temple Bar Development Programme* introduced a detailed mixed-use plan that included the vertical zoning of land-uses. This policy concentrated on the social urban realm and encouraged active ground floor uses such as retail, bars, clubs, galleries and other cultural facilities to help animate the streets and provide a boost to the evening economy and the safety of the quarter.

Thus, culture was seen as the key to the place promotion exercise and to changing the image of the quarter. The emphasis in Temple Bar has been on enhancing the ambience and character of its alternative cultural activities as opposed to creating more conventional tourism attractions. The importance of culture to Temple Bar is demonstrated by the 1991 survey carried out by TBPL and Nexus Europe Consultancy which identified 33 per cent of businesses in the quarter being involved in cultural consumption or production.

The Cultural Development Programme is one of four programmes for the quarter which TBPL is implementing; the others are Property, Retail and Residential. Nevertheless, it is the major cultural developments which are acting as the flagship projects and attracting the media attention in the revitalization of Temple Bar with funding for these coming from a combination of Government, TBPL, European Union, and other public sources as well as a considerable amount of private sector investment. In discussing the cultural projects, Montgomery (1995a, p. 161) notes that 'Each of these developments is seen as a strategic "chess-piece" in the area's overall development, and they are a mix of consumption and production spaces.'

Conclusion

In Temple Bar, tourism and culture have provided the focus and commercial base underpinning the other strands of the revitalization strategies, such as increasing the quarter's residential community and the retail element. As Lim (1994, p. 26) observes, initially there were 'obvious fears that the quarter will be transformed into an urban theme park that is both artificial and sanitised'. However, the cultural identity of the quarter is now so well established that these fears have been allayed and the character is evolving naturally. Indeed, the Development Programme (TBPL, 1992, p. 31) emphasizes the importance of allowing the cultural activities to develop at their own pace and 'has its basis in the organic development of the area as a place of artistic creation and animation.'

It is often difficult to separate the economic impact upon a distinct quarter from a city's total tourist experience because some of the attractions, facilities and infrastructure are based outside that quarter. However, in Temple Bar the visitor attractions are grouped into a tourist district. The primary impacts of clustered projects appear to have a greater impact on changing the image obsolescence of an area and therefore investor's behaviour. Thus, there seem to be benefits in locating tourist attractions within a distinct and identifiable quarter – as with Castlefield and Temple Bar – where they can create a strong destination pull. The concentration of these activities into a tourism quarter creates a clear focus for both visitors and investors alike. Law (1994, p. 128) states that: 'The argument for concentration is that tourists prefer a compact, walking city, and that a clustering of facilities makes a city more attractive to potential visitors because the total is perceived to be greater than the sum of the parts. With a critical mass of facilities and therefore tourists, higher thresholds will be reached to support secondary activities like hotels, catering and retailing.' Indeed, numerous linkages and external economies emerge from the presence of visitors with spending on food, accommodation, local products, and other goods and services potentially having a multiplier effect on the local economy (Mathieson and Wall, 1982; Kotler et al., 1993).

The success of the revitalization process in Temple Bar is partly identifiable from the following statistics: in 1992, there were only two hotels, 27 restaurants, 100 shops and 200 residents in the quarter; in 1996, it is forecast that there will be five hotels, over forty restaurants, 200 shops, 2000 residents, twelve cultural centres, and over 2000 people employed in the quarter (Montgomery, 1995a, p. 163).

In Temple Bar, particular emphasis has been put on attracting private investment which will coincide with the needs of the area. This is essential as many of the small cultural activities on which the character of the quarter depends are reliant on tax incentives and other forms of support which are short-term in their nature. Such a reliance still creates potential problems of the long-term commercial viability of many businesses and therefore the character and attractiveness to visitors in the future. Thus, despite the successes so far there is still some way to go before the original identity and the ambience upon which the quarter depends in terms of tourism is safeguarded.

CONCLUSION

The three case studies in this chapter demonstrate how many deindustrialized towns and cities can promote and develop tourism in historic quarters if they focus on unique or interesting assets and can provide the facilities necessary to support the attractions. Nevertheless, as Law (1994, p. 26) states: 'In the post-industrial world cities must compete to attract new activities to replace those they have lost. In this race cities do not start from the same position nor do they have an equal chance of being successful. Some inherit better resources, some are better located, and some have sites of greater potential.' In order to advertise and market their image these quarters require both tourist attractions and the appropriate infrastructure. Attractions include conference and exhibition facilities; arts, museums and heritage facilities; leisure activities; and special events. For tourism to play a major role in the revitalization the existing facilities have had to be improved and new attractions added and the totality of the visitor experience considered. This included the supporting infrastructure which enhances attractions and assists in the process of attracting tourists, such as shopping, catering and accommodation, plus transport and tourism agencies and environmental improvements. This multiplier effect is emphasized in Hewison (1987, p. 98): 'As SAVE Britain's Heritage 1982 pamphlet *Preserve and Prosper* makes clear, tourism by itself will not provide all the funds necessary for preserving old buildings. Indeed the costs of tourism . . . will sometimes exceed the revenue from visitors . . . Yet if the buildings themselves do not profit from tourism, other aspects of the economy do . . . The main economic benefit will be derived by transport, accommodation, catering and retailing businesses. In this context the historic building is a classical example of the loss-leader.'

By having an overall strategy for tourism in each of the quarters, the public agencies involved have been able to implement successful tourism and culture-led revitalization strategies. However, as Karski (1990, p. 17) warns: 'tourism development is not a universal panacea for economic and environmental ills . . . it is only one component of a wider set of economic and planning initiatives'. Many of the towns that based their revitalization on tourism in the 1980s are discovering that there are many external variables involved in the industry that they cannot control. As Bianchini and Schwengel (1991, p. 219) observe: 'A related problem is that tourism . . . on which cities are basing their regeneration strategies may well not be able to guarantee long-term economic viability, since they are liable to suffer from increasingly fierce inter-urban competition and from economic downturns which are outside the control of the city itself.'

Lowell, Castlefield and Temple Bar demonstrate many of the problems that are encountered in developing tourism in historic urban quarters (see Law, 1994, pp. 170–171). The main issues are:

* The problems of all cities potentially becoming alike and not developing their distinctive and special qualities.
* Increasingly fierce inter-place competition for the tourist market, not just from historic or even urban areas. This is related to the problem of relying on the long-term viability of a purely tourism-based revitalization strategy.
* Balancing the conflict between promoting and resourcing tourism for visitors versus providing for the local community.
* Environmental issues such as the sustainability of tourist development in cities, in terms of pressure on infrastructure, congestion and pollution which have become increasingly important.

Nevertheless, tourism is more than a component of local economic policy since investment for tourism brings other benefits for the local community such as facilities, attractions and environmental improvements with tourist spending at those facilities helping to make them more economically viable.

The three quarters considered in this chapter have each seen their industrial and commercial inheritance as an asset which could be exploited to attract visitors and therefore help to revitalize a distinct area of the city. In recommending proposals for other such quarters it is important to consider that each of the quarters is unique in terms of its physical, historical, heritage and economic inheritance. The experience gained in the development of tourism strategies and the exploitation of their potential as visitor attractions are unlikely to be directly transferable elsewhere.

The considerable experience gained from tourism-led revitalization initiatives over the past twenty years, nevertheless offer some lessons that may have wider applications, particularly in terms of the principles applied as well as the techniques, devices and the process of tourism revitalization. The case studies demonstrate three different approaches to tourism-led revitalization with differing degrees of success. Both Lowell and Castlefield have become quarters where the consumption of culture – through museums, visitor centres and interpretive trails – is prevalent. In Lowell, it has drawn upon the industrialization of the city in its promotion of tourism and the subsequent development of the National Historic Park. Castlefield has similarly developed the industrial inheritance of the area but it is based less on the history of the quarter itself and has become a more conventional tourism quarter. In contrast, Temple Bar has based the quarter's promotion to visitors on the appeal of its cultural ambience and character as a centre for the production of culture. Temple Bar has focused on creating life and vitality in the quarter which are essential qualities of urban revitalization. Nevertheless, each of the case studies in this chapter demonstrates that the promotion of tourism and culture-led revitalization can play a catalytic role in the wider revitalization aims of the city as part of an integrated package of measures.

5

HOUSING-LED REVITALIZATION

INTRODUCTION

In historic urban quarters, especially outside shop and office hours, residential uses can help to create a 'living heart'. The twenty-four hour life brought by residents is a crucial contribution to the vitality of an urban quarter, creating greater indigenous demand for facilities in the city centre and, thereby, increasing the number and mix of uses within the quarter. Thus, to revitalize historic urban quarters, many cities are attempting to attract residential uses. Equally, while seeking a physical conservation and renovation, some historic urban quarters are trying to retain their residential uses and, indeed, the original population. The flight of population from the central areas of cities to peripheral suburbs left inner districts of many cities with declining residential functions. However, the 1980s and early 1990s have seen increasing numbers of residents returning to central locations, particularly to newly revitalized historic urban quarters.

This chapter examines the revitalization of historic urban quarters where the quarters are or have become predominantly mixed use through retaining or acquiring a substantial proportion of residential uses. Some of the quarters strove to retain their existing population – a form of functional conservation – while others sought to attract a new population willing to live in, or attracted to, the centre of the city. The chapter begins by discussing the key issues with regard to residential conversions and development including the issues of displacement and gentrification. The case study examples are: the Marais quarter of Paris; central Bologna, New York's SoHo; Glasgow's Merchant City and London's Shad Thames. Apart from the Marais quarter and central Bologna, the quarters featured in this book have typically not had a strong tradition of residential use. The Merchant City and Shad Thames are also discussed in Chapter Seven.

CITY CENTRE LIVING

With the increasing decentralization of many activities and the development of high quality new office space, there is surplus office and industrial space that is vacant and may become derelict and blight the city centre. Conversions to other functions, especially residential use, is a way of ensuring that these buildings are in active use. As Ashworth and Tunbridge (1990, p. 114) observe: 'The historic city needs the residential function as the only practical alternative to widespread vacancy.' Furthermore, the 'compact city', with higher residential densities, more public transport and a mixture of uses, has been considered a more sustainable urban form. The suggestion is that this will reduce the amount and length of car journeys. In addition, residential development in and around the central area might also alleviate development pressures on greenfield sites and in peripheral locations. However, while a potential supply of residential stock exists, what is equally – if not more – important is an effective demand for that stock.

There are two principal attractions to living in the city. The first is the historic character and allure of the residential space available; the second is the convenience of the location. The two factors may be mutually reinforcing but, as Ashworth and Tunbridge (1990, p. 115) note, there is an important distinction between those who live in historic premises and those who – although resident in the same properties or areas – have a different set of motives and priorities. The first group value the historic character as such and live there because of it; they often invest in the properties and support its conservation. By contrast, the second group is relatively indifferent to the historical character, placing a higher priority on the area's centrality and accessibility – and perhaps most importantly – its low rents and/or flexibility of tenure.

In the UK and the USA, in particular, the dominant image of the residential environment has been that of suburbia. However, in New York around 1970, for certain sections of the residential market 'the bare, polished wood floors, exposed red brick walls, and cast-iron facades of these "artists quarters" gained increasing public notice, the economic and aesthetic virtues of "loft living" were transformed into bourgeois chic' (Zukin, 1989, p. 2). Currently a romance and charm – together with a certain social cachet and air of distinction – attaches itself to the inhabitation of former industrial spaces. However, they have not always been considered chic nor comfortable: 'Until the 1970s … making a home in a factory district clearly contradicted the dominant middle-class ideas of "home" and "factory", as well as the separate environments of family and work on which these ideas were based' (Zukin, 1989, p. 58). Nevertheless, beginning in New York, a desire for loft living has arisen. The initial loft spaces in SoHo had been raw industrial spaces that the first tenants adapted to residential use, and these 'unfinished' spaces that could be tailored to individual requirements were an attraction in themselves.

In the historic urban quarters featured in this book, although lofts and loft-type spaces are common, they are not the only type of housing. Often it may be new build housing or standard residential conversions. The benefits in this instance derive from the central location. In the late twentieth century, there is growing demand for central area housing. Gans (1968) in 'Urbanism and Sub-Urbanism as Ways of Life' discussed the relationship between people's 'life stages' and their geographical locations. As more people delay having children and with a greater proportion of active pensioners more people inhabit the life stage where the vitality and life offered by city centre living is attractive. Thus, there is increasing demand for city centre living as many people are prepared to live in city centres provided that it is safe and comfortable. These demographic factors are coupled with a fashionable lifestyle. In the UK, the DOE (1987b) supports this observation; attributing the trend towards housing in urban areas to a rise in the demand for distinctive homes; a need to provide housing in cities for young and business people and because building societies have become more willing to make mortgages available on converted properties.

Creating a vibrant 'urban village' in an area without a tradition of residential population needs a critical mass of development and takes a number of years to occur. Zukin (1989, p. 14) notes: 'Originally, it seemed that loft living attracted two types of residents: suburban parents whose children had grown up and fled the nest and those grown up children who were setting up their first apartments.' As many central areas do not have an infrastructure that would support residential uses, the initial residents are pioneers. It is likely, however, that only limited segments of the housing market would find city centre living attractive.

What has also been observed is that women in general, and gay men and women in particular, often have a greater preference for city centre living than other social groups. This has been shown to be true for New York, where there is a greater proportion of women than men with the exception of the western edge of TriBeCa where gay men led and dominated the gentrification process (see Smith, 1987). Zukin (1989, p. 72) noted the feminism and gay activism of many visible loft dwellers in SoHo. 'Quite a few of the first generation SoHo residents who took part in the movement to legalize artists' living lofts there (1969–71) or whose lofts were pictured in magazines were men or women who lived alone or gay (primarily male) couples.' Initially, such social groups had sought the anonymity of the city centre, later it became a base for their solidarity. Markusen (1981, p. 32) attributes this to the breakdown of the patriarchial household: 'Households of gay people, singles, and professional couples with central business district jobs increasingly find central locations attractive . . . [The profile of new inhabitants] corresponds to the two-income (or more) professional household that requires both a relatively central urban location that enhances efficiency in household production (stores are nearer) and in the substitution of market-produced commodities (laundries, restaurants, child care) for household production.' In part, this may be because women are relatively more affluent than they had previously been. Equally, it also reflects the necessity of juggling the demands of an often more complex lifestyle.

By its very nature housing-led revitalization almost inevitably results in a change in the functional and social character of the quarter. This is often termed gentrification where lower income residents or uses are displaced by higher income residents or uses. Appleyard (1979, p. 31) cogently describes how the process of gentrification gradually develops. The pioneer migrants only marginally affect the area's life and character, and are usually welcome. Nevertheless, as they do not want to live under the same conditions, as the existing inhabitants, they often improve their dwellings. As more are attracted, although retaining much of its orginal character, the neighbourhood becomes socially mixed. Equally, it also becomes 'chic' and relatively safe even for more conventional sections of the middle classes. Real-estate speculators begin to become actively involved in buying, converting, and selling. The area loses its 'life' and 'integrity' and – perhaps more than the original working-class population – the 'pioneers' resent the destruction of character caused by the 'gentrifiers'. The old bars and wine shops fold, to be replaced by boutiques, art galleries, speciality shops and high-priced restaurants. The passing of the area's traditional character is mourned by everyone, especially those who initiated its demise. Appleyard (1979, p. 31) notes that 'Ironically many of the complaints about gentrification come mostly from the pioneers.' As noted in Chapter Two, such displacement occurs in and between all sectors not just the residential sector.

CASE STUDIES

Unlike the British and American quarters, on the continent of Europe there is a longer established tradition of mixed use urban quarters or *quartiers*; the mixed use of which includes both workplaces and residences. As a mix of uses (work, residential, leisure, etc.) has been seen to be a key contributor to traditional urban vitality (Jacobs, 1961), residential development usually expands the range of uses within the historic quarter bringing both benefits and possible conflicts. Due to developments in transport, the general move of population away from living in town and city centres, and the corresponding peripheral expansion of most urban areas through suburbanization, has also led to the separation of workplace and residence. This was exacerbated by Modernist planning theories and practices that sought to functionally zone activities. However, in the SoHo quarter of New York, Zukin (1989, p. 68) notes how, living lofts, especially in an on-going manufacturing area, re-create the 'mixed use' of earlier urban neighbourhoods: 'symbolically, the mixed use in loft living reconciles home and work and recaptures some of the former urban vitality'. This vitality of mixed uses is arguably more desirable to create where residential uses invade traditionally industrial and commercial areas, as is currently happening, rather than industrial and commercial uses invading established residential areas.

Due to industrialization occurring in a different way, in the continental *quartiers* there are also fewer of the larger scale warehouses that are found in British and American cities. Thus, the building form and townscape found in such continental quarters is different. As will be discussed in both the Marais quarter and central Bologna, the revitalization and physical rehabilitation of the quarter was also an attempt to resist gentrification and the displacement of the original population. Thus, in effect, this is a social – or functional – conservation of the existing population as well as a restoration of the historic fabric. In contrast to the Marais and central Bologna, the American and British quarters examined in this chapter are not traditional residential areas. Nevertheless, by becoming increasingly mixed use, they are also becoming more similar to the continental European idea of the *quartier*.

MARAIS, PARIS

The Marais is a distinctive quarter of Paris, punctuated with magnificent sixteenth-and seventeenth-century *hotels particuliers* – town houses built for wealthy patricians. These palatial *hotels particuliers* nestle into a maze of narrow streets, alleyways, and courtyards, jostling with more modest dwellings (Figure 5.1). The contrast between these monuments and the more mundane and anonymous texture gives the Marais its physical character. The Marais also had a distinct functional character. 'It has always been and still is a centre of highly specialised skills: jewellers,

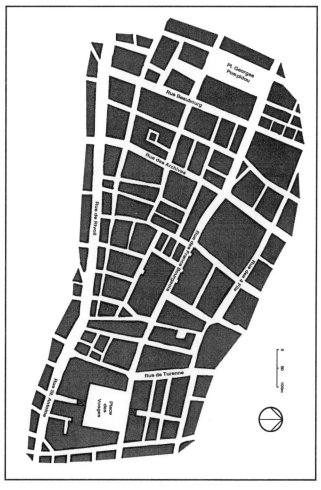

Figure 5.1

Plan of the Marais quarter, Paris.

clock smiths, gunmakers [in medieval times – swords and armour]; the special crafts associated with haute couture; lace, ribbons, buttons, artificial flowers, etc.; fine hardware, etc., etc.' (Fitch, 1990, p. 67). Many of these specialists still work in the area; their shops, workrooms, and studios still line the streets of the quarter. Formerly, many of these people also lived in the quarter. However, increasing prosperity permitted them to leave the substandard residential accommodation of the quarter and move to more modern housing in the suburbs. In the early 1960s, the danger was that – sooner or later – they would also move their workplaces out of the Marais.

The Marais – the French word for swamp – was originally marshland and was largely unbuilt until the mid-sixteenth century, when building plots were made available to the nobility and the bourgeoisie. Stimulated by the building of the Place Royale (now the Place des Vosges) by Henri IV from 1605, development intensified during the seventeenth century (Figure 5.2). Unlike the pattern of terraces facing onto the square of the Place Royale, the *hotel particuliers* built in the Marias during the seventeenth century took the form of separate, self-contained palaces walled off from the neighbourhood. Other houses built in the Marais at the same time were for those of more modest means: ground floor rooms were often used to house shops and workshops, while the residential accommodation consisted of lettable rooms rather than self-contained apartments.

Figure 5.2

The Place des Vosges (formerly the Place Royale), built by Henri IV from 1605–1612.

By the end of the seventeenth century, the Marais was becoming relatively crowded. New suburbs were developing at St Germain to the south and St Honore to the west. The prevailing winds meant the air was fresher there, and the fashionable rich soon found these locations more attractive. The King also moved his court to Versailles. However, middle- and lower-middle-class communities continued to grow in the Marais. Following the Revolution in 1789, property seized from the church and from aristocrats was sold at auction. Purchasers in the Marais were mainly artisans, tradesmen and shopkeepers, who adapted their newly acquired premises to serve as small workshops, business premises and modest living quarters.

During the nineteenth century, the area declined into a poor artisan quarter with multiple occupation and industries crammed in and around the *hotels*. As the craft-based industries increased and the population became increasingly dense, existing buildings were subdivided and additional stories built. Every available space at ground floor was used to build workshops and factories, while the courtyards – many of which were private pleasure gardens – were roofed over. Nevertheless, sanitary provisions remained very primitive. The process has strong similarities with that in the Jewellery Quarter described in Chapter Six.

In addition to this physical intensification, the Marais has a long history of blighting by – ultimately aborted – road building and clearance proposals. Being first blighted by road building schemes in the early nineteenth century, it has the longest history of any of the examples in this book. As an attempt to sanitize Paris, road widening schemes were drawn up from 1820 onwards. Simultaneously, legislation was introduced prohibiting improvements to any buildings that stood in the way of approved road widening lines. Although many road widening schemes were proposed, few were implemented but the legislation remained in force. Thus, many buildings in the Marais were effectively condemned to further dilapidation. Following a severe cholera epidemic that swept Paris in 1832, widespread water-supply, street drainage and sewage-disposal improvements were made. Unfortunately, as buildings subject to road widening were not allowed mains connection, much of the Marais was denied the benefit of these actions. Furthermore, between 1853 and 1870, the extensive Second Empire remodelling of Paris by Baron Haussmann proposed cutting two new thoroughfares through the Marais. Although neither of these roads was actually built, the demolitions planned to clear the routes further blighted the area.

Towards the end of the century, mortality from tuberculosis in Paris reached epidemic proportions. An investigation in the 1890s identified exceptionally high numbers of tuberculosis cases in six areas, termed *Ilots Insalubres*. *Ilot Insalubre No.1* was situated on the western fringe of the Marais, while *Ilot No.2* covered a fifteen hectare zone in the very heart of the district. The number of *ilots* was later increased to seventeen. Many people concluded that slum clearance was the only solution, including Le Corbusier whose 1925 Plan Voisin for Paris proposed the demolition of most of central Paris (see Figure 3.1). A significant part of *Ilot No.1* was demolished in the early 1930s (the site remaining empty until the building of the Pompidou Centre). Further clearance was prevented by the depression of the 1930s and then by the Second World War. Despite inoculation proving an effective method of eradicating tuberculosis, the *ilots* remained earmarked for demolition.

The conservation and revitalization of the Marais

Following the initial experience of post-war redevelopment, the proposed demolition in the Marais and elsewhere eventually provoked a campaign to save historic Paris from the bulldozer. Writing in the 1940s, the preservationist Georges Pillement argued that districts of special historic character, like the Marais, should be preserved and enhanced (Ellis, 1990, p. 27). He argued for a major restoration and renovation of the Marais, proposing a method of *curettage*: sweeping away the 'parasite' buildings and other accretions that had accumulated since the Revolution so that courtyards and gardens could be reinstated.

By the early 1960s, there were 74 000 people living in the Marais at a density of 585 people per hectare as compared to approximately 300 per hectare in Paris as a whole; 70 per cent of the households lacked an inside toilet, and 85 per cent of the total ground area (including roads) was built over, compared with about 55 per cent for Paris as a whole (Ellis, 1990, p. 28). However, its historic qualities were not going unnoticed. Preservationist groups had acquired some of the quarter's notable buildings and had begun to restore them. Although legislation governing the preservation of historic buildings in France originated from the mid-nineteenth century, it was not until 1962 that legislation to preserve the historic character of districts such as the Marais was introduced. In 1965, the Marais was designated France's first *secteur sauvegrade* or conservation area, covering some 120 hectares (310 acres): 'To ensure that the district's picturesque historic character would be conserved and enhanced, formal approval was required from the State for all future changes to buildings in or bordering the *secteur*. Moreover, the State was given absolute power to enforce any demolition or preservation of any building or part of any building' (Ellis, 1990, p. 28).

In addition to its status as a *secteur sauvegarde*, the Marais had a wealth of 'listed' buildings: 176 *monuments classes* and 526 *monuments inscrits* (Dobby, 1978, p. 75). The French tend to list far fewer buildings than in England. While England is perhaps 'over-listed', France is 'under-listed' and – allowing for the difficulty of comparison – it is usually assumed that were the French buildings in England, they would all be Grade I (Dobby, 1978, p. 73). The consequence of having so few buildings defined in this way is that they are subject to closer control and attention. For both categories, restrictions cover not just the building or land but also the immediate area up to 500 m – the *zone protege* and subsidies are relatively generous. The higher classification, *monument classe* requires an agreement between the owner and the state following designation. This allows the owner to obtain a contribution from the state amounting to 50 per cent of the cost of necessary repairs and maintenance. In return, the building cannot be changed without ministerial consent and some public access has to be allowed. Depending on the amount of public access, between 50 per cent and 75 per cent of the remaining cost can be set against tax. Grants for repairs to *monument inscrit* of up to 40 per cent may be offered by the Minister (Dobby, 1978, pp. 73–74). Reflecting their particular spatial character and properties, many of the *Hotel Particuliers* have been converted into museums, for example: Musee Picasso; Musee Carnavalet; Musee Kwok and the Musee de la Serrureria.

The 1962 *Secteur Sauvegarde* legislation required a strategy plan to be drawn up within two years of designation. In the interim, no work likely to alter the structure or appearance of a building was allowed. Once the strategy had been produced and agreed, no new construction or alterations could take place without permission. Owners receive 20 per cent grants and 60 per cent loans towards the required works, but if owners refuse their property can be expropriated. The public subsidy for these works has been considerable. Even in 1966, the cost of conservation in the *secteurs sauvegarde* was estimated to be more than £1 million per acre (Dobby, 1978, p. 75). The plan concentrated on physical rehabilitation and restoration of the quarter's historic environment, prior to the accretions, additions and overbuilding of the

Figure 5.3

The Marais quarter is an area of mixed uses and vitality.

nineteenth century. In accordance with Pillement's concept of *curettage*, it proposed 'extensive clearance of "parasite" buildings, including some 1,000 dwellings and workspaces utilized by 10,000 people' (Ellis, 1990, p. 28). As Dobby (1978, p. 75) decribes, the intention was for the quarter to revert 'to something like its appearance in 1739 – the courtyards, squares and gardens of the famous Plan Turgot – but with car parking in garages beneath.'

Finally published in 1969, the strategy's implied social destruction was profoundly unpopular. Subsequent modifications to the plan took a less determined physical approach to the renovation with provisions that respected and recognized the Marais's lively atmosphere and social mix. The aim was not just to physically rehabilitate thousands of buildings but also to stabilize and preserve the traditional demographic mix of the area. Furthermore, a more flexible approach was adopted towards *curettage* in order to encourage small businesses to remain in the area. For instance, the demolitions deemed desirable for the restoration of the Marais's architectural ambience could be postponed to allow for the continued use of certain buildings by enterprises that were considered to make a positive contribution to the district's lively atmosphere (Ellis, 1990, p. 29).

Conclusion

Despite the physical conservation and renovation that has occurred in the Marais quarter, the most controversial issue has been the change in its functional character as a result of displacement and gentrification. Despite its relatively successful – albeit costly – physical renovation, in terms of its aim of retaining the social mix and indigenous population, the revitalization process has only had a limited success. As demonstrated by the use of the slogan 'conservation equals deportation' in elections in Paris in the late 1970s, the Marais has acquired notoriety as an example of dramatic social change. Burtenshaw *et al.* (1991, p. 156) state: 'the sequence of restoration, higher rents and social change has been well-established with 20,000 residents moving out and a rather smaller number moving in since the project began. Whether higher land values are a result or a cause of the replacement of working-class housing and small workshops by high rent apartments is not clear, but the change in the function of the area is' (Burtenshaw *et al.*, 1991, p. 156). Furthermore, Dobby (1978, pp. 75–76) observes that there has been criticism that conservation in France and, especially in Paris, was 'having a similar effect to Haussmann's clearances under the Emperor Louis Napoleon, in that working classes are again being driven to the periphery, through loss of accommodation and increased rents'. Nevertheless, it is debatable how many of the indigenous population would have remained even without the programme due to the general historical process of the suburbanization of inner city residents.

CENTRAL BOLOGNA

Central Bologna has much in common with the Marais quarter. Eighty thousand people live in the historic core of the city which is divided into four *quartiers*. As in the Marais quarter, the issue has been to stop the existing population being displaced

– or otherwise choosing to go – to the city suburbs. The form of the *centro storico* of Bologna is that of an irregular hexagon approximately two kilometres across. Its perimeter was formerly the line of the city walls – some of which still survive. Within this hexagon, the road pattern reveals a grid-iron Roman plan surrounded by a radial Medieval plan.

In the early 1960s, like many old Italian cities, the centre of Bologna was in a poor physical condition. Despite its romantic streetscapes, most of the housing was substandard. Like that of the Marais, the population of the area was largely indigenous; many families had lived there for generations. However, due to the poor living conditions, younger and more mobile members of the community were leaving it in increasing numbers. The communist-controlled city authorities were also concerned about the changing nature and function of the city centre which threatened the architectural unity that had characterized it historically; a visually harmonious combination of a residential tissue interspersed with larger buildings: palaces, convents and churches.

Following spectacular growth in the 1950s, the 1960s saw a stabilizing of the city's population. The municipal authorities had been planning for a city of 1.2 million inhabitants in 1955. However, in the early 1960s, as the city authorities tried to halt the further growth of the city, this was revised down to 600 000 and later to 500 000. In the process, the Japanese architect Kenzo Tange's plan for Bologna Nord – a new city on Bologna's periphery to house deportees from the centre – was vetoed.

In 1969, Bologna adopted an overall, long range programme of development through the adoption of a new master plan for the city. The planning approach adopted has been described as 'both authoritarian and rigidly conservative/ conservationist' (Cantacuzino and Brandt, 1980, p. 3), while Appleyard (1979, p. 37) notes that Bologna's slogan was 'conservation is revolution'. The city authorities took the position that both the environment *and* the inhabitants of the *centro storico* were important. As Fitch (1990, p. 76) describes, the city saw the necessity to intervene to 'preserve *both*, the container and the contained, by improving the physical environment, increasing the level of services and amenities, and promoting democratic participation in all decision-making'. The principal aim was the total rehabilitation and restoration of the existing built fabric of the city, together with adequately integrated social services and equipment, and, more generally, the creation of a more liveable environment. In addition, as well as to better integrate transport and land-use patterns, the whole conservation process was linked to the maintenance of the pre-existing functional and social patterns. This approach was proposed as an alternative to new speculative development and further peripheral development of the city.

The 1969 plan was based on a comprehensive and thorough survey of the city's buildings and open spaces. The task of formulating the guidelines for '.. a correct methodology of urban renovation' (Bandarin, 1979, p. 192) was assigned to Professor Leonardo Benevolo, a prominent Italian planner and architectural historian. The key concept of the Benevolo proposals was that the architectural typology – like the façade or the style of the buildings – was a characteristic to be preserved as part of the historic heritage (Bandarin, 1979, p. 192). The 1969 plan had identified thirteen areas, which had become overbuilt and unattractive for private investment. Of the thirteen, five were selected as pilot areas, affecting approximately 6 000 people. All thirteen have now been completed.

The city authorities originally proposed a programme to expropriate property in the central city, rehabilitate it with public funds and thereafter treat it as public housing. In 1971, a new law – 'Legge sulla Casa' – was passed to enable authorities to expropriate unbuilt and built up real estate at indemnities below market value (Cantacuzino and Brandt, 1980, p. 7). The first detailed rehabilitation plan was released in October 1972. However, in addition to the funds from central government being insufficient for this course of action, it aroused intense opposition from homeowners. Real estate in central Bologna was in the hands of small landlords who

Figure 5.4

Renovated street in central Bologna.

made their living renting rooms to students; if these landowners were deprived of their livelihood by expropriation of urban property at rural prices, the neighbourhood councils threatened a massive exodus from the Communist Party (Cantacuzino and Brandt, 1980, p. 7).

A revised programme was agreed in March 1973. Expropriation remained for vacant dwellings and those at risk, but the city authorities converted the main programme to one of subsidy and concentrated on a long-term covenant to protect tenants from rent increases or eviction. Private owners were guaranteed municipal subsidy for rehabilitation on a sliding scale in inverse proportion to their own resources and the size of holding. The receipt of subsidies was dependent upon the offer of the restored accommodation to the original tenants at the unrestored rent.

Conclusion

With its twenty miles of characteristic arcaded streets, spacious boulevards and squares, Bologna is now one of Italy's best preserved historical centres, the largest after Venice. It is also in uniformly better physical condition than Venice. A larger number of residents have stayed but during the renovation the number of family houses was reduced and the number of flats increased. Thus, the area's social composition has also changed with more students and single person households. The historic centre of Bologna has also become a centre for tertiary uses. The historic centre is now an area for housing, university activities, cultural and tourist functions, small trades and businesses. Industry that had been within the central area has moved to the outskirts, taking advantage of the opportunity of selling urban land at urban prices and buying argicultural land at agricultural prices.

SOHO, NEW YORK

SoHo, a quarter of Manhattan, is the area best known for loft living. The author of the most comprehensive account of the phenomenon, Sharon Zukin (1989, p. 3) observes: 'During the early 1970s, New York City became both the harbinger and the model of loft living.' The name SoHo is a 1960s invention derived from the quarter's location *So*uth of *Ho*uston Street, a major east–west thoroughfare dividing Greenwich Village and SoHo. The area is unique for its abundance of mid-nineteenth century cast-iron architecture. The technique was an early form of modular construction using prefabricated façades and frames. Although cast-iron lost its popularity in the 1880s as steel-skeleton construction and safe high-rise lifts were developed making buildings of much greater height possible, the concentrated development period was vital in establishing the particular character and unity of the quarter.

One of the attractions of cast-iron was its facility to imitate the more expensive stone traditionally used in the construction of the more elaborate commercial buildings. Some of the moulding is so good that the only way to tell a cast-iron façade from a masonry façade is with a magnet. The popularity of cast-iron was due to its low cost and the speed with which cast-iron forms could be produced, compared

Figure 5.5

One of the most significant works in the quarter is the Haughwout building at 488–492 Broadway
designed by John P. Gaynor and completed in 1857.

with the time required by stone masons and carvers to produce similar effects. The
façades themselves were imitative of masonry buildings, exhibiting extensive use of
classical ornamentation, often in 'Italianate' and 'French Second Empire' styles. The
area also displays several buildings by James Bogardus, who constructed cast-iron
buildings all over the USA, including the St Louis waterfront.

The SoHo area of Manhattan had originally been a residential area. However, by
the end of the nineteenth century, most of the houses had been torn down to make

Figure 5.6

Broome Street, SoHo. Broome Street and Green Street contain the largest continuous arrays of cast-iron façades anywhere in America.

way for factories whose façades hid sweatshop conditions so appalling that the City Fire Department later dubbed the area 'Hells Hundred Acres'. Until the end of the nineteenth century, SoHo was New York's centre for mercantile and dry goods trade. In the twentieth century, it changed to light manufacturing, particularly in textiles. Throughout this period, SoHo was also one of the largest sources of employment for the waves of immigrants settling in New York.

In the 1950s and 1960s, the area was blighted by a planned expressway which would have wiped out not only SoHo but other distinctive and vibrant New York neighbourhoods such as Little Italy and Chinatown. In addition, SoHo's location between the Financial Centre in Lower Manhattan and the concentration of corporate headquarters in Mid-Manhattan made it vulnerable to grandiose redevelopment plans to establish better physical links between the two. From the 1950s, due to the planning blight and for a variety of other reasons, an increasing number of small firms and businesses began to leave SoHo. Nevertheless, some firms elected to remain. As Zukin (1989, p. 5) argues this was due, firstly, to the benefits of agglomeration and clustering of firms which maximized convenience for commerical customers while firms could save money by depending upon the supplies and services of their neighbours; and secondly, production expenses were relatively low. Until the late 1960s loft rents were cheap and stable, while the urban labour supply, particularly for the less skilled jobs, was plentiful and cheap. Nevertheless lofts were increasingly becoming vacant.

There was one group of people willing to move into the empty and vacant lofts; seeking low rent space where they could live and work, but also large relatively open spaces with high ceilings able to accommodate the increasing size of their work, artists found the vacant lofts ideally suited. Thus, landlords who had had great difficulty in getting business rentals, gladly accepted artists. Landlords were enthusiastic to have artists as tenants. Part of their enthusiasm was due to the fact that if the still scheduled expressway was ever approved and the buildings condemned, their compensation would depend on the number of tenants in the building (Gratz and Frieberg, 1980, p. 15). As long as the expressway was a possibility, city officials ignored the fact that the artists were living illegally in buildings zoned for industry. Similarly, violations of building and fire-code regulations were largely ignored by the city enforcement agencies. Thus, albeit unintentionally, the area's functional restructuring was being permitted to happen.

This led to the first wave of displacement as rising rents for residential use forced more manufacturing firms out of the quarter: 'the new residential rents were higher than existing manufacturing rents . . . the growing demand for lofts by residential tenants encouraged further rent increases' (Zukin, 1989, p. 6). However, if artists could outbid them, this testifies to the general weakness and marginality of those firms. A further wave of displacement was also beginning to develop as the demand for living lofts expanded to sectors of the general housing market with no connection to the arts. Their demand encouraged landlords to increase supply as though they were operating in a conventional housing market based on new construction.

In 1969, the expressway proposal was abandoned. This was largely through the actions of historic preservationists – Friends of Cast-Iron Architecture – who were concerned about the possible loss of the unique concentration of cast-iron fronted buildings in SoHo. However, the artists were united with the preservationists in a coalition of common purpose but different interest: the artists to protect their homes and workplaces; the preservationists to protect the buildings. The artists assisted the campaign by organizing the media attention and publicity, and by carrying out much of the original research work. In 1973, SoHo became the first commercial district in New York City to be officially designated an Historic District by the Landmarks Preservation Commission.

At about the same time, the city authorities moved to allow and legalize what was already effectively a *fait accompli* – artists working and living in buildings zoned for industrial use. There was already concern that legalization would encourage further displacement of businesses and, possibly, of the artists themselves (Gratz and Frieberg, 1980, p. 12). In 1971, when the city first legalized the use of lofts by artists, two crucial restrictions were established: first, large industrial buildings were barred from residential conversion while, in smaller buildings, the first two floors were reserved for commercial uses; and secondly, non-artists were prohibited from moving into SoHo, and an Artists Certification Committee was set up to screen new residents (Gratz and Frieberg, 1980, p. 12). However, there is general agreement that the city failed to enforce the regulation requiring SoHo residents to be artists. The definition of what was – and was not – an artist was not clear and anecdotal evidence exists of professionals creating portfolios of artwork virtually overnight to establish their credentials as artists and, thereby, secure tenancy.

Slightly later than the artists moving in to live and work in the lofts of the SoHo area, art galleries also started to open up. For the reasons that the loft spaces were attractive to artists as studios, they were also attractive as galleries. In 1968, the first SoHo gallery was opened; by 1978, the area had seventy-seven galleries (Zukin, 1989, p. 91). The art galleries made a significant contribution to the character of the quarter by introducing a street level activity. Simultaneously, restaurants, cafés and bars were opening up to cater for the increasing residential population. Although to some degree the proliferation of galleries reflects the general expansion of the 1960s art market, the dramatic increase in the number of galleries in SoHo between 1972 and 1977 'testifies to the market value of the new art and the new neighbourhood' (Zukin, 1989, p. 91).

By the early 1970s, a more mainstream housing market – albeit still generally illegal – was becoming established in SoHo. By 1975, loft rents had become competitive with apartment rents and, as individual units, lofts were no longer cheaper than conventional apartments (Zukin, 1989, pp. 6–10). As non-owners, the artists were vulnerable to changes in the rental market where there were few rent controls or limits placed on rent increases and few guarantees of lease renewal. As landlords sought to maximize their profits and returns, artists were forced out by vastly increased rents at the end of their lease period. Furthermore, artists were not entitled to any reimbursement or compensation for the cost of any improvements they had made to the lofts during their period of residence. Indeed, landlords could charge 'key money' to new tenants reflecting the value of those improvements. These factors further stimulated the market with lofts changing hands more frequently.

By the mid-1970s, the development of a more mainstream housing market in SoHo had attracted the attention of professional developers. Until 1975 or so, living lofts in New York suffered from what Zukin (1989, p. 11) terms a 'murky legal status'. Statutes that had mitigated against loft living – local building codes and zoning restrictions – while not being enforced still remained on the books. The entry of professional developers into the market demanded an end to this situation. To minimize their risks and protect their investments, such developers wanted assurances form the city authorities in terms of the way that planning and zoning policies for SoHo would develop. First, both developers and their financiers required the legal status of loft conversions be regularized; no residential market could be firmly established if tenants ran the risk of being evicted. Similarly, developers were reluctant to become heavily involved in residential conversions if the city was to return to policies that supported manufacturing industry. Furthermore, developers did not want to rehabilitate old buildings if the possibility of more lucrative returns through redevelopment might still be available. Thus, by the mid-1970s, developers were proposing eliminating all legal restrictions on floor size, and buildings that could be converted to residential use, and removing the legal barriers against loft living by non-artists (Zukin, 1989, p. 13).

The legalization of the housing market in SoHo effectively determined how SoHo would continue to develop the further deindustrialization of Manhattan. The New York Real Estate Board's 1975 report on loft buildings made the point that such buildings were no longer viable in manufacturing use: 'The area's manufacturing activity shows no signs of recovery, and its tax base is eroding.' Nevertheless, the Board did find a favourable prognosis in residential conversion: 'Demand for apartments, exceedingly strong for buildings already converted . . . could be expected to support a considerable residential expansion' (from Zukin, 1989, pp. 11–12).

Although perhaps not to the extent or as quickly as developers would have desired – various assurances and commitments were gradually made that confirmed SoHo's status as a residential and mixed use quarter. Thus, the entry of professional developers had ensured that SoHo would be functionally restructured, becoming a mixed use area with an increasing amount of upmarket housing with some artists and manufacturing firms hanging on. Nevertheless a 1977 study by the New York City Planning Commission found that 91.5 per cent of all loft conversions in Manhattan were illegal while only 8.5 per cent were legal (Zukin, 1989, p. 11). Another effect of the development of a more mainstream housing market was that, in the interests of greater profits, what had previously been 'lofty' lofts, now became loft-apartments. These were relatively conventional apartments but with sufficient industrial features and character to retain the notion of a 'loft' but on a greatly reduced size. As Zukin (1989, p. 10) notes a private study of loft buildings in 1977 found that the average rent per square foot in living lofts was $2.28 a year, but the average in converted loft-apartments $7.68.

Conclusion

It is significant that the revitalization of SoHo through a housing-led restructuring was not a planned process. Effectively, it was a market-led restructuring that was initially illegal but tolerated by the city authorities who ultimately and effectively legalized the existing situation. However, that legalization also changed the nature of the revitalization, leading to the displacement of the initial residential population – the artists – and creating a highly expensive but more mainstream residential market. From the street, there are few signs of the rehabilitation and conversion of loft buildings; very few façades have in fact been restored and many appear to be in very poor condition (see Figure 2.2). Some have been painted, but as Gayle (from Gratz and Frieberg, 1980, p. 14) observes: 'there has been no replacing of leaves on Corinthian capitals or recasting of missing pieces of columns or cornices and no urns have been put back on the cornices'. In addition, the presence and number of trucks on the streets testify that it is still, in fact, a significant industrial area.

Following the influence of SoHo, many American cities now have residential communities in historic warehouse districts: for example, Portland's Skidmore Old Town and Philadelphia's Old Town. In these cities, the process has been different. As Gratz and Frieberg (1980, p. 15) note: 'Not many cities have the artist population of a New York City, and not too many have New York's high-rent, low-vacancy rate.' Thus, as these cities have not generally had a residential property market as strong as that of Manhattan, the restructuring of these areas for residential uses has generally been – to a greater or lesser extent – a planned process.

By the 1970s, artists displaced from SoHo had moved south into TriBeCa and other parts of Manhattan and Brooklyn. TriBeCa is another 1960s invention; an acronym for: *Tri*angle *Be*low *Ca*nal Street (Figure 5.7). Lying to the south of Canal Street to Chambers Street and west from Broadway to Hudson, it is a quieter quarter than SoHo and one of Manhattan's fastest growing neighbourhoods. Although, it lacks the

Figure 5.7

TriBeCa, New York.

consistent architectural character and townscape of SoHo, it is an eclectic combination of renovated cast-iron fronted warehouses and new condominiums, innovative art galleries, new clubs and restaurants.

THE MERCHANT CITY, GLASGOW

Planned in the last quarter of the eighteenth century, Glasgow's Merchant City was the first extension westward from its overcrowded and squalid medieval High Street. This 'New Town' extension was based on the wealth of the trade interests of Glasgow's merchants during the eighteenth century and constituted the first significant growth of the city since medieval times (City of Glasgow District Council (CGDC), 1992, p. 1) (Figure 5.8). The Merchant City's historic townscape is largely

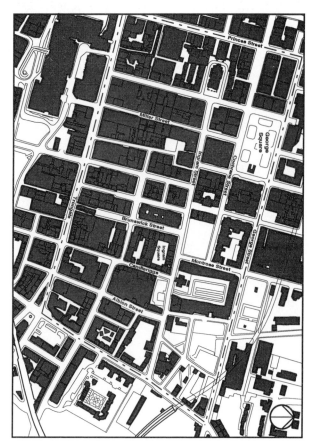

Figure 5.8

Plan of the Merchant City, Glasgow.

Figure 5.9

View up Hutcheson Street terminated by the Hutcheson Hospital. Within the Merchant City, there are significant townscape qualities arising from the terminated vistas and the powerful sense of contained space and an intimacy of scale rarely found elsewhere in Glasgow.

intact. Its buildings cover a range of architectural styles spanning a period of over 250 years: 'Today, Georgian town houses mix with Victorian splendour and handsome early twentieth century warehouses to form a mixture of height, colour, and detail held together by the continuity of building frontages' (CGDC, 1992, p. 2). Sixty per cent or 105 buildings in the quarter are listed. In terms of layout, the Merchant City was the precursor of Glasgow's ubiquitous grid. However, rather than being the open-ended grid of Victorian Glasgow, the grid is off-set creating a series of carefully controlled vistas, terminating on key buildings (Figure 5.9). As the city's planning department (CGDC, 1992, p. 2) describes: 'The contrast between the heart of the area and its edges largely explains the sense of place that is felt in the area – a City within a City.' As Johnson (1989, p. 48) states: 'Once entered the Merchant City is a closed, fairly static series of spaces.'

The decline of the Merchant City

Until the mid-1960s, the dominant land use in the Merchant City was wholesale distribution which accounted for about a quarter of all wholesale distribution in Glasgow. Together with public and civic buildings, wholesale distribution made up over 60 per cent of the area's built floorspace, while less than 7 per cent of property was vacant. However, over the next fifteen years, commercial patterns in the Merchant City altered radically to the point where over a third of all property fell vacant and economic activity became depressed.

The area was suffering from planning blight, locational and functional obsolescence. The eastern edge of the area was blighted by Glasgow East Flank motorway proposals which required the demolition of some areas to the west of High Street. In addition, in 1969, the University of Strathclyde presented plans to expand its campus south of George Street requiring the public acquisition of land in order to assemble development sites, and thus, further blighted the Merchant City. The high concentration of warehouses and related uses caused major traffic congestion in both the Merchant City and surrounding areas. This was a sympton of the area's functional obsolescence as 'the unusual pattern of streets in the area seriously affected the operational viability of wholesale distribution when compared to contemporary site and building preferences' (CGDC, 1992, p. 1). In addition, the buildings themselves were functionally obsolescent and unable to cater for the contemporary demands of warehousing and distribution. In 1969, as a means of coping better with demand and relieving local traffic problems, the Fruit Market at Candleriggs was relocated to Blochairn. Businesses dependent on the market activity were effectively made locationally obsolete, causing a substantial number of them to move or to cease trading completely. Furthermore, due to competition from abroad, the Merchant City was increasingly unable to support its clothing and textile firms.

The combined effect of this obsolescence was to set in motion a chain of events that led to increases in vacant property, the acceleration of decay and ultimately to the demolition of buildings. By the late 1960s and early 1970s, the area had declined sufficiently far that an Outline Comprehensive Development Area (OCDA) was designated. This permitted the acquisition and clearance of derelict buildings by the local authority. Together with site acquisitions associated with the abortive University plans, this meant that much of the Merchant City came into public ownership (CGDC, 1992, p. 1).

The conservation of the Merchant City

During the early 1970s, efforts to encourage new uses into the area met with only limited success. Those uses that did locate in the Merchant City did so because of the very low property rents and values (CGDC, 1992, p. 1). The area continued to deteriorate physically, with many important – often listed – buildings becoming structurally suspect and at risk. As a consequence the architectural and townscape quality of the Merchant City was in jeopardy. In 1976, to try to arrest any further loss of architectural qualities and in recognition of its special features, the whole of the Merchant City was included in Glasgow's central conservation area.

By 1980, the problems of the Merchant City were clear: large-scale redevelopment was unlikely and the East Flank Motorway proposal was still causing blight and development uncertainty. As a result over a third of all property in the area was vacant or under-used; the physical fabric of the Merchant City and its townscape quality were in danger because of under-use and neglect (CGDC, 1992, p. 2). Furthermore, given its proximity to the city centre, the rundown appearance of the Merchant City was blighting the city centre in particular and, more generally, inhibiting new initiatives promoting Glasgow, such as the 'Glasgow's Miles Better' campaign.

The further passage of time, nevertheless, meant that some of the threats to the area were removed. For example, Strathclyde Regional Council's *Structure Plan* (1981) reduced the status of the East Flank Motorway to an expressway with improved traffic management. In addition, the route was altered so that it passed east of High Street, thereby by-passing the Merchant City.

The revitalization of the Merchant City

Given the local authority's major landholding in the area, they were a key party in leading the revitalization process. The district council owned about 40 per cent of property in the Merchant City including 60 per cent of the vacant property. However, as the major landlord, it was receiving little return on its assets. In view of the vacant property, the Merchant City required a new economic role around which to base a revitalization. As many of the buildings were empty, there would be few problems of displacement.

Accordingly, the district council decided on a housing-led revitalization. This approach would also be assisted by restrictive planning policies that limited the competitive supply; the *Structure Plan* and Glasgow District Council's *Local Plans* aimed 'to encourage housing to be built on vacant sites in urban areas by limiting the availability of land in suburban and rural areas' (CGDC, 1992, p. 2). In addition, Glasgow had had very bad experiences with peripheral housing estates. Thus, in response to the changes in the road proposals, the lack of market interest in the area and given the housing objectives for the city centre, the district council undertook a feasibility study of some of its commercial property in the Merchant City to assess the scope for conversion to housing and ways of encouraging private developers.

From these investigations, it was found that conversion to housing would be structurally practical and acceptable standards could be achieved. Nevertheless, given the estimated selling prices, it would not be economically viable. Since there was no established market for housing, developers were not willing to become involved without the cushion of gap funding by the public sector. Fortuitously at this time, housing legislation in Scotland was also amended. Local authorities were given wider powers to offer financial assistance and to make grants to developers to help with the cost of conversion. The district council was able to offer conversion grants at an average rate of over £5 000 per house. In addition, it made its own property available at attractive prices and was flexible in the consideration of planning standards, such as the provision of parking spaces. As the city's planning department (CGDC, 1992, p. 3) observed: 'This range of incentives was intended to provide assistance and a level of security for potential developers by helping to make up some of the shortfall and by taking a promotional view of proposals.'

The first demonstration project was the Albion Building, on Ingram Street. This was a listed four-storey warehouse, built *circa* 1890. At the time, although the ground floor was in partial use as a bank, it was largely vacant. In 1982, planning consent was granted to convert it into 23 flats for sale (19 one-bedroom and 4 two-bedroom) with a shop on the ground floor. The public subsidy for the project was significant. In addition to the transfer of its property for a nominal sum, the district council's conversion grant amounted to 30 per cent of the total cost.

As all the project's houses were sold before the construction work had been completed, the project demonstrated that there was a market for residential uses in the Merchant City. As the city's planning department note, the project 'introduced housing into the Merchant City for the first time in over 100 years'. A number of developments followed based on similar financial arrangements: conversion grants plus cheap transfers of property. By 1987, 550 flats had been completed and another 1 250 were in the pipeline (Johnson, 1987, p. 40).

Ingram Square development

The most significant project in the Merchant City, however, was the Ingram Square development. This project introduced a new style of joint venture between the public and private sectors. Instead of the grant plus property arrangement, a formal development partnership was formed involving the district council and the public sector Scottish Development Agency (SDA) as part investors in the project with a private developer (CGDC, 1992, p. 3). A complete city block, rather than a square, Ingram Square is located in the heart of the Merchant City. Before redevelopment started, the block contained fourteen individual buildings, mainly warehouses, workshops and offices, with a few retail shops at street level (Johnson, 1987, p. 40). Ingram Square now contains a total of 240 flats (both conversions and new-build), twenty shops, parking for 108 residents' cars and a large communal garden.

The project was initiated by Kantel Developments (Edinburgh) (KDE); a firm set up in 1980 by two architects who had become 'expert at using their architectual skills to see opportunities missed by others, picking up marginal projects and making them viable by astute packaging of private and public funds' (Johnson, 1987, p. 41). In 1984, their attention had been drawn to the listed Houndsditch building, built in 1854 and standing on the corner of Ingram Street and Brunswick Street (see Figure 7.7). In isolation the building was difficult to convert; in combination with the other buildings in the block a more satisfactory scheme could be developed with a shared central courtyard. Many of the other buildings on the site, including a gap site on Wilson Street, were owned by the city council.

Although a market for housing in the Merchant City was becoming more established, development costs still outweighed estimated sale value. Thus, public sector gap funding support was still necessary. However, the scale of the project put it beyond the reach of the *ad hoc* partnerships previously devised. Accordingly, KDE, the district council and SDA set up a joint development company called Yarmadillo. The equity input placed in Yarmadillo came from each of the three partners (Johnson, 1987, p. 41). KDE contributed ownership of the Houndsditch building plus working capital of £1.35 million raised by a bank loan. Glasgow District Council contributed

Figure 5.10

Ingram Square development.

£1.2 million (£5 000 per dwelling) in housing improvement grants. It also contributed its property in the block, the cost of which was to be recovered from future profits, if any. The SDA provided a £1 million interest free loan and a further £230 000 towards the cost of environmental improvement. With the council's encouragement, KDE and the SDA prepared a joint feasibility study. The resulting design proposal received planning permission in 1984.

The City of Glasgow Planning Department (CGPD, 1992, p. 3) regard the Ingram Square project as the most significant for the revitalization of the Merchant City for a number of reasons: raising the scale of development from a single building to a complete street block; introducing the building of new houses rather than solely conversion; and offering solutions to more complex problems such as the partial use of buildings and car parking. The Ingram Square development also diversifies the quarter's population by including an element of student housing for Strathclyde University.

Conclusion

The housing-led revitalization of the Merchant City has been relatively successful. The district council's efforts in promoting and supporting with public subsidies conversion work turned the liability of owning dilapidated and often empty buildings, into the positive advantage of being able to control the pace and quality of development and to achieve the conservation and revitalization of an historic quarter of importance to Glasgow. Since the first housing conversion in 1982, more than 1 200 flats have been created in the quarter providing a substantial indigenous population and a demand for other facilities. The district council's intention had been to taper out subsidies as the demand and market for housing in the quarter become established. However, the property recession of the early 1990s has slowed the pace of development in the quarter.

The most recent developments in the Merchant City are the result of the implementation of the 1995 *Glasgow City Centre Public Realm Strategy and Guidelines* (Strathclyde Regional Council, 1995). In the Merchant City this will mean the widening of footways. A policy also exists to strengthen the area's links with the city centre by creating 'the Wynds'. This is to be a pedestrian route through the area, increasing permeability by creating arcades through some buildings. Equally, some of the initial policies to enable housing uses to gain momentum in the Merchant City stored up problems that now have to be addressed. One of the most significant is the problem of car parking. While 53 per cent of the Merchant City population have cars, only 23 per cent have private off-street space (CGDC, 1995). The on-street parking problems in the Merchant City stem from early developments that were permitted with lower than normal parking standards; the parking space requirement of one per unit had to be dropped as unfeasible. The shortfall has been partly met by a new multistorey car park for residential use on Candleriggs. The CGDC are currently trying to increase the amount of off-street parking especially through the investigation of more basement parking.

SHAD THAMES, LONDON

Shad Thames is the area immediately to the east of Tower Bridge on the south bank of the River Thames (Figure 5.11). The western extent of dockland influence is marked by Tower Bridge which forms 'a symbolic cultural and physical junction between the industrial monumentality of the docks and the commercial monumentality of the City' (Slessor, 1990, p. 39). The buildings on the eastern bank of the inlet of St Saviour's Dock generally mark the eastern extent of the quarter, although some developments are now occurring on the eastern side of Mill Street. The area is covered by the Tower Bridge Conservation Area and the St Saviour's Conservation Area and has been described as the 'only part of London (with the possible exception of Wapping) in which the Victorian character survives as a significant entity' (LDDC, 1987, p. 49). The narrow street which gives its name to the area, Shad Thames, runs parallel to, but inland from, the Thames. Within the heart of the building complex known as Butler's Wharf, it turns sharply and again runs parallel to, but inland from,

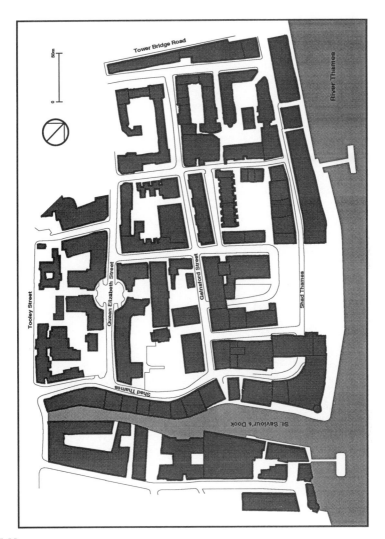

Figure 5.11

Plan of Shad Thames.

St Saviour's Dock (Figure 5.12). Once the mouth of one of London's 'lost rivers' – the neckinger – St Saviour's Dock is now a tidal inlet, densely surrounded by warehouses.

During the twentieth century, some sites were redeveloped and there was also a series of poor quality new developments around and among the more substantial Victorian warehouses. By the late 1970s, many of the warehouses had been derelict since the closure of the docks in the mid-1960s. Although there had been plans for their demolition and replacement with a commercial development along the river

Figure 5.12

Shad Thames, the street which gives its name to the quarter, is a dramatic canyon formed by warehouses either side of a street; it is crossed at a variety of levels by lattice wrought iron bridges built to carry barrows from warehouses immediately alongside the river to those further inland.

edge, very little demolition had actually occurred. In the late 1970s, a small artist community was squatting in the main building of the Butler's Wharf complex and in other buildings in the area.

The revitalization of Shad Thames

Although the first rehabilitation project in the quarter had begun by 1980, a major catalyst for the revitalization of the area was the establishment of an urban development corporation (UDC), the London Docklands Development Corporation, in September 1981 (see Oc and Tiesdell, 1991). UDCs reflected a fundamental policy shift in the UK transferring the initiative for urban renewal away from local authorities and towards the private sector through single function agencies, unencumbered by diverse local authority responsibilities and under the direct control of central government. Under its terms of reference, the primary objective of a UDC was: 'to secure the regeneration of its area . . . by bringing land and buildings into effective use, encouraging the development of existing and new industry and commerce, creating an attractive environment and ensuring that housing and social facilities are available to encourage people to live and work in the area' (Local Government, Planning and Land Act, 1980).

UDCs effectively established a temporary emergency planning regime, empowered and resourced to achieve their single objective of regeneration. UDCs were also intended to play a facilitative role. Rather than directly financing and constructing residential, industrial and commercial projects, UDCs were to physically regenerate and service land. By being entrepreneurial and fast-moving, it was considered that UDCs would be able to respond to opportunities as they arose. This resulted in a commercially realistic and flexible mode of planning, but primarily one oriented to the short-term needs of private capital. Thus, in Shad Thames the onus was on private sector developers to spot the evident potential for the conversion of the vacant waterside warehouses to residential uses within easy walking distance of the City of London.

The key project that initiated the housing-led revitalization of Shad Thames was New Concordia Wharf by Andrew Wadsworth (Figure 7.9). In 1979, Wadsworth, then aged 22, had moved to London from Manchester. Fed up with living in Fulham and Kensington, he started looking for a warehouse on the river. In September 1979, he found New Concordia Wharf, a Victorian grain warehouse built in 1885, and situated east of Tower Bridge on the corner of St Saviour's Dock. It took a year to persuade the owners, who also owned the adjacent Butler's Wharf site, to sell, but in December 1980, Wadsworth managed to acquire the 120 000 sq ft building. By this time, Wadsworth had also formed the Jacobs Island Company.

In April 1981, planning consent was granted for a conversion scheme. Rather than just residential units, Wadsworth's intention was to produce a mixed use development. He also insisted that the building be converted to shell stage only to allow future users to fit out their own spaces. The final scheme consisting of 60 flats (including 27 different variants of type, size and shape); 20 000 sq ft of workshops/studios; 3 000 sq ft of offices; 3 500 sq ft of restaurant space, mostly on the ground floor; a swimming pool; jetty; communal roof garden; caretaker's flat; laundry room and basement car park. In February 1982, however, the building was spot listed requiring listed building consent to be obtained. This was granted five weeks after application. Work began on site in May 1982 and was completed in May 1984. Despite the reservations of financing companies, most of the residential shells were sold before the building works had been completed (Baumgarten, 1984, p. 56). The project had a major effect on Docklands as a whole. Within five years, virtually every waterside warehouse in Docklands had been converted or was in the process of being converted or plans were in hand for conversion.

Figure 5.13

Butler's Wharf, the largest building in the Butler's Wharf complex, dominates the Thames-side elevation of Shad Thames. Its riverside elevation has a bold architectural treatment with prominent end pavilions with rusticated quoins, massive bracketed cornices and pedimented parapets. To the east of Butler's Wharf is the Design Museum.

The revitalization of Shad Thames was effectively led by its major landowners: the Butler's Wharf Consortium – made up of Sir Terence Conran as the major shareholder, together with Jacob Rothschild, Lord McAlpine and Conran Roche – and Wadsworth's Jacobs Island Company. The major landholding in the core of Shad Thames was held by the Butler's Wharf Consortium. In 1984, this consortium purchased an option to buy five hectares of riverside property called Butler's Wharf, including seventeen buildings, the largest of which was Butler's Wharf itself (Figure 5.13). Butler's Wharf is a considerable group of warehouses either side of Shad Thames extending up to the western bank of St Saviour's Dock and 150 yards inland. As the complex was an assortment of warehouses of variable quality and in various stages of decrepitude, it was acquired for less than £5 milllion.

Other land parcels around the fringe of the Butler's Wharf complex were bought up by Wadsworth's Jacobs Island Company. The Jacobs Island Company's landholding included the 4.75 acre, former Anchor Brewery, site adjacent to Tower Bridge. The inland area of this site was sold off with covenants which determined the use, design and completion date for its development. The masterplan drawn up entailed the demolition of existing buildings and the creation of the new public square and mixed use development known as Horsleydown Square (Figure 7.15). Wadsworth also held the waterfront site next to New Concordia Wharf, now called

China Wharf, which has been developed for residential use (Figure 7.9); the warehouses on a three-acre site on Jacobs Street/Mill Street next to New Concordia Wharf, which were converted to residential use, and a site on Queen Elizabeth Street that has subsequently become 'The Circle' development, a largely residential new build development (Figure 7.17). Following the lead of the Butler's Wharf Consortium and the Jacobs Island Company, other large developers became involved in Shad Thames, such as Rosehaugh who developed the Vogans Mill complex on the east side of St Saviour's Dock.

As the area was largely urbanized at the start of their operations, the LDDC considered that no urban design framework was necessary (Edwards, 1992, p. 93). The retention of many historic buildings, and the maintenance of the old street pattern and pedestrian routes encouraged new development to add to, rather than destroy, the pattern. Thus, as the largest landholders in the quarter, the Butler's Wharf Consortium and the Jacobs Island Company were the effective masterplanners for the quarter and could determine both the form and nature of development. As Edwards (1992, p. 93) describes: 'They have directly or indirectly established standards of design and construction for others to follow, and by disposing of land on leases as against freehold the company has, like a traditional estate developer, kept control of the area.' Thus, as seen in other areas of the London Docklands, such as Canary Wharf, developers with large land holdings had a vested interest in closely controlling the quality of each individual development and its contribution to the whole, in order to sustain and reinforce the composite value of the area. To enhance its attractivity, an element of functional diversity was also introduced into the area. Although many of the sites have predominantly housing uses, they also include a small element of other uses, such as restaurants, offices and shops on the lower floors. Shad Thames is emerging as a notable restaurant quarter serving a wider community. In addition, the London Design Museum was located on Shad Thames (Figures 5.13; 7.16), while residential accommodation for students at the London School of Economics diversifies the social mix of the area.

Conclusion

The quarter developed very quickly; the length of the river frontage between Tower Bridge and St Saviour's Dock was largely revitalized through residential conversions between 1983 and 1989 stimulated by the booming house market in London and in Docklands in particular. However, a lot of residential properties came on to the market at the same time, just before the residential property market collapsed. In the early 1990s, several development companies went into receivership, including the Butler's Wharf consortium. As a consequence, the future for Shad Thames is uncertain.

The remaining development opportunities in the Butler's Wharf consortium's considerable land holding are now being marketed by the receivers. However, it is questionable whether the new owners will exert the same sensitivity or degree of control over new developments in the area. There are still some parts of the quarter which need rehabilitation. The largest development opportunity is Spice Quay; the

Thames-side site between Butler's Wharf and the Design Museum. This had been the site of a Grade I listed building which has been moved and reconstituted elsewhere in the quarter. The latest plans for this site are for a 325-bed hotel. In 1991, the Butler's Wharf Forum was created involving local businesses and residents, the LDDC and Southwark Borough Council, with the aim of stimulating public–private partnerships to complete the infrastructure provision in the quarter, including a footbridge to link the two sides of St Saviour's Dock, thereby extending the riverside pathway.

Despite the impact of the property recession, the housing-led revitalization of Shad Thames benefited from the prospect of a strong residential market – subsequently reflected in the very high price of the flats created – as a consequence of its historic buildings, waterside location and its close proximity to the City of London. In many ways the manner in which Shad Thames developed was the result of a very permissive planning authority that, in effect, allowed the area's largest landholders to pursue revitalization in the way they thought best. Such an approach relies heavily on the quality and sensitivity of developers, and the likelihood of it occurring with the same results elsewhere is highly questionable.

CONCLUSIONS

Two of the key issues in housing-led revitalizations arising from the case studies are: first, displacement and gentrification, as shown in the case study examples of the Marais quarter, central Bologna and SoHo; and secondly, as in any restructuring, the creation of a robust market for the new use.

The precise relationship between conservation and change in the functional character of neighbourhoods is imperfectly understood. As Burtenshaw *et al.* (1991) question: 'Is it the expenditure on renovation and rehabilitation that encourages richer residents to acquire city-centre properties in a socially selective, "back to the city" movement, thus displacing lower income groups? Or is it the movement of the working class, more or less willingly, to newer and more comfortable suburban locations that leaves a vacuum which in turn is filled by people more willing and able to bear the costs of renovation and maintenance?' (Burtenshaw *et al.*, 1991, pp. 142–143). They conclude that while social and functional change and the conservation of the physical fabric of cities are intimately related, the chronology of cause and effect is generally locally determined. Thus, if, for example, the existing population simply wants better housing and quickly, a *functional* as well as a *physical* conservation – as in the Marais quarter and central Bologna – that includes the retention of the existing population, may be misconceived. Given choices, the desire for better housing may outweigh the attachment to the historic quarter. In Bologna, a greater proportion of residents were prepared to remain in the historic area as a result of greater subsidies to live in the city; better services and the physical environment of the city centre – which is generally higher than in the Marais.

The displacement and gentrification issues in SoHo are more complex. SoHo is not the more typical instance of the displacement of low income resident by higher income resident. Instead there was initially a functional gentrification where one higher value use or function displaced a lower value use or function. As Zukin (1989, p. 5) describes: 'the real victims of gentrification through loft living are not residents at all. Before some of the residents were chased out of their lofts by rising rents, they had displaced small manufacturers, distributors, jobbers, and wholesale and retail sales operations. For the most part, these were small businesses in declining economic sectors' (Zukin, 1989, p. 5). As in the gentrification of the Marais quarter, and however undesirable in terms of the functional change it might be, the restructuring of SoHo is part of the inexorable economic evolution of cities. To resist this restructuring might frustrate attempts to generate the investment required to conserve the quarter physically, leading to the deterioration and/or loss of the historic fabric. However, as in all housing-led revitalizations, there are issues concerning the loss of employment space and the role of, and need for, the retention of low-cost commercial space where small manufacturers can incubate, grow and mature.

It is important to note that SoHo was a market-led development, not a planned process. Initially, as the restructuring began, a blind eye was turned to violations of zoning and building codes. Nevertheless, later there was official support for housing developers. It was the interest of the large developers that confirmed SoHo as a mainstream – albeit highly expensive – residential area and which led to the displacement of artists as residents and the further displacement of manufacturing industry. This would only occur where there was a commercial incentive to convert the property to a new use. Thus, a key factor in the housing-led revitalization of SoHo was the strength of the New York housing market. In Manhattan in the 1970s, it was no joke that people looked through the obituary columns for apartments that might become available to let.

In both the Merchant City and Shad Thames, prior to the housing-led revitalization there had been high levels of vacancy. Thus, there have been fewer instances of displacement and gentrification. In retrospect, Shad Thames was an evident market opportunity offering the possibility of distinctive housing, much of it in converted industrial buildings in waterside locations, and within easy walking distance of the City of London. The challenge was for developers to create the financial packages that would realize that potential. Although the housing created was very expensive, the conversions were undertaken without major subsidies. The area, however, suffered as a result of the fall in the property market in the early 1990s with a number of developers going into receivership. Nevertheless, the housing market in the area has again begun to recover. By comparison, the Merchant City was a planned process led by the local authority and involving considerable public subsidies to encourage the functional restructuring of the quarter, provide a use for historic buildings and, through the creation of a viable residential market in an area with no tradition of such uses, bring people to live in and near the city centre. Although now established, like other locations, it remains vulnerable to the fluctuations of the property market.

6

REVITALIZING INDUSTRIAL AND COMMERCIAL QUARTERS

INTRODUCTION

This chapter discusses historic urban quarters that have traditionally been industrial or commercial quarters but have suffered various forms of obsolescence. Physical and structural obsolescence and – to an extent – functional obsolescence can be addressed by refurbishment and conversion. This creates a better stock of property in an area, however, a demand for the utilization of that property is also required. As discussed in Chapter Two, this often relates to the area's locational obsolescence – its lost competitiveness and competitive advantage as a location. The quarters in this chapter have also experienced locational obsolescence as a result of the changing economic structure of the country as well as the changes in the local economy. Such areas have therefore declined as their traditional functions have moved elsewhere to cheaper, more convenient locations. Although, many areas suffer from locational obsolescence, in historic urban quarters the capacity for responsive change is limited. In considering the functional regeneration, restructuring or diversification of these quarters, it is useful to bear in mind the example of Lowell where functional restructuring was achieved through attracting new industrial/commercial activities as well as tourism. In the USA, there are other examples of the functional restructuring of historic mill towns through the attraction of high-tech industries, when it has been recognized that their role as centres of textile or steel industries has become obsolete. Maynard, Massachusetts, and Pittsburgh, Pennsylvania, are two examples of this realization of the consequences of the changing world economy.

This chapter examines four historic industrial warehouse quarters with distinctive townscapes and clear local images as major areas of employment in the past. Nottingham's Lace Market and Birmingham's Jewellery Quarter are trying to maintain their positions as centres of production, while also diversifying and competing for positions as centres of consumption. In both of these quarters, an attempt has been made at a revitalization through functional conservation and regeneration. More determinedly in the case of the Lace Market, more relaxed in the case of the Jewellery Quarter. Bradford's Little Germany has had one historic period as a major centre for production but is now trying to re-establish a position as a centre of production and/or consumption through functional restructuring. Denver's Lower Downtown, formerly the centre of the town, was made obsolete by the migration of the CBD. It is now being revitalized to complement the new CBD. Many of these quarters have also attempted to diversify their economic base through residential and tourism developments. As noted in the previous chapters, tourism-led and housing-led revitalizations have direct and indirect impacts, and can significantly re-image places. However, as will be seen in the following case studies, efforts in industrial/commercial revitalization have less visible impacts and the success is more measured.

CASE STUDIES

THE LACE MARKET, NOTTINGHAM

The Lace Market is a unique British cityscape containing some of its finest nineteenth-century industrial architecture. Few areas of Britain compare; the Little Germany quarter of Bradford – discussed later in this chapter – is the nearest equivalent. Until the nineteenth century, what became the Lace Market had been a residential area of large mansions and well laid-out gardens. In the 1850s and 1860s, there was an explosion of factory building as the area became the world centre for the lace industry. By the late Victorian period, without significant change to the street pattern, the area had been filled with model factory buildings (Figures 6.1 and 6.2).

Lace making reached its peak in Nottingham just prior to the First World War when there were about 200 lace making firms in the area (Crewe and Hall-Taylor, 1991). Thereafter, both the lace industry and the area went into decline. The decline was exacerbated by wartime bomb damage and post-war 'improvement' schemes that left raw and jagged edges of buildings to define newly widened roads. The nadir was reached in the 1950s and 1960s, when it became little more than derelict urban space and temporary car parks on otherwise abandoned sites. Nevertheless, although covering a smaller area than in its nineteenth-century heyday, much of the Victorian townscape has survived. It thus provides a geographic focus for revitalization.

Although the lace industry has virtually disappeared from the area, what distinguishes the Lace Market is the number of textile and clothing firms that exist within the historic townscape, preserving a functional link with the area's past through similar skills in the labour force. Research by Crewe and Hall-Taylor (1991) identified particular reasons for the continued concentration of clothing and textile firms in the Lace Market. One reason is the employment within the industry of skilled and predominantly female labour, usually reliant on public transport, preferring a location that is a single bus ride from home and which offers scope for other

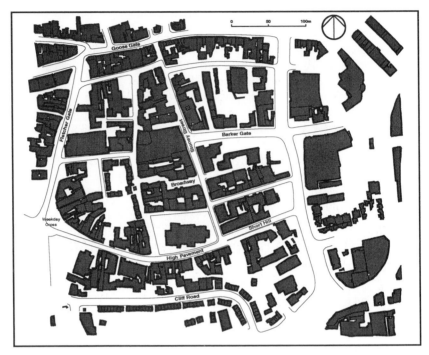

Figure 6.1

Plan of the Lace Market. On an elevated site to the east of Nottingham city centre, the Lace Market is variously defined: to the south there is a cliff escarpment; to the east and north-east the area slopes away into St Anns. To the north, the area becomes the eastern part of the city centre, and to the west across Fletcher Gate are the main retail areas of Nottingham city centre.

activities, such as lunchtime shopping. Another reason is the close networking and interrelation of firms within the Lace Market, as a result of their historic proximity within a small area of the city and the amount and scale of sub-contracting among firms. The agglomeration of similar and inter-related firms has resulted in a strong local allegiance to the area. Nevertheless, due to obsolescent premises – for example, production lines spread over several floors as a result of the narrow plots – many firms would like to move out but do not have the necessary capital to make that move.

This is distinctly different to, for example, Bradford's Little Germany where the traditional uses had already vanished from the historic landscape. Thus, an important distinction must be drawn between the 'physical' conservation of the built environment – the 'built heritage' – and the 'functional' conservation (and regeneration) of the traditional activities of the area – the 'living heritage'.[1] This is the particular challenge presented in the Lace Market.

[1] These terms are used in the 1991 Tibbalds Colbourne Karski Williams Ltd (TCKW) report on the Lace Market.

Figure 6.2

The Lace Market, Nottingham. The quarter's character is derived directly from the nature of the activities that took place in the buildings. The warehouses and factories were utilitarian structures: lace buyers need to see the product in good light, while the fine nature of the lace-making also demanded good lighting. Large windows in load-bearing masonry construction were a significant engineering achievement. The Lace Market's scale is also atypical of English cities. The tall warehouses, built of the distinctive red-orange Nottingham brick, stand squarely up to the edge of the pavement to create canyon-like streets.

The conservation of the Lace Market

The preservation of the historic Lace Market began with its designation as a conservation area in 1969, rescuing the area from further devastating road building and redevelopment plans. Its status was upgraded in 1974 to a conservation area of outstanding national importance, making it eligible for building improvement grants under Section 10 of the 1972 Town and Country Planning (Amendment) Act. This two-tier categorization of conservation areas in the UK has subsequently been abolished. In 1976, the Lace Market Town Scheme was established giving city council, county council and Department of the Environment assistance for repairs to buildings.

From the early 1970s, the city's planning policies attempted a 'functional' conservation by seeking to protect not only the physical landscape but also the traditional industrial character of the Lace Market by resisting the conversion of warehouses to office use. The city council sought to preserve the diversity of the city's economic base. It was therefore not just a conservation policy but – perhaps more importantly – a local economic policy. As recently as 1989 in their *Lace Market Development Strategy*, the city council made a policy commitment to retain 500 000 square feet of textile accommodation within the Lace Market. However, this policy had always been threatened by the encroachment of office development which would fundamentally change the area's distinctive functional character and make it more vulnerable to the fluctuations of the more volatile office property market. Although, in a dynamic property market, differentials do fluctuate, during the 1980s rents for office space had often been four times those for manufacturing.

A more positive encouragement for the physical conservation of the Lace Market has been its status as an Industrial Improvement Area (IIA) since 1979. The report advocating the Lace Market's designation recognized that the area had undergone some improvements since its designation as a conservation area ten years previously. However, it also noted that it was still characterized by a generally run-down and neglected appearance. Buildings were in need of repairs and facelifts and working conditions inside the factories were poor. Powers to establish IIAs were contained under the Inner Urban Areas Act of 1978, with grant-giving powers to enable local authorities to assist local firms in external and internal improvements and conversions. The approach is short-term and concentrates on restoring confidence to stabilize or revitalize the area's economy. The poor image and reputation of run-down areas make them unattractive to work in and discourage investment.

The Lace Market is regarded as one of the more successful Industrial Improvement Areas (DOE, 1988a). By 1982, more than 100 buildings had been renovated under the various grant schemes. This has been beneficial for the physical conservation of the Lace Market. However, the individual and piecemeal basis of the grant regime diluted the impact on the area. Furthermore, as the emphasis is on physical improvements to the building stock and environmental improvements, the IIA, in common with the Town Scheme and other grants, is an example of a concern for physical conservation. This improves the physical image of the quarter but may have little impact on the economic base of the area other than a temporary stabilization.

The functional regeneration of the Lace Market

Local economic revitalization and development approaches often attempt to encourage local employment initiatives by providing assistance to those industries that are already well established in the area. Nottingham City Council has implemented and adopted various initiatives and strategies to assist the agglomeration of clothing and textiles industries in the Lace Market. As a quarter of manufacturing employment in the Nottingham travel-to-work area is in the clothing and textiles sector efforts to assist this sector are of major significance, particularly in the Lace Market which is the largest single concentration.

The Nottingham Fashion Centre (NFC) was established in 1984, at the instigation of Nottingham City Council and funded initially under the Urban Programme. It was an attempt to provide a coordinated response to the common problems facing the clothing and textiles industries (DOE, 1988b). It is therefore an example of the city council – albeit at arms length – becoming constructively involved with local economic development. The NFC was promoted as a way of enhancing the marketing capacity of local small- and medium-sized manufacturers to generate more trade. Since many firms had not developed their own marketing functions, they were particularly vulnerable to decisions made by their few main clients. The Centre also sought to provide an attractive focus for the clothing industry and to maintain a high profile in the local media and trade press. The NFC is part of a wider package of initiatives taken by the city council to assist the clothing industry. These include: equipment, technical and business advice; workspace schemes dedicated for the clothing industry; and a programme to help firms to restructure and become more competitive (DOE, 1988b, p. 90).

Despite the support for the clothing and textiles industries through the 1980s and the city's conservation strategy, functional restructuring of the area continued to occur. Between 1971 and 1989, in addition to a number of warehouses converted into restaurants and small businesses, sixteen warehouses were converted into offices with a further nine at that time (1989) under conversion (Crewe and Hall-Taylor, 1991). Local businesses were displaced as the benefits of the rehabilitation of the area were capitalized into rising property values and higher rents affordable only through conversions to office use. Nevertheless, in the absence of economic restructuring, it is questionable whether even a physical conservation would have taken place except through significant public subsidy.

The inherent weakness of the city council's functional conservation strategy and the attempt to protect the traditional industrial character of the quarter was its over-reliance on the regeneration of the clothing and textile industries to provide the finance to preserve and revitalize the area. The strategy was further undermined by a relaxation of national planning legislation. The changes introduced by the 1987 Use Class Order brought many of the office and light industrial uses into a single use class removing the need for planning permission for the change of use. In addition, the 1988 General Development Order removed the necessity for planning permission for changes between particular use classes.[2] The effect was that planning controls could no longer be used to prevent development which converted warehouses and manufacturing premises into offices.

---

[2] For example, development which changed the use of a building from Class B2 (general industrial) or Class B8 (storage and distribution) to Class B1 (business) no longer needed planning permission.

The functional diversification of the Lace Market

By the late 1980s, there was an emerging acceptance by the city council that market-led restructuring of the area's economic base was inevitable. The encroachment of office uses appeared irresistible and accordingly the city authorities modified their approach. The city's new approach was intended to be in sympathy with the character of the Lace Market, yet able to accommodate functional diversification without a large-scale displacement from the Lace Market of traditional activities or detracting from the qualities of the physical environment. The first such initiative came from Nottingham Development Enterprise (NDE); a public–private partnership company, initiated by the city council and embracing the expertise, finance and resources of the public and private sectors in order to produce a coordinated approach to local economic regeneration. Established in 1988, its major role was to identify specific opportunities to benefit Greater Nottingham's local economy and to initiate those projects most appropriate to meet that objective. NDE persuaded the DOE to 75 per cent grant aid a study of planning and economic development opportunities in the Lace Market.

In September 1988, a team of consultants led by Conran Roche was commissioned to prepare a development strategy for the Lace Market. Its brief was to marry physical conservation with a limited functional restructuring. Considerable market pressure for office development which would entrain some potential benefits was recognized. Increased rents would generate the income to enable the physical maintenance and conservation of the area, but would also threaten the survival of smaller textile firms with their low rents and narrow profit margins in an area in which they were strongly dependent. Hence provision would need to be made to protect them against the threat of displacement. Conran Roche's report was based on the prospect of rising property values and proposed four flagship developments: the New Lace Market Building and the Adams Hotel; East Broadmarsh; Barker Gate Gardens; and Plumptre Street Textiles (Figure 6.3). Flagship proposals of this nature were a direct reflection of the 1980's concern for property development projects which – it was claimed – would fundamentally revitalize the economic base of an area (see Healey *et al.*, 1992; Solesbury, 1990; Turok, 1992).

Conran Roche's report was adopted by the City Council as the *Lace Market Development Strategy* (Nottingham City Council, 1989). The city also took up the recommendation for a public–private body to oversee the development. The Lace Market Development Company (LMDC) was set up in September 1989, intended to have a five-year life. The LMDC was a joint-venture company with 50 per cent local authority ownership and four developers with equal shares. The LMDC was intended to be an explicitly property-led regeneration agency. Unfortunately in the interval between publication of the Conran Roche report and the formation of LMDC, developers had also identified the opportunities and bought up the land, thus tying the hands of the LMDC. The LMDC's activities were further hampered by coming into operation concurrently with the onset of the recession in the property and construction industries.

The *Lace Market Development Strategy* was an attempt to resist the indiscriminate market-led economic restructuring of the Lace Market. However, the city was still

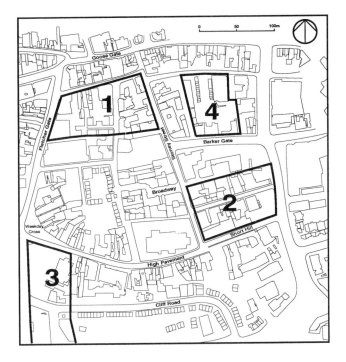

Figure 6.3

Flagship proposals from the 1989 *Lace Market Development Strategy*:
(i) This development – the Lace Market Building – would act as a focal point and gateway to the Lace Market, providing speciality retail themed to fashion – reflecting the observation that Nottingham does not have a distinctive shopping quarter – and office accommodation. The adjacent Adams factory would be converted into a luxury hotel, with high quality retail space on the ground floor and high quality apartments on the upper floors. The space between these two developments would become a public open space with additional car parking provided below.
(ii) The acquisition of a number of buildings around Plumptre Street to house at affordable rents firms relocated from the Adams factory and other displaced textile firms.
(iii) The eastward extension of the existing Broadmarsh Centre to the south-west of the Lace Market, with two floors of retail and residential apartments on upper floors.
(iv) Barker Gate Gardens to the south would be converted to residential development, while those of poorer quality to the north would be replaced with new residential development.

attempting to protect the city centre's other office areas and the diversity of the area's economic base by resisting the market's attempts to address the obsolescence of the area. In February 1991 the city council attempted to reassert planning control over changes of use in the Lace Market by submitting an Article 4 Direction to remove building owner's permitted development rights for changes from industrial to office use. However permission was refused by the Secretary of State because there was insufficient justification for the removal of permitted development rights and – in any case – the changes had been introduced as deregulatory measures to improve efficiency and widen choice in the use of commercial buildings. Later, the city council contested and – lost on appeal – two planning applications involving the conversion of properties on Stoney Street to office use. This was overwhelming evidence that planning policy could no longer control functional change in the area. It could be argued that a market-led restructuring could have turned the Lace Market's fortunes around. The city council are now showing signs of taking a more pragmatic approach, but this change may have come too late as the property boom of the late 1980s in the area could have attracted significant investments.

The inability to control market-led restructuring of the Lace Market forced the city council into a belated consideration of the need for further functional diversification. As discussed in Chapter Four, the exploitation of the area's heritage and character – both physically and functionally – for tourism development is an economic diversification ostensibly able to synchronize with the area's existing economic base. One of the suggestions of the Conran Roche report had been the designation of the Lace Market as a British version of US national historic urban parks. Consultants were commissioned in October 1990 to develop this idea in order to help persuade the Department of the Environment to designate the Lace Market as Britain's first national heritage area.

The precedent cited in the Conran Roche report was Lowell. However, the direct transfer of Lowell's experience to the Lace Market was not appropriate. At Lowell, the historic built environment remained largely intact, but the buildings were derelict and disused. For the Lace Market where traditional use remained, the consultants' proposals therefore placed emphasis upon both the physical and the functional conservation of the area (TCKW, 1991). Their report recognized the importance of the overall environmental quality if the area was to be perceived as a tourist attraction rather than as a decaying Victorian industrial area and proposed a comprehensive urban design strategy. This made recommendations for urban 'healing' (the restoration of the traditional urban form in terms of identifiable urban spaces, streets and squares), as well as the retention, reinforcement and promotion of traditional Lace Market activities. Another part of the strategy identified the need to establish a strong and recognizable corporate image and identity for the area. The report, however, was unable to persuade the Department of the Environment to embrace the concept of national heritage areas.

Even without the threat of extensive commercial development, a strategy based on preserving and promoting the clothing and textile industries and increasing the tourism potential of the area is not without problems or conflicts. From the clothing industry there are concerns that increased promotion of the area as a tourist attraction would trivialize and undermine the textile manufacturers' hard-earned reputation for quality. Furthermore, few tourists will be attracted to an industrial area in poor repair. Before a tourist industry can develop, a critical mass of facilities such as visitor attractions, restaurants, car park improvements, accommodation and – as significantly – environmental improvements must be in place. This will involve substantial investment. Some of these are already underway, such as, improvements to Weekday Cross, the latest phase of Nottingham's Heritage Trail that links the Castle to the Lace Market, balancing these tourism attractions and drawing people through the town. On High Pavement, next to the existing Lace Hall Museum, the Shire Hall site received a substantial grant from the European Regional Development Fund for development as a Museum of Law.

A substantial functional diversification and restructuring of the Lace Market could create a mixed function urban quarter. The 1992 *Strategy Review* noted that, as a consequence of the recession, the scope for alternative viable uses, apart from office uses, had increased and identified an opportunity: 'housing development potential on some sites, including an "urban village" quarter' (Nottingham City Council, 1993a, p. 5). In essence, this would require a number of residential developments and conversions to residential use to supplement the existing uses and to increase the local demand for retail uses. There is already a small amount of residential development in the Lace Market. In the late 1970s and the early 1980s, three of the larger derelict sites within the Lace Market had been developed for housing, two by the city council and one by a housing association. There are also a small number of 'loft' and 'penthouse' conversions at the upper end of the housing market. However, the prospect of large-scale residential development was not central to the revitalization strategy.

The future of the Lace Market

At present the Lace Market is at a watershed. The downturn in the property market after 1989, placed on hold the prospect of large-scale property development, while in 1991, the city council was specifically advised not to include the Lace Market in its first round City Challenge bid. Thus, the Lace Market lies outside the boundary of Nottingham's successful bid for the neighbouring areas of Sneinton and St Anns. The 1992 *Lace Market Development Strategy Review* recognized that major flagship developments were less likely to be viable, and that phased projects, interim uses and innovative funding packages were likely to be needed (Nottingham City Council, 1993a). The city council also recognized that it was no longer feasible to use planning powers to retain Lace Market premises for industrial use. Instead it has adopted a policy of positive business support measures concentrating on sustaining and developing viable businesses to meet current market conditions (Nottingham City Council, 1992).

Currently, there is a significant surplus of vacant floorspace for both industrial and office use in the Lace Market with more than one-third of the office stock standing vacant. If other city centre and city fringe sites are developed for office use, then the pressure for office development might be eased on the Lace Market over a longer period. But, the building of high quality office space around the city centre is having a knock-on effect which is further marginalizing the Lace Market as an office location, leading to increased vacancy and dereliction unless other uses are found. The second review of the Lace Market Strategy (September 1995) notes that 'Although there has been considerable achievement in certain areas, notably tourism, there are still serious issues relating to the Lace Market' (p.1). The Quarter still has high levels of office vacancy, the remaining clothing and textile companies face serious difficulties, attempts to attract housing have not been successful due to lack of adequate financial support and key buildings, like the Adams building, are lying vacant and deteriorating. As a consequence of continued difficulties faced by the Lace Market the City Council have amended planning policies 'to facilitate mixed uses' (p.2) while retaining their commitment to the clothing and textile sector. The City Council also continues in its commitment to conservation and environmental improvement.

In the UK, recently revised national planning guidance places increased emphasis on keeping historic buildings in active use as the best way of preserving them (DOE, 1994). It is suggested that where the original use is no longer viable that local planning authorities consider the capacity for change. Thus, if the building is economically obsolete in its existing use, then new uses should be found for the building. Such consideration is belatedly being taken on board in the Lace Market as the probability of revitalization through regeneration and conservation appears remote.

THE JEWELLERY QUARTER, BIRMINGHAM

Birmingham's Jewellery Quarter lies to the north-west of the city centre. It is separated from the city centre by the Great Charles Street Expressway and the Birmingham and Fazeley Canal. However, these physical barriers have helped to preserve it from the pressures of development, creating a relatively peaceful enclave only minutes from the city centre (URBED, 1987, p. 3) (Figure 6.4). Although around St Paul's Square – Birmingham's only Georgian square – the historic townscape is largely intact, much of the historic fabric has been destroyed. There are only fragmentary reminders of how the quarter had once been. However, rather than its physical landscape, the distinction of the quarter is the activities located there. As Victor Skipp, in his book *The Making of Victorian Birmingham* (1983, p. 52), states: 'Here we have something that must be virtually unparalleled elsewhere in twentieth-century Britain. For the Jewellery Quarter is an efficiently functioning modern industrial zone in which, not only are there whole streets of workshops and small factories which look much as they must have looked a century ago, but in a considerable number of cases they are still being used in much the same way' (from URBED, 1987, p. 4). As URBED (1987, p. 4) note: 'few other areas have survived so extensively for so long in what is largely the same use . . . it is the activities rather than the buildings which are its unique feature'.

Until the mid-eighteenth century, the area was a large estate owned by the Colmore family and was an attractive area with streams and a large pond. An Act of Parliament in 1746 enabled the estate to be developed. In 1779, St Paul's Church was built – unofficially named the jewellers' church – and shortly afterwards St Paul's Square was also laid out. Although, the area had been a centre for metalware production from the 1580s, the jewellery industry did not become significant until the late eighteenth century. Until the mid-nineteenth century, the area remained a residential area and predominantly unindustrialized. However, at this time, due to a rise in the demand for inexpensive jewellery and the discovery of gold in California and Australia, the jewellery industry began to grow.

The area had a ready supply of craft skills, and as jewellery making is a relatively small-scale activity, entry to the trade was relatively easy with low start-up costs. As the families moved to more salubrious residential areas, the former residential area was turned into a series of workshops: houses were converted

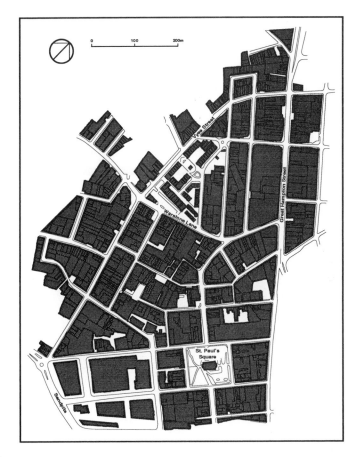

Figure 6.4

Plan of the Jewellery Quarter. The area traditionally considered as the Jewellery Quarter is approximately 100 acres (40 hectares).

and extended, new streets were cut across gardens and new workshops were built on vacant lots. All the gardens became built up with these workshops and the area became very densely packed (Figure 6.5). The workshops were among the most dense and badly arranged in Birmingham (Children's Employment Commission Third Report, 1862). This cramped environment became a characteristic of the Jewellery Quarter. Nevertheless, as it was highly skilled work and well paid, the trade expanded. By 1866, the jewellery trade was one of the largest industries in Birmingham, employing 7 500 people and the conversion of houses to workshops was well underway.

The trade continued to expand such that by 1886 about fifteen thousand people were employed in the area. The close interdependence of specialist skills meant that the industry remained concentrated in the quarter. Although there were some larger premises, the typical unit of production was the small artisan workshop or small

Figure 6.5

Houses converted to industrial premises in the Jewellery Quarter.

factory (Figure 6.6). In 1887, the British Jewellers Association was set up, and in 1890, the School of Jewellery. Both are still in the quarter and the school is assisted by local jewellery craftsmen who teach on a part-time basis. Jewellery manufacture in Birmingham reached its peak in 1914. By this time, it was the city's second industry employing over 20 000 people in the Jewellery Quarter alone. Due to the loss of the foreign markets and increased competition from overseas, the industry declined after the First World War. The industry continued to decline and by the 1960s the Jewellery Quarter area was left shabby and run down, suffering from severe decay and decline.

Figure 6.6

Industrial buildings in the Jewellery Quarter. The scale of the Jewellery Quarter is very different from that of the Lace Market.

Plans were proposed for the wholesale clearance of the quarter and the building of slab blocks of multistorey factories to replace the working slums. 'Even the manufacturers' association had espoused the idea that the replacement of the "warren of workshops and houses" by parallel rows of flatted factories set among lawns would be practical' (Pearce, 1989, p. 49) (see Figure 3.5). Nevertheless, the City of Birmingham had other priorities, in the 1950s and 1960s large-scale clearance and redevelopment of inner-city areas left the Jewellery Quarter relatively unscathed. The small scale of the buildings and fragmented ownership has prevented large-scale redevelopment. The local authority had originally acquired its current large landholding in the quarter to promote a large-scale redevelopment scheme and to concentrate the industry in about a third of its then area. Although, only part of these

Figure 6.7

The Hockley Centre and 1970s retail development in the Jewellery Quarter.

redevelopment plans was ever implemented, the area remained blighted by the proposals. The city council did implement the first phase of a plan to provide a purpose-built centre to house the trade by redeveloping a triangular site between Vyse Street, Worstone Lane and Hockley Street, compulsorily acquired in 1963. The intention was to house many of the jewellery firms that traded on the site in modern purpose-built premises, whilst freeing up the ground floor for retail space. The scheme also had provision for a multistorey car park to relieve the parking problems being experienced by the inner city area. The building was originally known as the Hockley Centre and is a seven-storey factory block. The building still exists but is under the management of a private firm and has been renamed 'The Big Peg' (Figure 6.7).

The effect of this development was summed up by the *Birmingham Evening News* in January 1973: 'Because of the new complex, many small firms had to move out of the area to other parts of the city because of expensive rents. The units are too large for one-man businesses and are more suited to light engineering. There is also a high cost for firms to equip the workshops.' Arguably, this upheaval contributed to the further decline of the industry which had employed 8 000 people in 900 firms in 1965, but only 4 000 people in 600 firms by 1985 (Pearce, 1989, p. 49). This example demonstrates how an ill-conceived planning decision initiated to preserve the jewellery industry actually contributed to its decline.

The functional regeneration of the Jewellery Quarter

The 1973 *City of Birmingham Structure Plan*, superseding the 1960 *Birmingham Development Plan*, introduced policy changes that were to begin the process of turning around the fortunes of the Jewellery Quarter. Two specific aims and objectives of the plan formed the basis for the Jewellery Quarter policy guidelines. These were, firstly, to encourage the growth of existing and the establishment of new industries and other sources of employment; and, secondly, to conserve and enhance the natural, architectural, historic and other qualities of the environment (Birmingham City Council, 1973, p. 15). To facilitate the preparation of a more detailed city centre local plan, further studies were undertaken, their findings were used to draw up the Birmingham *City Centre Local Plan* which eventually appeared in 1984. Prior to its publication, however, other policies and initiatives had been implemented to encourage the revitalization and functional regeneration of the Jewellery Quarter.

As an initial step in abandoning its policy of wholesale clearance, the City Council had declared a conservation area around St Paul's Square in 1971. In 1980, the City introduced two further conservation areas covering substantial parts of the Jewellery Quarter to preserve the remaining townscape and to prevent further dispersal of the industrial community: Key Hill conservation area (1980); and the Jewellery Quarter conservation area (1980). At the same time, it also extended the St Paul's Square conservation area. The intention of the conservation areas was to preserve the townscape but also to prevent further dispersal of the jewellery industry.

In 1980, the City Council designated the Jewellery Quarter as an Industrial Improvement Area. The Council noted that Birmingham's historical legacy was a wealth of old industrial buildings which were affected by poor environment, vacant sites and premises, poor access and servicing facilities, together with a high incidence of crime. Despite these factors, the council considered that such areas had potential to regenerate their local economies. The IIA designation gave owners a financial incentive to improve their buildings. By 1989, more than 370 projects had been carried out, costing nearly £11 million, almost 60 per cent of which came from the private sector. The *Birmingham Evening Post* reported in August 1989 that had it not been for the IIA designation and the resulting physical improvements to the quarter's building stock, many of the buildings would have been legally obsolete and simply closed down on health and safety grounds. It was also considered unlikely that the displaced firms would have been able to afford rents elsewhere in the city.

The policies applied in the 1980s recognized the emerging patterns of land uses within the quarter and effectively divided the Jewellery Quarter IIA into two distinct

Figure 6.8

St Paul's Square, Jewellery Quarter. This part of the Jewellery Quarter has been identified as a mixed use area with considerable scope for residential developments.

areas: the St Paul's Square area and the Jewellery Trade area. In the Jewellery Trade area the development of offices was not encouraged. In the area around the St Paul's Square, the City Council adopted an approach of functional restructuring by allowing the development of offices, but at the same time the amount of development was limited to protect the City Centre Primary Office Area. In addition, the 1984 *Local Plan* while not having a specific policy for the Jewellery Quarter, did identify that within the mixed use area around St Paul's Square there was considerable scope for residential developments if environmental standards could be met (Birmingham City Council, 1984, p. 15) (Figure 6.8). This approach to dealing with the issue of the possible displacement of industrial uses by offices uses contrasts with the blanket presumption against office conversion in the Lace Market. Equally, it should also be recognized that development pressures were different in the two locations.

The 1984 *City Centre Local Plan* (Birmingham City Council, 1984, p. 9) noted that industrial uses occupied 40 per cent of the central area. The Jewellery Quarter was one such area offering significant locational advantages to enterprises in the form of access to good communications, proximity to the city centre services, and a large potential labour supply with established links between firms. Thus, within the Jewellery Quarter, a policy of industrial improvement was pursued.

Although still the major source of employment in the area, the jewellery industry had declined since the First World War and faced further challenges: 'the industry is being hit by cheaper and in many cases more design conscious competition from abroad. Margins are under pressure from large buyers, including mail order catalogues and High Street multiples' (URBED, 1987, p. 5). 'Though the quarter primarily is the centre of the manufacturing jewellery industry, and therefore is largely competing in the middle-priced market, it still practises traditions of craftsmanship and specialization which have disappeared in other industries. The streets effectively form the production lines with most of the firms employing only a handful of people each' (URBED, 1987, p. 5). In addition to being strongly concentrated in the Jewellery Quarter, the jewellery industry was also becoming more concentrated within the quarter itself with most of the firms located in an area of approximately 35 acres.

Many of the firms are on long leases, and generally paying very low rents. Although landlords are reluctant to invest in the buildings, there are few pressures to move. Thus, the industry benefits from the continued concentration and economies of agglomeration. An additional benefit for the Jewellery Quarter has been the strong community spirit among the jewellers. This community spirit has played a crucial part in preserving the functional role of the area and maintaining the pool of skills needed to service the industry. The Jewellers Association was set up to represent the jewellers' interest in the area. The Association is committed to the area, keen for it to be improved and is in regular contact with the city council. The unity that exists amongst the jewellers has ensured that functional conservation and regeneration has been considered by the City Council when revitalization policies were adopted for the area.

The functional diversification of the Jewellery Quarter

From the early 1980s onwards there has been a discernible change in parts of the jewellery industry 'To cope with the recession and improve cash flow, manufacturing firms started to go into retailing, turning their front rooms back into showrooms. These have been joined by others who are largely importing jewellery and selling it from what were built as factory units' (URBED, 1987, p. 6). In 1982, there were only two retail outlets, this had swelled to nearly eighty by 1987 and over 100 today, mainly in Vyse Street, Warstone Lane and the Jewellery and Silver Centre. Nevertheless, in 1987, URBED (1987, p. 6) reported that 'many established firms regret the changes that have taken place, and the "cheap" image that most of the shops present'. Equally, the jewellery shops represented the main visitor attraction of the quarter, and suggested further potential for tourism development.

In 1987, the consultants URBED were commissioned to report on the potential for tourism development. They noted particular emerging patterns of use within the quarter. These were a 'Golden Triangle' (Warstone Lane, Vyse Street and Spencer Street), the 'market place' for jewellery; an 'Industrial Middle', where larger manufacturing firms are concentrated, centred on the blocks between Victoria Street and Frederick Street; and thirdly, the area around St Paul's which was 'becoming a "smart place", with offices for design companies, and the existing wine bar and restaurant are likely to be joined by a number of others, until the area could achieve a critical mass as a place to eat and drink' (URBED, 1987, p. 9). Significantly, the consultants did note that 'it would be wrong to see the entire Jewellery Quarter as a major general tourist attraction' (URBED, 1987, p. 25). URBED's report identified three types of attractions: the retail jewellers, the potential of the St Paul's area as a 'smart place' and the quarter's intrinsic historic character. However, as with most historic urban quarters, the historic attractions have to be made accessible through, for example, museums, factory tours and discovery centres. These facilities have and are being developed in the quarter. Nevertheless, as in the Lace Market, there are conflicts between the manufacturing firms and the demands of tourists and tourism. 'In the past the only people in the area were connected with the trade, and a stranger would be quickly recognized. This will never be true again and the level of crime generally has risen, making insurance harder and more expensive to obtain' (URBED, 1987, p. 7).

The future of the Jewellery Quarter

The *Birmingham Unitary Development Plan* (UDP) was approved in February 1991, becoming the sole statutory land use plan for the city until the year 2001 and superseding the 1984 *City Centre Local Plan*. The UDP develops the city's policies for the Jewellery Quarter taking into account the changes that have taken place in Birmingham, its city centre and in the Jewellery Quarter itself. The UDP recognized the Jewellery Quarter as a long established light industrial and commercial area and continued the commitment to the IIA stating that 'every effort will be made to support the manufacturing and industrial presence and non-industrial activity in the heart of the area will be discouraged' (Birmingham City Council, 1991, s.15.76) (Figure 6.9).

The UDP was itself significantly influenced by the 1990 *City Centre Design Strategy*, the final report of the Birmingham Urban Design Studies (BUDS). This was 'essentially a long term view about how to make the centre of Birmingham a more "user-friendly" place' (BUDS, 1990, p. 1). Although produced by consultants, it also represented the culmination of various urban design discussions and ideas for Birmingham that had currency through the 1980s. The strategy advocated a quarters concept for the central area of Birmingham recognizing 'a number of distinct quarters . . . of . . . potentially homogeneous townscape character' (BUDS, 1990, p. 50). The quarters concept has since been adopted as policy. Significantly, in this document, the area discussed so far as the Jewellery Quarter is actually divided into two quarters: St Paul's and Environs and the Jewellery Quarter. Area-based urban design frameworks are being prepared for each quarter (see Figure 3.6).

Figure 6.9

The Argent Centre, Jewellery Quarter. This former industrial building – its size and scale are atypical of the Jewellery Quarter – has been converted into managed workshops units.

The 1991 UDP notes that its success will depend upon the sustained reversal of the spiral of decline which set in during the 1970s. The long-term revival of the city's economy and the renewal of those parts of the city most affected by that decline will continue to be crucial (Birmingham City Council, 1991, s.2.7). The UDP intends to break the concrete collar around the immediate city centre and extend the city centre into the surrounding area, coupled with policies that seek to achieve a balanced mixture of uses, particularly housing. Consequently, with regard to the Jewellery Quarter the UDP notes 'the introduction of the residential element in St Paul's Square and its environs has contributed towards quality housing provision in the city centre. Further opportunities exist in surrounding streets and alongside the canal for additional domestic scale housing' (Birmingham City Council, 1994, s15.77). In addition, more emphasis was placed on encouraging the growth of development to link the Jewellery Quarter with the central core of the Birmingham. It was also noted that Great Charles Street/Queensway physically isolates the Jewellery Quarter from the city core and proposed: 'The re-introduction of surface crossings at Newhall Street and Ludgate Hill is proposed as part of the conversion of Great Charles Street to a local distributor and tree lined boulevard. This will enable greater integration of the Jewellery Quarter' (Birmingham City Council, 1991, s.15.69). The City Council have made many environmental improvements to the area by way of pavement improvements, car parking, litter bins and sign posting. The UDP notes that these improvements should further be enhanced and 'development in the Quarter itself should recognize and retain the unique character of the area and be sensitive to its surroundings. New development should generally be two to three storeys in height' (Birmingham City Council, 1991, 15.74). The new railway station on Vyse Street will further improve the Jewellery Quarter's linkage with the rest of the city.

LITTLE GERMANY, BRADFORD

On the edge of Bradford's city centre, Little Germany constitutes one of the finest collections of Victorian warehouses in Britain (Figure 6.10). Where the quarter differs from the Lace Market and the Jewellery Quarter is that the original industry has disappeared from the area. Thus, there was no opportunity or desire to pursue a functional conservation and regeneration of the area. The need was for an economic restructuring; new activities needed to be attracted to the quarter.

Little Germany was originally Bradford's merchant quarter. A major turning point for Bradford came with the advent of the Industrial Revolution. This change was largely due to the changes within the textile industry of worsted manufacture and the growth of a highly organized and intensively capitalized iron industry, especially after 1760 (Firth, 1990). By 1850, Bradford had been transformed from a small market town with a population of approximately 16 000 at the turn of the century to a thriving industrial/commercial centre of approximately 100 000: 'the wool capital of the world' (Bradford Economic Development Unit (BEDU), 1991a).

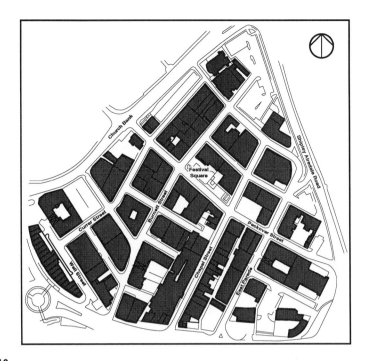

Figure 6.10

Plan of Little Germany, Bradford. Covering approximately twenty acres, it consists of eighty-five buildings, of which fifty-five are listed; the highest concentration of listed industrial buildings in England.

During this period of growth, an increasing number of foreign merchants, particularly German, came to reside in Bradford. By the mid-nineteenth century these merchants were able to invest in high quality buildings, many of which are now of architectural and historical significance. Thus, the Little Germany quarter was created and largely constructed between 1854 and 1874. This concentrated period of construction and development contributed to the quarter's architectural unity (Figure 6.11).

However, the area's boom abruptly ended with the outbreak of the First World War when the German merchants were forced to leave Little Germany. This quickly contributed to the area's decline and, more indirectly, that of the textile industry as a whole. The decline continued through the twentieth century. By the late 1960s, most of the remaining textile merchants had moved out of Little Germany and there were few remains of the area's original activities. Many of the buildings lay largely vacant and abandoned as they proved unsuitable for modern manufacturing warehousing purposes. Fortunately, the majority of the buildings in Little Germany escaped the clearance for comprehensive redevelopment which swept away many of Bradford's other Victorian buildings.

Figure 6.11

Little Germany, Bradford. Little Germany was largely constructed between 1854 and 1874. This concentrated period of construction contributes significantly to the quarter's architectural unity. These elegant buildings, with their decorative façades, reflected the power and prestige that the merchants commanded in the international markets. Within the quarter, the warehouses' grandiose architecture reflected the merchants' rivalry and one-upmanship.

The conservation of Little Germany

Little Germany's fortunes began to change in 1973 when it was designated a conservation area by Bradford City Council. In conjunction with the listing of the fifty-five buildings, this move was the first positive step towards securing the quarter's physical conservation. Since the early 1970s, a range of policies and initiatives has been applied to the area to foster its economic revitalization.

The area is strongly defined, but physically isolated from the activities of the city centre by the city's ring road. Equally, however, the ring road provides the quarter with good accessibility to the motorway network. The construction of the road system, together with a series of other improvements to existing roads, caused considerable blight, particularly for Bradford's older industrial areas which surrounded the city centre. Although the ring road scheme was irreversible, the abandonment or modification of other road schemes during the 1970s helped to eliminate further blight. Rather than comprehensive redevelopment the City Council adopted the view that small infill development, within the existing street pattern, was the best means to encourage private sector initiatives and to minimize planning blight.

Significantly, in contrast to the Lace Market and the Jewellery Quarter, there was no opportunity or desire to attempt a policy of securing a functional conservation and regeneration within the area. As the textile warehouses in the area were in a major decline, a functional regeneration would have been both inappropriate and commercially unrealistic. In terms of efficiency, production process innovation, and the cost of labour in other countries, notably in the Far East, the competition was too strong for Bradford and consequently Little Germany.

As the *Bradford City Centre Local Plan* (Bradford CC, 1984) signifies, both the city and county councils were committed to the revitalization of Bradford's old industrial areas. Their approach was 'to bring land forward for development, to stimulate new industry and assist existing businesses'. As a positive attempt to assist these central industrial areas, the City Council declared two Improvement Areas. Little Germany was in the Forster Square Commercial Improvement Area, which was declared in 1982. Considerable public funds were provided in the form of grant-aid to individual firms, as well as towards highway and environmental improvements. These public sector, 'pump-priming resources' were used to lever-in additional private sector investment. In all, about 25 per cent of the major buildings in the area have been improved though not all of these improvements were funded under the CIA. However, with the termination of Urban Programme funding in 1993 the CIA was subsequently discontinued. Little Germany was also included within the Inner Bradford Economic Priority Area, to which 'first priority' was to be given in the allocation of public resources to secure economic development.

With specific reference to Little Germany and the Cathedral Conservation Area, the council also permitted alternative uses to establish themselves within these predominantly industrial warehouse areas, such as small retailing outlets, cafés and motorcar showrooms, examples of which can be found in Little Germany. This approach was seen to be of particular relevance for these areas. Encouraging mixed-uses in multistorey buildings was seen as a way of bringing the buildings back into productive use, as well as giving greater vitality to such areas.

The council at the time also recognized that, in the light of continued de-industrialization, growth in office space within the city was needed to accommodate the increasing employment in this service sector. This directly contrasts with the Lace Market where office conversions were resisted. An appropriate location for such offices was the city centre or those areas nearby, such as Little Germany where vacant buildings could be renovated and converted to office uses. However, in 1984, when the council set out to encourage major office development on seven sites, only one was located in Little Germany, the Church Bank site. The conversion of existing purpose-built warehouses to offices was not always a straightforward process. Many had become obsolete, making them either undesirable or impractical for potential developers to consider moving into. Many buildings would have had to undergo considerable internal changes to make them suitable to the demands of the market as well as ever more stringent legal requirements. Though demand for such space at the time was low, the Council still tried to maintain its planning principles and design standards, as well as avoiding the unnecessary break-up of the city's architectural heritage. In recent years, the cost of renovation has been significantly increased by the VAT on building repairs.

The revitalization of Little Germany

The first concerted efforts, however, towards physically revitalizing Little Germany, began with the city council funding a major programme of stone cleaning in the area. Another project, undertaken to generate confidence and a feeling of dynamism within the area, was the development of Festival Square as a much needed public open space in the heart of the area (Figure 6.12). This was used for a festival in 1986 which has since grown to become the annual Bradford Festival. Today, it still enjoys

Figure 6.12

Festival Square, Little Germany. Festival Square was developed as a much needed public open space in the heart of Little Germany in the mid-1980s. Two key development projects face onto the square: Merchants House and the Design Exchange.

the same prime-status within the area. Following this in 1986, private sector consultants, URBED, were commissioned by the City Council, the English Tourist Board and English Heritage to draw up a Revitalization Strategy for the area.

The strategy identified the need for extensive environmental improvements including the provision of improved street lighting, in a style sympathetic to the quarter's industrial heritage, and the laying of new stone pavements. Parking was noted as a particular concern in the area. Subsequently, a 140-space car park was built in the northern corner of the quarter, and a permit system was introduced to enable on-street parking.

In 1987, the Council developed two important demonstration schemes in the heart of the quarter. Merchants House in Peckover Street, was a high quality office conversion, while the Bradford Design Exchange, was a conversion of three buildings, at the corner of Burnett Street and Peckover Street, to form gallery, studio and office space. An application by the City's Economic Development Unit successfully attracted £1 million worth of grant aid from central government under the Urban Programme to help finance the Merchants House scheme. Each of the schemes faces onto Festival Square. These schemes were intended 'to show the private sector what could be achieved with sensitive and imaginative refurbishment' (BEDU, 1991a, p. 24). As with other revitalization initiatives, their development was designed to generate confidence and create a positive, upbeat image for the area. The work on these two projects was largely responsible for attracting private investment to secure the rehabilitation of a further fourteen buildings. Over a four-year period, the combined sum of this public sector pump-priming and private sector investment came to more than £20 million (BEDU, 1992).

By 1990 much of this work was nearing completion, although, there was also a feeling that the area's recovery was not sufficiently advanced to enable it to become self-sustaining. It was, therefore, seen as vitally important to build on the momentum achieved by trying to attract further private investment into the area, as well as to secure additional general physical improvements. However, the inevitable desire to scale-down public sector involvement at the expense of increased private sector activity forced the city council to reduce the financial and staff-time investment that was needed for continued revitalization of the quarter. The search began for an agency of some kind to continue the coordination of the revitalization of the quarter.

URBED had proposed a locally-based Action Team be set up. This was similar to the Lace Market Development Company. However, while the LMDC had a pronounced property focus, the Little Germany Action Team had a broader remit. The aim of this agency was to secure concentrated efforts within Little Germany to take 'the vital next step towards self-sustaining regeneration' (URBED, 1992). 'Little Germany Action' was the name given to the initiative and, while initiated and managed by URBED, it was funded by the public sector, Leeds/Bradford City Action Team and British Telecom's 'Community Programme', and supported by Bradford City Council, Bradford Chamber of Commerce and English Heritage.

The initiative was based on a model developed by URBED through its work in Birmingham's Jewellery Quarter. The key features of the initiative were the ability to bring together and co-ordinate the public and private sectors; to apply concerted efforts over a short, defined period; and to develop a shared 'vision' and to draw upon experience – where necessary – from elsewhere. Support for the vision was further sought through the re-establishment of the Little Germany Improvement Association, which had existed for a brief period in 1986. The Action Team's intended strengths were that it would promote action on the ground, rather than producing reports and strategies, and that it would work closely with local people to ensure that initiatives were effective and tailored to their needs. The vision was based on an analysis of the economy of the area and the companies and organizations in it. It therefore sought to build on the area's strengths and to identify possible growth areas 'to create a diverse and healthy local economy and a vibrant, lively area' (URBED, 1992, p. 5). Building support for the vision was an important stage and involved regular contact, discussion and consultation with people, groups and companies, both within and outside the area.

Little Germany Action operated within the area from July 1990 until July 1992, a period which coincided with an economic recession. It had two full-time staff and a very small budget of £160 000 over the two years. It was established with six main aims: to encourage creative business to set up and grow in the area and to promote design and cultural activities in the area; to raise additional funds, particularly from the private sector; to help existing businesses in the area with growth potential to expand; to foster investment to bring empty or under-used property into productive use; to develop Little Germany's potential as a place to visit; and to help and encourage local people to play a more active role in the area and its future.

The main task for the Little Germany Action Team (LGAT) was to develop the four main strands of the Revitalization Strategy for business development, cultural development, tourism development and residential development. It was recognized that business activity was one of the most important aspects to be addressed. Commitment was made to promoting this sector and to ensuring that no other part of the strategy harmed existing local businesses. A working partnership was, therefore, sought between LGAT and local companies. A number of initiatives were undertaken over the two-year period. First, throughout the two years, Little Germany Action acted as a drop-in centre for local businesses and also for those seeking to move to the area. Business Fact Sheets including a register of available space in the area were made available to local companies. Agreement was reached with the Bradford Enterprise Centre to establish business surgeries in the area. LGAT updated and computerized the property register for the area listing all local buildings, their floor area, ownership and vacant space, to put companies in search of space in touch with building owners with space to let. A Business Watch Scheme was launched specifically to deal with crime and security in the area. Following research conducted to identify local training requirements, a need was identified for desktop publishing skills. In response the Design Exchange now provides desktop publishing facilities and local companies have been eager to utilize the service.

Many of the companies assisted by Little Germany Action have been involved in design and the arts, an indication of the appeal of the area's historic character to creative businesses. LGAT also offered services and organized a number of other related initiatives over the two years. In the first instance, it provided independent help and advice as well as an influential lobbying voice for the quarter's cultural organizations, many of whom experienced severe difficulties over the two-year period. Following the opening of the Design Exchange, LGAT organized a series of meetings of the Design Forum. This brought together a wide range of people from the fields of design and industry to promote the Design Exchange as well as to encourage debate about the area. LGAT also instigated the Sculpture Trail. The motive behind this being that additional attractions other than the fine buildings were needed to attract visitors to the area. This was conceived as an outdoor cultural attraction, which would project a positive cultural image. A sculpture competition was organized; the winning sculpture has since been installed at the top of Chapel Street.

LGAT facilitated the refurbishment of the Playhouse, a scheme largely undertaken to promote its revival following the British Film Institute's decision to locate elsewhere in the city in 1991. LGAT undertook initial design work and brought in local architects to work on the scheme. A grant of £25 000 was secured from the Urban Programme with a further £25 000 contributed by the Playhouse itself. LGAT also actively sought the development of affordable studio space in the area for working artists. In addition, there was a programmed 'Summer Season', the most significant of LGAT's initiatives in co-ordinating and bringing together local cultural venues. Such was the success of this work that Little Germany was the runner up in the Arts Council/British Gas 'Working for Cities Awards' for the use of arts in regeneration in 1992. By the end of the project's life, the area was able to boast three cinema screens, three theatres, three exhibition venues, two radio stations, graphics, darkroom and recording facilities, 7 000 square feet of artists' studio space, five bars with cabaret and music venues, Bradford Cathedral with its programme of summer recitals, and the Bradford Arts Club. Whilst LGAT cannot claim direct credit for these facilities, it did play a significant role in supporting and co-ordinating them and, most importantly, welding them together to form a cultural quarter. However, the impact of this area as a cultural quarter is not as significant as that in Temple Bar, discussed in Chapter Four.

In spite of Bradford's much heralded tourism initiative (see, for example, Kotler *et al.*, 1993), Little Germany has yet to play a full role in the city's tourist industry, despite the potential with its architectural and historical heritage, on a par with places such as Titus Salt's model industrial village, Saltaire, also in Bradford. Tourism was seen as an important area for LGAT to develop. There were, however, two main areas of concern. The aim was not to turn the area into a contrived theme park heritage experience, such as Wigan Pier, with actors appearing in historic costumes to make the place come alive. There was concern by local companies that increased visitors to the area would take up already scarce parking, make access more difficult and lead to potential security problems. Thus, the aim was to develop the area's visitor potential in a way which was complementary to the existing activities within it. LGAT undertook a number of initiatives, including commissioning signboards to orientate visitors, to highlight the places to visit and explain some of the quarter's history. In order to interpret the heritage of the area, a series of guided walks was organized as part of the 'Summer Season'.

In order to draw and hold visitors in the area for any period of time, it was recognized that accommodation must also be available. A number of proposals for hotel development in the area were made, strongly supported by LGAT, and practical assistance was offered to a number of developers interested in developing Austral House on Well Street. However, this has yet to materialize. LGAT also ensured that the area was featured in travel and visitor information produced for Bradford as a whole.

Encouraging residential development in Little Germany has been difficult, particularly as it is not an established residential location and the early residents would be pioneers. Discussions were held with the University of Bradford to assess the possibility of student accommodation in Little Germany, but the capital costs of building conversion, combined with the complexity of the area's buildings, made the proposition unviable. Other propositions for residential development in the area have been site specific. For example, the Downs Coulter building had been gutted by fire. The Council subsequently spent £80 000 on a scaffold-structure to support the remaining façade. In order to recover this outlay, it secured the right to market the site and the North British Housing Association converted it into 38 single-parent dwellings.

The future for Little Germany

Little Germany Action came to an end in July 1992. Since then, much of the revitalization momentum has been lost as the property recession has continued. LGAT contributed a lot of activity and energy producing a significant impact in addressing the quarter's image obsolescence, projecting a more positive image and profile for the area. However, there are few tangible achievements. The two demonstration projects, while successful in themselves, remain somewhat isolated. One of LGAT's most substantive contributions that will be greatly missed was their on-site management and day-to-day stewardship of the quarter. In combination, the various measures taken by LGAT helped generate a positive and successful image for the area, to generate confidence in the quarter and externally in the minds of prospective inward investors. In many ways, LGAT was performing a role analogous to that of town centre managers.

At present, the quarter is not covered by any blanket policy designations, with assistance now being of a project-orientated nature. The situation is one where businesses or developers bid for funds, assistance being available from either English Heritage, by way of Conservation Area Grants, and/or the European Economic Regional Development Fund (ERDF) since the area is officially an ERDF Objective Two Area. The present strategy means that, whilst securing area-wide revitalization remains the objective, this must be achieved by site- and building-specific and project-orientated initiatives. This case study illustrates Bradford's attempts to revitalize Little Germany with moderate public expenditure through management of its physical assets. It could be argued that Little Germany has suffered from policy conflicts in Bradford, being marginal to the main ambitions of the city which directed a number of key developments to other parts of the city.

LOWER DOWNTOWN (LODO), DENVER

LoDo – the *Lower Downtown* of Denver – is an historic warehouse district located at the north end of the Sixteenth Street Mall (Figure 6.13). As the city's birthplace and the original location for many of its institutions, it represents the largest concentration of historic buildings in the Denver Region. Containing a mix of offices, shops, restaurants and housing, it is also becoming a centre for Denver's arts and design community. Most of the buildings are three- or four-storeys high, of orange-red brick and constructed around the turn of the century. As the demand for new energy resources soared, real estate in the Denver downtown boomed in the late 1970s and early 1980s. The revitalization of Denver's Downtown was centred on the Sixteenth Street Mall, a mile-long spine running from the State Capitol and Civic Centre and running into LoDo. This is a successful attempt by the city to attract people to the city centre in competition with suburban malls and their free parking. However, as Collins *et al.* (1991, p. 70) note 'creation of the 16th Street Mall carried a price: rebuilding was so extensive, Denver lost much of its unique character. To be sure, it still had the mountain setting to give it a sense of place, yet preservationists felt that preserving Lower Downtown was critical to maintaining that sense'. LoDo also represented a human scale environment that juxtaposed with the nearby towers of the CBD.

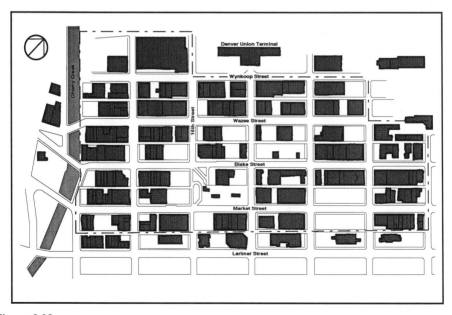

Figure 6.13.

LoDo or Lower Downtown, Denver. LoDo is a twenty-five block area bounded by Speer Boulevard and Twentieth Street, Larimer Square and the Central Platte Valley.

In the 1970s, LoDo suffered from a high level of vacancies. It was described by the *Denver Business Journal* as a collection of 'wornout warehouses, rundown hotels, and seedy bars' (from Collins *et al.*, 1991, p. 68). However, during this period preservationists began to identify historic buildings in the LoDo and to build public support for the idea of an historic preservation district. The original 1974 zoning ordinance for the area that contained LoDo envisioned a mixed use quarter. This ordinance was amended in 1982 providing additional incentives for residential development and historic preservation. Significantly, however, it failed to contain any controls over demolition or design standards for new construction. Although preservationists had supported the new ordinance, they had also expected proposals for design and demolition controls to be submitted to the city council which did not occur (Collins *et al.*, 1991). Between 1981 and 1988 an estimated 20 per cent of the building stock of LoDo had been demolished (Roelke, 1992, p. 7). Thus, the initial challenge was the physical preservation of the quarter.

In 1984 Mayor Pena instituted a major city centre planning effort. This was a collaborative process involving all the major stakeholders. Significantly the discussions took place during a lull in Denver's building boom. The process culminated in the 1986 *Downtown Area Plan* which recognized the importance of LoDo and the need to protect it. Historic preservation was one of the ten components of a downtown constitution. More specifically, the plan stated: 'The district must be preserved and redeveloped through a package of actions that stimulate new economic demand . . . and protect its historic character by preserving the existing buildings and promoting compatible infill development' (from Roelke, 1992, p. 3). The plan included a comprehensive package of recommendations for preserving and revitalizing LoDo, including the designation of LoDo as a local historic district with design and demolition review procedures. Although, political support for this was tenuous at first, the city council ultimately approved historic district status for LoDo in March 1988 (Collins *et al.*, 1991, p. 90).

The emerging revitalization of the area is a result of the robust *Downtown Area Plan* of 1986. This plan states that:

> Lower Downtown is an asset to the entire city and region, the last remaining historic commercial district in the Downtown core . . . [It] could be one of Denver's great landmarks . . . To function in that fashion, a strong, critical mass of older buildings in the area must be preserved, restored and reactivated. The preservation of only the 'best' or most historic buildings will not meet the need.

The plan also recommended various other measures. Many of these relate to the physical conservation of the quarter. First, there was a presumption against and control over demolition. In order to preserve the physical character of LoDo a critical mass of historic buildings had to be preserved, restored and reactivated. The onus was placed on the property owner to demonstrate the infeasibility of renovating or re-using an historic building. To stop the problem of historic buildings being replaced by surface level car parks, even when demolition was permitted, a replacement structure had to be agreed for the site. Between April 1990 and March 1992, twenty-six applications for rehabilitation and nineteen applications for minor repairs were approved, while only one new construction and two demolitions were approved (Roelke, 1992, p. 6). Secondly, minimum design standards were to be developed and enforced to ensure compatibility between new and old buildings. Thirdly, there were revisions to the zoning code to reduce density bonuses previously offered for building atria and plazas that conflicted with the district's traditional visual character. Conversely, to encourage a more diverse mix of uses within the quarter, developers could obtain density bonuses, if housing, underground parking or street level stores were provided. There were also reduced parking requirements for restored historic buildings. These new controls raised a certain amount of controversy and the city committed itself to biennial reviews for the first six years following adoption to consider whether to retain or repeal the ordinance.

In addition, there was a commitment to public investments, civic design improvements and business promotion activities aimed at revitalizing the district. An important action was a commitment to remove an intrusive viaduct that represented a major obstacle to LoDo's revival. The plan also acknowledged the contribution of waterways to Denver's history and recommended that Cherry Creek be revamped to allow access for enhanced use of the water amenity (Roelke, 1992, p. 4). The LoDo revitalization has significantly benefited from investment in infrastructure. This investment in terms of environmental improvements, repairing of streets, new street lighting, street furniture and pedestrianization, together with rehabilitated buildings, provides a physical conservation that provides a platform for the economic revitalization of this historic quarter.

Due to its historic character, scale, existing housing, available services and proximity to the Downtown core, the *Downtown Area Plan* identifies LoDo as a prime residential quarter in the central area and recommends housing development at a scale compatible with historic preservation. Increasing numbers of historic buildings are being rehabilitated for residential use as medium priced lofts. There are also attempts to provide a more diversified housing mix to balance the existing upper middle class housing: the Denver Housing Authority has plans to undertake conversions to create low income housing.

'Revitalization of LoDo continues with the number of new businesses which have been proposed and established' (Roelke, 1992, p. 13). Roelke points out that the establishment of the historic district has meant that those with investments were protected from demolition and blight while restored confidence in the area is attracting an increasing number of businesses. For the established businesses, the ease of access, and ample parking attracts more vibrant commercial activity into the area. LoDo continues to attract entertainment and arts-oriented establishments, unique shops, arts, retail and restaurants. The *Downtown Action Plan* proposes that LoDo should not be a continuation of retail and financial districts and should develop its unique character to juxtapose with the 16th Street Mall.

The 1988 ordinance, which designated LoDo as a preservation district, also created the Lower Downtown Design and Demolition Review Board (LDDDRB) as a sub-committee of the Denver Landmarks Commission. This Board has the power to review all proposed alterations or modifications to building exteriors within the area. The Board has played a significant role in preserving the remaining buildings in the area and its visual character. The plan also recognized that in order to achieve the goals of conservation and revitalization, it was necessary to create easily accessible financial assistance and provide economic incentives for business development in LoDo. To enable this, a revolving loan fund (RLF) was established by the City and County of Denver and Historic Denver Inc., and made possible by a loan from the National Trust for Historic Preservation. Five lending institutions have also committed to review and participate in RLF projects. All projects must demonstrate that they would not be viable without the RLF loan. The RLF makes low-interest loans not grants and loan applicants must present evidence of repayment ability. The fund provides low interest loan assistance for building and façade renovation. It was initially administered by the Denver Partnership through the Lower Downtown Business Support Office. Roelke (1992, p. 19) notes that while many projects have been successfully implemented without the RLF's assistance, some important projects would not have been possible without it.

The future of LoDo

The fact that LoDo is an integral part of the Downtown area is a major factor in its revitalization. It benefits from – and contributes to – the Downtown revitalization. 'These sectors: downtown retail, housing, hospitality and entertainment, must and will work in unison to come to full potential' (Roelke, 1992, p. 11). LoDo contains a mix use of offices, retail, restaurants, housing and parking and a growing design community which creates a symbiotic relationship with the Downtown offices. Roelke (1992, p. 3) argues that 'because of LoDo's distinct character as compared to the central core of Downtown, revitalization should demonstrate the advantages of character and feel of the area. Activities, street life and shopping are important site attractions that businesses offer their employees. As a marketing tool for the central core, LoDo provides a major attractant to entice new business to Downtown. It is therefore vitally important that the success of the outer sectors occurs, in order to regain office market strength for the whole of Downtown'. LoDo is also expected to benefit further from two adjacent developments – Corrs Field Sports Arena and Elitches Amusement Park – which will increase demand for offices, entertainment, retail and residential.

CONCLUSION

The four case studies discussed in this chapter illustrate different approaches for areas which had commercial/industrial functions in the nineteenth century and have experienced varying degrees of physical and economic obsolescence in the twentieth century. Little Germany experienced the most dramatic downturn in its fortunes, the Lace Market experienced a much slower decline and the Jewellery Quarter, after losing its world lead in custom-made jewellery, is enjoying an improvement in its fortunes. The three British quarters, in addition to suffering economic decline as a result of changing world economy, were for a brief period in the 1950s and 1960s also adversely affected by road building schemes. Although in

Figure 6.14

Stoney Street, Lace Market, Nottingham. Industrial uses in the quarter tend to lack the capital to keep the buildings in good repair. Thus, there are often stark juxtapositions between shabby warehouses in industrial use and the pristine appearance of another converted to office use.

all three the road building schemes were only on the edges, they each experienced varying degrees of blight. Their fortunes changed after being declared conservation areas. They also benefited from IIA and CIAs being declared in various parts of them. Over the past two decades, all three local authorities have made efforts to revitalize them.

In the Lace Market and the Jewellery Quarter, the revitalization approach has to a large degree involved attempts at a functional conservation and regeneration. However, the weakness of local firms and businesses has compromised the physical conservation and revitalization (Figure 6.14). In the Jewellery Quarter, after a short period of clearance threat and consequent blight, physical conservation and functional conservation policies are creating the necessary environment for revitalization of the quarter. As the quarter never lost its specialist function, planning policies have successfully aided the recovery and revitalization and regeneration of the quarter through selective functional conservation and regeneration.

The Lace Market is the most physically distinctive of the four case studies. It is also the most interesting example of a local authority's determination to revitalize the quarter through functional conservation and regeneration. The various policies and initiatives in the Lace Market show a local authority taking a proactive role in both conservation and revitalization, seeking to make full use of central government grants and schemes, while simultaneously trying to ensure a revitalization which preserves the area's industrial character. However, despite the many reports and initiatives, and apart from the achievements of the IIA and a grant-aided multistorey car park on Stoney Street, there is little tangible evidence of anything other than a stabilization of the Lace Market's fortunes. Arguably it was the persistence of the city council's functional conservation and industrial planning policies, with minimum diversification throughout the 1980s and into the 1990s, which frustrated and delayed development in the Lace Market. In terms of anticipating market trends and conditions, the Conran Roche report was commissioned at least five years too late and the opportunities of the 1980s for property development have passed, as sites in more preferred locations of Nottingham city centre have become available. Equally, although the area has not been comprehensively revitalized, it can be argued that it has – at least – been 'saved' from comprehensive conversion to office space. The distinction of the Lace Market is not just its physical landscape but also the textile and clothing firms which, although not the original lace industries, preserve a functional linkage with the area's past. Thus, physical preservation in the Lace Market was considered a necessary but not a sufficient conservation. The key planning and conservation dilemma remains, to what extent should the exigencies of revitalization compromise the Lace Market's traditional industrial character, firms and businesses that are under threat from internal and external competition.

The Jewellery Quarter is fortunate to house a viable function in jewellery making and retail. What is also important is that belatedly Birmingham is planning to improve its links with the city centre and drawing up urban design framework for future improvements. Little Germany, on the other hand, has never had sufficient attention and, having suffered from road schemes, has continued to suffer through policy inconsistencies. For example, the location of the National Film Museum in Little Germany rather than in the city centre and improvements to the link to the city centre could have changed its fortunes significantly. However, what is significant in the case of Little Germany is the achievements made through what could be called 'quarter management', with only moderate expenditure.

Both LoDo and Little Germany have attempted, and achieved, some measure of physical conservation. In Little Germany, the local authority, realizing that functional conservation would be a fruitless attempt, has made a creditable effort to bring about revitalization through physical conservation and functional diversification/restructuring. While for the time being physical conservation has been achieved, it has been difficult to gather momentum in terms of an economic revitalization. However, Bradford City Council has not helped Little Germany, as its central area policies have undermined their efforts to revitalize this quarter. By contrast – and for various reasons – LoDo has been more successful in building on a platform of physical revitalization to achieve an economic revitalization – but it is still early days yet. LoDo in Denver is an example of a successful revitalization of an historic urban quarter. It clearly benefits from being an integral part of the Downtown Area Plan designed to regenerate the whole of the Downtown, as exemplified by the 16th Street Mall. LoDo benefits significantly from the revitalization of the Downtown and – in return – it contributes to the overall Downtown regeneration. The quarter shows significant signs of economic revitalization, the physical conservation measures undertaken to rehabilitate the buildings and the environment are pivotal in this revitalization. This success has been aided by the ordinance and the revolving loan fund. Unlike the Lace Market, there was never an opportunity or desire for functional conservation; the City of Denver sought to create jobs and create a vital and vibrant area by attracting those investments willing to take risks in this historic environment.

7

DESIGN IN HISTORIC URBAN QUARTERS

INTRODUCTION

The revitalization of historic urban quarters involves two processes which inevitably conflict: the *rehabilitation* of buildings and areas which seeks to accommodate the consequences of economic change and *preservation* which seeks to limit change and protect an historic building and an area's character. Nevertheless, as Lynch (1972, p. 39) states: 'The management of change and the active use of remains for present and future purpose are preferable to an inflexible reverence for a sacrosanct past.' Thus, physical change is inevitable in historic urban areas: 'An environment that cannot be changed invites its own destruction. We prefer a world that can be modified progressively against a background of valued remains, a world in which one can leave a personal mark alongside the marks of history'. Any intervention into the physical fabric of a building irreversibly changes its history for all time, becoming part of that history. The act of planning in historic quarters therefore is the process of managing change in a sensitive and appropriate manner to preserve the character of the locality while permitting necessary economic change. As Burtenshaw *et al.* (1991, p. 159) describe: 'There is a need to plan for cities which are capable of evolution and can welcome the future and accommodate the present without severing the thread of continuity with the past.'

This chapter discusses the challenges of design and change with regard to the spatial and architectural character of the quarters. It begins with a discussion of the issues surrounding the management and control of that change. It then examines the design issues concerned with rehabilitation and those concerned with new developments focusing on both their urban form and their architectural articulation. The principal case study quarters in this chapter are London's Shad Thames and Glasgow's Merchant City, previously discussed in Chapter Five.

DESIGN IN HISTORIC URBAN QUARTERS

The management of change

To manage change requires effective controls, but the degree and extent of controls is always a normative issue. The protection, maintenance, repair, restoration and rehabilitation of historic buildings and areas all involve choices and judgements between competing claims. Nevertheless, there is an inexorable tension between the exigencies of rehabilitation – necessary change – and preservation – the prevention of change – which must be reconciled.

The spirit of place – the *genius loci* – is an historic urban quarter's most important aesthetic attribute. This should be maintained. The continuity and development of the quarter's *genius loci* is therefore one of the most important design considerations in an historic urban quarter. The maintenance of the visual identity and continuity of an historic quarter's physical character is critically dependent on the preservation and, where necessary, the rehabilitation of the quarter's historic fabric wherever possible. As Gratz (1989, p. 57) states, the key challenge is to 'preserve and restore the physical fabric without resorting to fake history and period pieces. The genuine maintains the continuity of history'.

Accordingly, most conservation and preservation ordinances include a presumption against the demolition of existing buildings. In most countries, before demolition of an historic building is permitted, the onus is on developers to demonstrate that there is no other economic use. Such controls are often highly controversial, particularly in the USA where they are imposed at the local rather than at the federal level. However, the extent of the control over demolition – whether to retain all buildings, only those of special character or only the best – calls for careful judgement. At Shad Thames, there was a policy of selective demolition. A significant aesthetic risk was taken by the area's planning authority, the London Docklands Development Corporation, to permit the demolition of certain historic buildings of indifferent quality or in poor repair and of little architectural or townscape importance.

Similarly, in most conservation legislation and ordinances, there is usually a general presumption against change and usually controls restricting the amount and nature of change to buildings. The degree of control for any particular building can vary, but is usually more restrictive for 'listed' or 'landmark' buildings. Equally, such buildings usually have greater eligibility for grant aid and other assistance. Grant aid also usually requires a certain standard of workmanship – on penalty of the grant being withdrawn – and is usually paid in arrears to ensure the quality of the work.

The threshold between regulated and unregulated change is important as the aggregate effect of a large number of relatively small changes can, over time, result in the erosion of the character of the quarter. In the USA, at the local level most historic preservation districts have a Review Board which permits or refuses changes to the exterior of buildings. Such Review Boards place a discretionary layer of control over the zoning system. Except where required by a local ordinance, changes to historic buildings in the USA do not normally require

1. Every reasonable effort shall be made to provide a compatible use for a property which requires minimal alteration of the building structure, or site and its environment, or use a property for its originally intended purpose.

2. The distinguishing original qualities or character of a building shall not be destroyed. The removal or alteration of any historic material or distinctive architectural features should be avoided when possible.

3. All buildings, structures, and sites shall be recognized as products of their own time. Alterations which have no historical basis and which seek to create an earlier appearance shall be discouraged.

4. Changes which may have taken place in the course of time are evidence of the history and development of a building structure, or site and its environment. These changes may have acquired significance in their own right, and this significance shall be recognized and respected.

5. Distinctive stylistic features or examples of skilled craftsmanship which characterize a building, structure or site shall be treated with sensitivity.

6. Deteriorated architectural features shall be repaired rather than replaced, wherever possible. In the event replacement is necessary, the new material should match the material being replaced in composition, design, colour, texture and other visual qualities. Replacement of missing architectural features should be based on accurate duplication of features substantiated by historic, physical or pictorial evidence rather than conjectural designs or the availability of different architectural elements from other buildings or structures.

7. The surface cleaning of structures shall be undertaken with the gentlest means possible. Sandblasting and other cleaning methods that will damage the historic building materials shall not be undertaken.

8. Every reasonable effort shall be made to protect and preserve archaeological resources affected by, or adjacent to, any product.

9. Contemporary design for alterations and additions to existing properties shall not be discouraged when such alterations and additions do not destroy significant historical, architectural or cultural material and such design is compatible with the size, scale, colour, material, and character of the property, neighbourhood or environment.

10. Wherever possible, new additions or alterations to structures shall be done in such a manner that if such additions or alterations were to be removed in future, the essential form and integrity of the structure would be unimpaired.

Figure 7.1

The Secretary of the Interior's standards for historic preservation.

permits. Control over rehabilitation is, however, exerted through a system of financial and tax incentives to encourage owners to rehabilitate historic buildings to acceptable standards. This has meant that the standards to which owners must conform, if they wish to benefit from tax credits, have had to be defined and published (see Figure 7.1). The standards for rehabilitation are deceptively simple but they are also supplemented by guidelines which amplify the provisions and indicate the way in which they should be applied in particular cases. This combination of rehabilitation standards and tax credits, results in controls that can be quite exacting, for example, the detail of replacement windows (see Yeomans, 1994). These standards and guidelines are quite rigorous but do demonstrate a particular philosophy with which many are in general agreement. The policy is one that requires alterations to be clearly distinguished in order to avoid any suggestion of 'fake history' (Yeomans, 1994, p. 167). There is, however, some debate over the details of the provisions; points 3 and 9 are regarded as the most contentious (see Yeomans, 1994; Gleye, 1988).

In the UK, listed building consent is required for most changes to listed buildings, while any building's location within a conservation area will usually be a material consideration in applications for planning permission. Many local planning authorities have *ad hoc* advisory conservation area panels to advise over applications in conservation areas. In addition, as a matter of good practice, many local planning authorities consult with local amenity societies, such as the Victorian Society. At the national level, both the Royal Fine Arts Commission and English Heritage can make representations with regard to planning applications. However, many small-scale changes are regarded as 'permitted development' and therefore escape detailed planning controls (see, for example, Yeomans, 1994, pp. 159–178). Subject to the approval of the Secretary of State for the Environment, local planning authorities can remove the permitted development rights of property owners within conservation areas. Thus, development of a relatively minor nature that does not normally require formal planning consent is brought under planning control thereby increasing the range of activities and change which come under planning control.

Although excessive control is always possible, there will always be some who resent the tyranny of any stricture or limitation on their actions. Nevertheless, it is valid to appreciate the irony 'that current conservation planning controls would have frustrated the creation of most of the historic buildings they now protect' (Ashworth and Tunbridge, 1990, p. 9). Rogers (1988, p. 875) notes that it is disturbing to realize that had the conservativist outlook of today prevailed, the magnificent buildings adjoining St Mark's Cathedral in Venice may well have been denied planning permission on the grounds that their construction destroyed the pristine architectural environment. Equally, if there had been conservation areas in the past, there may not have been a Baroque Rome or Haussmann's Paris. Nevertheless, it would be misleading to suggest that the only options are total control or no control. Control and freedom do not exist in isolation: there is a perennial dialectic between them. The key issue therefore is the degree and magnitude of permitted change and the implementation of controls relative to the historic character of the quarter. The control of change in such areas needs to be a negotiated process involving the reaching of consensus. As people often have differing values, the preservation and conservation of historic artefacts inevitably involves a negotiation and decision-making process that has to resolve or choose between competing values; as Sir Hugh Casson (1984, p.ix) wrote: 'The essence of sound conservation is judgement.'

Visual continuity in historic urban quarters

The visual and physical continuity of historic urban quarters raises the issues of the 'robustness', permanence and resilience of the built fabric and other physical attributes of the quarter. Within Modernism there were ideas about the impermanence of buildings (see, for example, MacCormac, 1983b, p. 741). This had its roots in the potential of industrial production: buildings, like motor cars, could be just another mass produced product with built-in obsolescence, designed to be discarded once their immediate utility was extinguished. However, this attitude is antithetical to architecture's traditional place-making and place-defining qualities. It is the relative permanence of an urban space that helps establish its qualities as a meaningful place.

Aldo Rossi in *The Architecture of the City* (1966, 1982) describes as 'pathological' those built form elements which become frozen in a former time period and retard the process of urbanization: 'such a museum piece is like an embalmed body which only gives the appearance of being alive' (Eisenman, 1982, p. 6). However, he notes that historic built form elements within a city need not only be pathological, they might alternatively be 'propelling', 'serving to bring the past into the present and providing a past that can still be experienced' (Eisenman, 1982, p. 6). The survival of such elements through to the current period largely happened in an era of *laisser faire* prior to the emergence of comprehensive planning controls and state intervention in the property market to effect their survival. As Burke (1976, p. 117) states: 'Until recent years conservation was scarcely recognised as a subject for national government policy. Buildings and ground layout from the past survived fortuitously largely on their own merits, and chiefly because they continue to serve useful purposes.' This resilience may have been through economic necessity, but equally was an expression of certain aesthetic and/or cultural values, for example, the urban scene is sufficiently desirable to be retained rather than demolished.

The patterns of the infrastructure – streets and squares – generally have a greater resilience than buildings. Equally, the cadastral unit itself and its sub-divisions may also be more enduring than individual buildings. Nevertheless it is the buildings, and furthermore their façades – the external surfaces defining the public realm – that chiefly provide the sense of 'place' and 'time' and establish the quarter's physical character. Since the retention of the façade presupposes the retention of the pattern of street and squares, the cadastral unit and the historic plot division, it is therefore the façade which is arguably the most important layer of permanence. Where a particular urban scene has maintained a relative continuity over a period of time, however, the functions behind those external surfaces may well have varied. Often the physical fabric of a building outlives the functions for which it was created. Thus, the original function or purpose for which a building was designed is not a 'binding' constraint in terms of the maintenance of the quarter's visual character. This suggests a relatively 'loose fit' between form and function, such that function may alter independently of form. A loose fit of form and function is particularly true of warehouses – and of office buildings generally – the dominant building type in most of the quarters featured in this book. Nineteenth-century warehouses rarely require scholarly restoration and not only do they lend themselves to conversion, depending on their location, they offer a range of possible new uses: residential, commercial, retail, office or workshop and studio uses. The flexibility of such structures is congruent with the credo of 'loose fit long life'.

Taken to an extreme, Lynch (1972, p. 32) describes a design doctrine that distinguishes between 'inside and private' and 'outside and public' where 'only the external historical shell need be preserved or reconstructed. It can then shelter current, active uses, and internal physical modifications suitable to those new uses are allowed. "Outside" are public, historic, and regulated, while "inside" are private, fluid, and free'. While Lynch's interior–exterior, public–private dichotomy is a convenient distinction to make, it is an over-simplification and must be qualified; there is a reciprocal relationship by which the visual effect of the interior informs the exterior. For example, as Lynch (1972, pp. 32–34) describes, in restoring the Nash terraces around Regent's Park in London for modern offices, the façades were rebuilt according to the original designs, but enough of the former internal arrangements was also required so that the view from the street would also have the right sense of depth.

REHABILITATION IN HISTORIC URBAN QUARTERS

With respect to historic buildings, Fitch (1990, pp. 46–47) suggests a useful classification of 'levels of intervention according to a scale of increasing radicality' (see Figure 7.2).[1] 'Preservation' and 'restoration' are generally only of major importance when dealing with buildings of exceptional architectural or historical quality. Most of the buildings that are considered in the case studies do not come into this category. 'Reconstitution' and 'replication' have occurred in some of the case studies considered in this book, but such actions are rarely respectable except in certain, very specific situations. The term 'rehabilitation' has been used in this book as a generic term to include restoration, refurbishment and conversion. Rehabilitation includes not only the most dramatic cases of change requiring a certain amount of internal and external alteration, but also bringing the building into line with the expectations of contemporary users, for example, in terms of safety and comfort standards. As Lynch (1972, p. 32) notes, even this poses questions of the building's aesthetic integrity: 'To what degree does contemporary utility, however discreetly provided, rupture the sense of historical integrity?'

There are various levels and degrees of rehabilitation. Appleyard (1979, p. 26) discusses 'surface' and 'deep' rehabilitation. His preference is for deep or 'gut' rehabilitation including both external and internal rehabilitation; a very purist concern for the aesthetic and architectural integrity of the entire building, Implicitly, deep rehabilitation must also retain the building's original function; it is therefore a 'refurbishment'. While deep rehabilitation of this nature may be desirable, maintaining both the quarter's physical and functional character *and* the original

1 The precision of terms is important as the words are sometimes used interchangeably which can create a confusion of intention. In this book, for clarity, some of Fitch's terms have been amended; his original terms are shown in parentheses.

PRESERVATION
The maintenance of the artefact in its current physical condition. 'Nothing is added to or subtracted from the aesthetic corpus of the artifact.'
(Fitch, 1990, p. 46).

RESTORATION
The process of returning the artefact to the physical condition in which it would have been at some previous stage of its morphological development.

REFURBISHMENT (Conservation and consolidation)
The physical intervention in the actual fabric of the buildings to ensure the continued performance of its structure and fabric.

RECONSTITUTION
The piece-by-piece reassembly of a building, either *in situ* or on a new site.

CONVERSION (Adaptive use)
The adaptation of a building to a new function or use.

RECONSTRUCTION
The re-creation of vanished buildings on their original site.

REPLICATION
The construction of an exact copy of an existing building.

Figure 7.2

Scale of levels of intervention in historic buildings (adapted from Fitch (1990) original terms are shown in parentheses).

integrity of its architecture, it may not be possible for a variety of reasons; for example, the existing use may not be sufficiently profitable to yield the capital to make such a comprehensive refurbishment of the property.

By contrast, surface rehabilitation is primarily concerned with the façade of the building and its contribution to an area's townscape. Thus, surface rehabilitation is either a 'townscape' rehabilitation – where only the external shell of the building is refurbished – or an 'adaptive reuse', which Appleyard (1979, p. 26) pejoratively describes as a 'disembowelment'. As an alternative to the refurbishment or restoration of a building for its original or existing function, buildings can be converted or adapted to accommodate new uses, by which they are able to avoid a functional obsolescence in the original use. Conversion generally involves a greater degree of change than refurbishment and restoration. The capacity for change is, however, limited by a number of factors: the physical and spatial parameters of the existing building; the architectural character of the building and the constraints imposed by special historic building controls on permissable change; the planning policy context; the environmental consequences of the change of use, particularly in terms of traffic generation and management; and the reception of the commercial market and possible users and investors to the change of use.

Accommodating new and different functions can have a range of impacts. In considering the design of conversions, there will inexorably be conflicts and compromises with regard to the degree of change and the necessary respect for the building's architectural integrity and original character. At the limit, however, Lowenthal (1981a, p. 14) observes 'there is little point in "saving" the past if what is saved is debased or altered beyond recognition'. The degree of fidelity must, however, be balanced by considerations of viability.

Aesthetic integrity and the problem of façadism

In discussing any changes to an historic building, there are perennial debates about the proposed rehabilitation's fidelity with the aesthetic integrity of the historic structure and fabric. The critical dilemma is encapsulated even at the level of the minor repair: should the repair be made invisible as if no problem had occurred or should the new work be uncompromisingly new so that what is old and what is new is easily discerned. In many cases, as most old urban structures are the result of much adaptive reuse, the supposed purity and integrity of the original building may already have been compromised. Rehabilitation, therefore, often faces the problem of choosing which of the many pasts should be restored (Ashworth and Tunbridge,

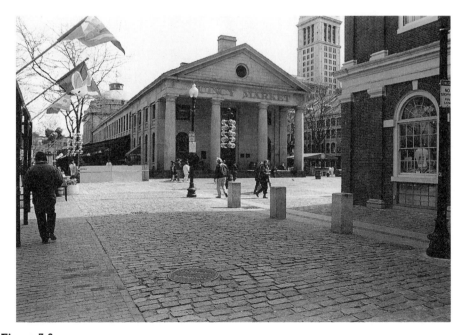

Figure 7.3

Quincy Market buildings, Boston. The proposed rehabilitation of these buildings provoked a debate about whether to leave the structures in their twentieth-century condition or restore the exteriors to their original 1826 design.

Figure 7.4

Retained façade on Ingram Street, Merchant City. Short of demolition, façadism represents the most extreme incidence of change to an historic building. Nevertheless, it can be a valid method of conservation that enables the retention of historic streetscapes.

1990, p. 24). This was the case in the rehabilitation of the Quincy Market buildings in Boston (Figure 7.3). The developer and the architect wanted to leave the structures in their much altered twentieth-century condition as examples of the organic growth of architecture, while others advocated restoration of the exteriors to their original 1826 rooflines and granite façades to conform with the architect's original design (Webb, 1976, p. 118). When the buildings were rehabilitated in the 1970s, all accretions of the intervening 150 years were stripped away to return the buildings (largely) to their original historic design. Nevertheless, as Barnett (1982, p. 50) states: 'while it is a successful adaptive re-use, it is not necessarily a happy example of historic preservation. In order to turn the old market into a modern retailing and food service environment, Thompson's design and the Rouse company management have changed the character of the buildings'. Similar criticism has been made of the conversion of the Covent Garden market buildings: 'the extent and quality of restoration has . . . removed the visible effects of its use as a market. This wear and patina is what one associates with an historical market and it can be disorientating to find it so entirely removed when the market is turned into an uncharacteristically elegant shopping centre' (Hareven and Langenbach, 1981, p. 121).

As stated previously, it is the façades which contribute most to the visual continuity of the quarter's character. Nevertheless, a concern for the façade of a building *in isolation*, can reduce conservationist concerns to a simpler concern for townscape. Short of demolition, façadism represents the most extreme incidence of change to an historic building (Figure 7.4). It therefore merits particular attention. In façadism, two principles come into conflict. The first is more pragmatic and conservationist: the preservation of street elevations is paramount and the building's chief conservation value is its contribution to the townscape. The second is more architectural and purist: buildings were originally designed as an aesthetic 'whole' which cannot be separated into interior and exterior except to the detriment of that whole. In the latter instance, façadism can refer to two distinct situations. Firstly, where a new building is built behind a retained historic façade, and secondly, to any new building where there is a functional and structural 'dishonesty': 'an absence of conceptual unity in terms of style and form between the exterior and the interior' (Richards, 1994, p. 20). Such buildings often do not command great respectability in modern architectural circles, being regarded by critics as lacking 'unity' and 'integrity'. A source of the architectural integrity line of criticism can be traced from John Ruskin's 'Lamp of Truth': 'which praises buildings for the structural honesty of their appearance' (Scruton, 1979). There is also criticism that façadism prevents new architectural styles from evolving, and reduces the design of buildings to mere two-dimensional elevations 'creating townscapes which are little more than stage sets' (Richards, 1994, p. 2).

Justification for façadism can be offered on the grounds that it is a valid method of urban conservation that enables the retention of familiar historic streetscapes or formal set pieces of urban design (Richards, 1994, p. 2). As many buildings only have utilitarian interiors, façadism permits the provision of up-to-date accommodation with all its comforts and conveniences (Richards, 1994, p. 2). Façadism therefore addresses the functional obsolescence of the building – by effectively destroying the building – while respecting its contribution to the continuity of the historic streetscene. It also allows contemporary architects to put exciting spaces behind historic elevations, for example, the Italian House in the Merchant City (Figures 7.5 and 7.6). In practice – and from the exterior – there may only be a marginal difference between the retention of the façade only and a comprehensive adaptive reuse.

Extended debate about the fidelity of a building's rehabilitation is – for the most part – ultimately arid and academic. It is only at issue when it concerns buildings of real architectural distinction or historic importance. The problem stems from turning a generally desirable aesthetic principle – the conceptual unity of the interior and exterior of a building – into a dogma. However, Brolin (1980, pp. 5–6) states: 'no virtue or higher morality is served by expressing interior uses "honestly" on the exterior. This is one moral preoccupation of Modernism which should be less important than the visual relationship between the building's exterior and its architectural context'. There is therefore little room for moral rectitude with regard to

Figure 7.5

rehabilitation of the majority of buildings. Similarly, it is not possible to prescribe universally the maximum level of permissable change to historic buildings. John Ruskin (1883, p. 143) argued against any change: 'We have no right whatsoever to touch them, they are not ours. They belong partly to those who built them and partly to the generations of mankind who are to follow.' It is easy to be too precious and purist in terms of rehabilitation. There needs to be some flexibility – and even expediency – because keeping the buildings in effective use is often the best way of preserving them. In most cases, what is important is that the intrinsic character of the building – whatever that might be – is respected. For example, in converting industrial buildings to residential use, it is important to resist the temptation to 'over-domesticate' them and thereby sever the link with their own history (Cunnington, 1988, p. 122). Pearce (1989, p. 79) states it is important that 'a warehouse should retain some of its rugged "warehouseness"'. If this has gone, the area is sanitized and its intrinsic qualities lost.

Figures 7.5 and 7.6

Interior and exterior of the Italian House, Merchant City. As demonstrated by this example, façadism permits contemporary architects to put exciting spaces behind historic elevations.

Many of the issues discussed above are raised lucidly in the rehabilitation of buildings in Glasgow's Merchant City and London's Shad Thames. The Houndsditch, in the Merchant City, is a new building built behind an historic façade. As Johnson (1987, p. 42) argues to convert the Houndsditch building to residential use, the only feasible way was to demolish and rebuild behind the retained stone façades. The existing building had three floors with very high ceilings. These would have been ill suited to the relatively small rooms required for residential use. Furthermore, as it would have compromised the visual character of the building, the architects were unwilling to run new floors across the tall windows. The solution finally adopted involved a new building behind the original façade. There are still three floors to the front, but two of them with inserted mezzanine gallery bedrooms thereby exploiting the height of the original windows but without running new floors across them (Figures 7.7 and 7.8).

Figures 7.7

The retained façade of the Houndsditch building. The façades meet at a corner which is marked only by an obliquely placed turret.

Also in the Ingram Square development, in Glasgow's Merchant City, the building on the corner of Wilson Street and Candleriggs and the building in the centre of the elevation to Brunswick Street were the first two buildings in the development to be converted to flats. The architects aimed to change the external character and image of the building through colour and the addition of a penthouse. In addition, a lightweight and visually unobtrusive steel framed penthouse was added to the top

Figure 7.8

The rear of the Houndsditch building contrasts significantly with the front.

floor of the Nova Building with a small gazebo at the west end symbolizing the change of use. Within the Merchant City, there has been an attempt to have non-residential uses at the ground floor level. Dwellings at street level in urban contexts are usually undesirable. However, ground and lower floors given over to car parking tend to deaden the life of the street. Thus, some element of mixed use within buildings is usually desirable with either shops or small offices on the lower floors.

As described in the previous chapter, Shad Thames is an example of a housing-led revitalization. Shad Thames has been able to absorb the residential function without its existing character being adversely affected. The conversion of New Concordia Wharf, the earliest of the warehouses in the area to be adapted to residential use, established 'a standard of taste and technical excellence for later architects to follow' (Edwards, 1992, p. 96) (Figure 7.9). The building remains a

Figure 7.9

New Concordia Wharf, Shad Thames. New Concordia Wharf has one gable end to the Thames and a long flank facing across St Saviour's Dock. The former dockside cranes were restored and other industrial features have been carefully repaired or replicated using evidence from Victorian photographs (Edwards, 1992, p. 96). The retention of these features maintains the memory of the working dock. Standing next to New Concordia Wharf, is China Wharf, a new-build mixed development of apartments and offices. Using a variety of idioms and references, albeit few that are readily identifiable, it contrasts sharply with the 'white box' Modernist developments of Shad Thames. Arguably, it is sufficiently different for it to be a juxtaposition rather than a continuity.

typical Victorian warehouse, with external loadbearing brick walls, arched windows, timber loophole loading bays. On the waterside façades of the buildings, balconies have been inserted where loading doors once opened. However, these do not visually jar; by respecting the original fenestration pattern, they have added detail where the eye anticipates greater visual complexity. The detailing of

Figure 7.10

Anchor Brewery, Shad Thames. The existing building's idyosyncracies have meant that it has been possible to convert it to residential uses without compromising its character.

the railings also carries the appropriate visual weight for the façade. Commercial pressure did force the developer to adapt the roofline by the insertion of a further floor and the addition of conservatories. Although preservation of the façade of historic buildings is paramount, the retention of the original roofscape is also important – particularly that part of the roof which is seen from the public realm. Roof top extensions that add extra floors will usually adversely alter the proportions and balance of the façade. Developers often want to insert extra space by a roof top extension and/or to cut back the existing roof profile to create roof terraces. With their associated paraphernalia of railings and temporary sun shades and umbrellas, such changes inevitably reveal the residential function and, unless handled carefully, can harm the visual character both of the area and the building.

The main Butler's Wharf building is an example of façadism (Figure 5.13). When completed, in 1873, it was the largest wharf on the Thames. The building was converted in the mid-1980s into ninety-eight apartments. The front and rear walls that front onto public spaces were retained and carefully restored. Its riverside elevation has a bold architectural treatment with prominent end pavilions with rusticated quoins, massive bracketed cornices and pedimented parapets. The addition of balconies where loading doors previously existed reveal the residential function but do not detract from the stateliness or monumentality of the building. However, to allow the construction of a rooftop storey and basement car parking, a new concrete frame was inserted into the brick shell of the existing building. To the rear, along Shad Thames, the cast-iron bridges have been repaired. Although the shops and restaurants animate the street scene, new openings have had to be formed to accommodate them. The detail of these new openings with yellow stock bricks and engineering brick dressings is sympathetic to the building. Edwards (1992, p. 95), however, is critical of the result: 'In the process of adaptation one cannot help feeling they have been oversanitized or at least given too liberal a dose of "Habitat" good taste. Butler's Wharf is not so much the preservation of a group of buildings as their restoration to a rather idealized and convenient version of the original.' Adjacent to Butler's Wharf, the former Anchor Brewery, has also been converted into sixty-two flats, office space and a health club. The existing idiosyncracies of this building have meant that it has been possible to convert it to residential uses without compromising its character (Figure 7.10).

One of the major problems of converting buildings to residential use is the provision of parking. Some newly residential quarters, such as New York's SoHo, have very low levels of car ownership. Planning authorities may relax the minimum provision requirement, but developers argue that parking spaces are necessary in order to be able to sell the properties. One solution is to insert underground car parks beneath the buildings; this was a method widely used in the renovation of the Marais quarter of Paris. However, it is often expensive and may technically not be possible. In the Merchant City, due to the initial relaxation of parking provision standards to encourage residential conversions, many early schemes did not provide sufficient parking. There is currently a shortage of off-street parking provision and a major problem of on-street parking in the quarter. Arguably, the provision of central parking facilities for residents should be seen as part of an area's public infrastructure that supports the residential function. In Philadelphia, a significant public action has been mounted to build more car parks in the Old Town quarter to improve the infrastructure that would be supportive of residential conversions.

NEW DEVELOPMENTS IN HISTORIC URBAN QUARTERS

While the rehabilitation of the existing historic fabric of the quarter is to be preferred, new development in historic urban quarters is inevitable; particularly if buildings have become physically or structurally obsolete. These are usually – but not always – infill developments. Architectural and urban space design in historic urban quarters is not – by definition – design on a greenfield site or where there is – or can be – a *tabula rasa*. More generally, MacCormac (1983b, p. 751) argues that 'design cannot isolate itself from vocabulary and precedent because they are inherent in the process of thought itself. There can be no Tabula Rasa'. All design interventions in such areas must respond to – or simply ignore – the existing context: they cannot remain indifferent. Such design may in fact be easier: 'Designers are aware that it is easier to plan when there are some commitments than it is when the situation is completely open . . . The fixed characteristics restrict the range of possible solutions and therefore ease the agony of the design search' (Lynch, 1972, p. 38).

Where demolition does occur, new development should preferably respect, complement and enhance both the urban form and the architectural character or identity of the quarter. The aim is to achieve a 'harmonious' relation with the existing context. Thus, new developments in historic urban quarters derive authority from their respect and sensitivity to the quarter's particular aesthetic qualities, both spatial and architectural. These are the two distinct levels where design control and/or consideration is required: firstly, in terms of the overall massing and urban form of the development. This might be regarded as the morphological or *spatial character* of the quarter. In each of the quarters featured there is a townscape where buildings enclose space rather than buildings standing freely in space. Secondly, the elevation of the proposed development which defines and encloses the external urban space and the public realm. This might be regarded as the *architectural character* of the quarter; a concern for the architectural articulation of the building's elevation or façade. As will be discussed later in this chapter, this issue can be approached in a number of ways. Three different approaches are identified, these are termed *contextual uniformity*, *contextual continuity* and *contextual juxtaposition*.

RESPECTING THE HISTORIC URBAN QUARTER'S SPATIAL CHARACTER

As discussed in Chapter Three, most contemporary or postmodern urban design is informed by a sense of history and local tradition. Given the ravages of the past century, the approach to the urban form of new development in historic urban quarters should generally be an urban healing approach. This approach prioritizes the continuity of building lines and street frontages in order to enhance street containment and enclosure. It generally permits little scope for the design of buildings as sculptures or objects in space – the building as a self-referential entity – without a positive design of that space. The only exception is where a low relief sculptural treatment of a façade or elevation does not detract from the street frontage or the containment of the street volume. A location where a highly sculptural or landmark building might be appropriate is at a significant point for the legibility of the townscape, such as a street corner or the termination of a particular view or vista. The landmark qualities might also be enhanced by a skyline projection (see, for example, Moughtin *et al.*, 1995). Most urban design guides for historic urban quarters, for example, the BUDS Study for the Jewellery Quarter, demonstrate this urban healing approach, stressing respect for the continuity of the street frontage, the grain and street pattern (Figure 3.6).

As the retention of the existing buildings wherever possible would keep the historic urban space and form intact, new developments should generally retain the overall massing, form and 'footprint' of the buildings that previously occupied the site. In plan and section, figure–ground diagrams are a useful tool to explore this. This need not be a slavish adherence, merely that the spirit of the spatial character be respected. Richard MacCormac has likened this approach to repairing a hole in an old rug so that the repair becomes invisible and contributes to the new whole. In this respect, the amalgamation of individual street blocks should also be resisted as it coarsens the grain of the quarter. In terms of the size of urban blocks, both Jane Jacobs (1961) and Leon Krier (1984) are in favour of small blocks for increased urbanity.

In terms of achieving a harmonious relation with the existing context, the size and scale of a building are arguably more important than its particular architectural language: 'Style, in terms of presence or absence of period trimmings, is of almost no consequence set alongside the appropriateness or not of the bulk and grain of a building' (Pearce, 1989, p. 166). This raises the issue of the appropriate scale in redevelopment: whether to retain the scale of the demolished building or respond to the scale of the remaining buildings.

The Merchant City consists of a mix of six- and seven-storey warehouses and three- and four-storey residential buildings. If lower buildings have been demolished, what should be the appropriate scale of new development? In the Ingram Square development, in the design of the new building on the corner of Brunswick Street and Wilson Street two options were available (Johnson, 1989, pp. 48–51) (see Figure 7.12): either to respect the existing scale of Brunswick Street – largely that of the original three- or four-storeys – or to acknowledge the height of the 1930s warehouses further to the south. The developer's preference is usually – of course – for a larger building. Respecting the height of the warehouses was chosen for the corner block which is eight storeys, with the height dropping to five storeys further along Wilson Street. Matching the height of the warehouse to the south helps to maintain the symmetry of the view looking east down Wilson Street, however, the change in scale between the new building and its neighbour on Brunswick Street is very abrupt and less successful.

To appreciate and identify precisely an historic quarter's particular spatial character, sensitive observation and research are required. The spirit and character of the spatial containment varies from quarter to quarter. The American examples in this book are typically grid layouts where the qualities of the buildings *en masse* create the townscape rather than the qualities of the space itself. In more irregular layouts, such as Shad Thames, there are more picturesque qualities deriving chiefly from the character of the space. However, in some instances the spatial and architectural character of a quarter are memorably fused as, for example, in the Lace Market, Broadway (Figure 7.11).

Glasgow's Merchant City is also a grid but the grid is offset. As a result, there are significant townscape qualities arising from the terminated vistas and the powerful sense of contained space. The important buildings and set pieces like the Trades House and the Hutcheson Hospital are intended to be viewed *en face* (Johnson, 1989, p. 48) (Figure 5.9). In this context, the corners of buildings are not

Figure 7.11

Although it contrasts with the predominantly straight and narrow 'canyon' streets of the Lace Market, Broadway is a magnificent fusion of architecture and urban space. The effect, however, has been diminished by the poorly designed and executed paving scheme.

architecturally emphasized as this would set up competing diagonal accents. In a spatial analysis of the Merchant City, Walker (from Johnson, 1989, p. 48) wrote: 'Corner units are noticeably the conjunction or, to be more accurate, the juxtaposition of façades and gable or façade and façade, ie they are plannar abutments maintaining the rectilinear aesthetic of the grid rather than three-dimensionally sculptural elements responsive to oblique perspective.'

However, the spatial character of the Merchant City has not always been respected by the urban form of new developments, for example, the landmark building in the Ingram Square development at the junction of Brunswick and Wilson Street (Figure 7.12). The corner of this building is marked by a circular projecting tower feature rising the full height of the building and topped by a circular glazed drum. The tower

Figure 7.12

New build element of the Ingram Square development at the corner of Brunswick Street and Wilson Street. This is generally a well-mannered example of contextual continuity. However, the introduction of the tower element sets up a diagonal emphasis which is alien to the spatial character of the Merchant City, while the change in scale between the new building and its neighbour on Brunswick Street is rather abrupt.

element sets up a diagonal emphasis which is alien to the Merchant City. Other corner treatments in the Merchant City, such as those of the Houndsditch (Figure 7.7) and the Nova building, are relatively simple and restrained; 'articulating' rather than 'celebrating' the junction (Johnson, 1989, p. 48). In addition, as Johnson (1989, p. 51) has described, when viewed from the west the flimsy and lightweight scale of the attenuated verticals of the tower's upper windows have 'an unhappy relationship with the grimy but dignified Ionic south portico of the Sheriff Court'. By the use of corner tower element, this landmark building introduces an architectural tradition that is common in the rest of Glasgow, but unfortunately alien in the specific local context of the Merchant City.

A quarter's spatial character can also be enhanced by area-based improvements. A key component of the spatial character is the design of the floorscape, the spaces between the buildings and the three-dimensional objects – street furniture and so on – within those spaces. High quality, well-maintained spaces between buildings can also produce positive externalities that enhance the economic value of the surrounding buildings. Some of the floorscape improvements in Seattle's Pioneer Square (Chapter Three) and Denver's LoDo (Chapter Six) have already been described. In many historic urban quarters, there have been schemes to improve pedestrian comfort, such as street closures, traffic calming and the widening of pavements. Such schemes are generally better where they demonstrate an awareness of and sensitivity to how people actually use urban public spaces. The Merchant City is currently undergoing a programme of environmental improvements as part of Glasgow's *Public Realm Strategy.*

RESPECTING THE HISTORIC URBAN QUARTER'S ARCHITECTURAL CHARACTER

Having created new forms and massing that respect the quarter's spatial character, the walls that define those spaces have to be articulated architecturally. As noted earlier, there is rarely a place for highly sculptural buildings in historic urban quarters. The issue is therefore primarily one of elevational design. Generally, the vertical and horizontal rhythms, the arrays and patterns of solid and void, masonry and glazing on building elevations are more important than the precise details of the building's architectural style. To maintain the grain and scale of the quarter, the amalgamation of historic plot divisions should be resisted. Where this is not possible and sites are assembled into larger packages, the scale of the historic plot divisions should be respected in the elevational designs to ensure consistency with the quarter. Together with the consistent use of materials, such patterns and rhythms, contribute to and establish the architectural character of the quarter.

A pertinent question, however, is whether there is any discernible architectural coherence and/or homogeneity within the quarter. Some quarters possess a relative architectural homogeneity and coherence. Much of this has resulted from a concentrated development period and the functional requirements of the buildings combined with either the constructional limitations of locally available materials, for example, in the Lace Market or Bradford's Little Germany, or from the extensive use of a particular constructional method, for example, the cast-iron fronted buildings in New York's SoHo. The limitations of traditional construction methods and materials normally result in a relative homogeneity of scale within a quarter. However, a major change since the quarters were constructed in the nineteenth century has been further development in the technology of building materials and construction methods. Thus, the circumstances which created the existing or historic architectural tradition are likely to have changed. As, for example, the Lace Market is no longer a nineteenth-century lace making area, contemporary designers are not bound or limited by the construction techniques and materials of that period or the necessity to recreate the physical landscape; equally, they may choose to respond to it. The issue is therefore one of restraint and the extent to which the designer *chooses* to imitate, interpret or ignore the historic architectural tradition.

Although distinctive in other ways, some quarters do not have a consistent architectural character to which to respond. Alternatively, their original coherence has been lost or fatally weakened through insensitive incremental development, such as, Birmingham's Jewellery Quarter or Manchester's Castlefield. The strength of the quarter's particular architectural homogeneity and character will determine the appropriate design response.

ACHIEVING CONTEXTUAL HARMONY

The chief quality sought in the design of new developments in all historic urban quarters is 'harmony'; the creation of 'a visually integrated – [but] not necessarily homogeneous – townscape' (Brolin, 1980, p. 16). Richard Rogers (1988, p. 874) argues that – contrary to generally held opinion that contextual harmony can only be achieved by imitating neighbouring styles – such harmony can be achieved by several means. Rogers identifies two methods of attaining a contextual harmony: firstly, through *contextual uniformity* and, secondly, through *contextual juxtaposition*. This notion of juxtaposition is compatible with Modernist ideas of design. There is also a third way of *contextual continuity* or transformed/evolved tradition, this is compatible with certain postmodern ideas of urban design. These approaches will now be discussed.

Contextual uniformity

Contextual uniformity is the copying or imitation of the neighbouring styles. Examples of a contextual uniformity approach abound in the urban quarters featured in this book. An example of this approach is the multistorey car park located on a prime site in the heart of Nottingham's Lace Market (Figure 7.13). This approach is not without criticism. Lewis Mumford (1938) in *The Culture of Cities* warns of 'the monotony of a future that consists in repeating only a single beat heard in the past'. As a straightforward imitation of the architectural character of the quarter, it seeks to preserve what once was, rather than what might be, resulting in the dilution and weakening of the qualities it sought to retain. Furthermore, as Freeman (1976, p. 115) states, although historic areas need historical continuity, to choose 'to replicate the past is a decision that automatically eliminates the possibility of adding value to a project or area through sensitive and high quality new design . . . If it is poorly executed, the reproduction will be a sham that undermines the setting of nearby structures'.

This notion of contextual uniformity can also sink to a superficial and unchallenging 'pastiche' – a too literal copy of tradition. Pastiche disconnects style from construction – the building lacks any semblance of architectural 'integrity'. As

Figure 7.13

Multistorey car park on Barker Gate, Lace Market. The design of this car park respects the scale and massing of the Victorian Lace Market and is significantly better than many other post-1945 developments in the area. Nevertheless, it fails to replicate the depth and quality of detail found on the Lace Market's Victorian buildings. It therefore dilutes the historic character of the quarter. In this instance, part of the problem is the detailed design of the window returns which lack sufficient visual depth. In functional terms, the location of a car park in the heart of the quarter, while convenient, contributes little to the street life and vitality of the quarter.

Hewison (1987, p. 134) notes: 'The emotional equivalent of pastiche is nostalgia, which deliberately falsifies authentic memory into an enhanced version of itself. It is a strangely powerless emotion, a sweet sadness conditioned by the knowledge that the object of recall cannot – indeed, must not – be recovered.' Such designs 'blur the line between real and fabricated history, distorting the context in which what is genuine can be appreciated and understood' (Hareven and Langenbach, 1981, p. 121). Jameson (from Hewison, 1987, p. 134) condemns pastiche as 'speech in a dead language . . . Pastiche is . . . blank parody'.

Contextual juxtaposition

Rogers (1988, p. 875) argues that a harmonious order can result from 'the juxtaposition of buildings of different epochs, each one being the expression of its own time'. Rogers uses this argument to justify the insertion of the Pompidou Centre, adjacent to the historic Marais quarter of Paris, and the Lloyds Building in the City of London. To further illustrate his argument, Rogers (1988, p. 875) again cites the example of St. Mark's Venice, where 'people of vision had the courage to put a further building of quality next to an already perfect building, thereby radically altering the balance of the existing spatial context'. Nevertheless, as Kolb (1990, p. 177) notes this was not a negligent or accidental juxtaposition: 'Those who produced the buildings around the Piazza San Marco looked at the whole they were making. They did not make context-ignoring monuments or ironic rhapsodies.' This notion of contextual juxtaposition is congruent with the ideas of the Modernist and the challenge of the zeitgeist. As previously described, the Modernist argued that as a result of technological advances, the future always means a fundamental break with tradition.

Shad Thames contains several examples of a contextual juxtaposition approach to the design of infill development. For the most part the developments respect the principles of good contextual urban form. They have their own aesthetic integrity and are empathetically and uncompromisingly of their period with few stylistic concessions to the surrounding local context. Nevertheless they both enhance and establish a new character at Shad Thames. As Edwards (1992, p. 91) states 'old and new buildings stand side by side in happy communion'.

Contrary to first appearances, the white Modernist cubes of the Design Museum and the Clove Building are adaptive reuses of mid-century concrete framed warehouses. In the former case the original structure is very well disguised, while in the latter the structure is expressed externally. 'The Design Museum establishes a crisp Modernist counterpoint to the rustic warehouses of the south Thames. It is both gleaming white and a stepped cube, thereby making direct reference to the International Style' (Edwards, 1992, p. 96). The Clove Building is another white Modernist adaptation of a mid-century concrete framed warehouse (Figure 7.14). By contrast, Saffron Wharf is a new build scheme, facing onto Shad Thames and to St Saviour's Dock (Figure 7.12). The building is sleek but unremarkable; as Slessor (1990, p. 43) notes: 'much of its appeal is generated by the *frisson* of discovering such a poised, sleek cube among the earthy conglomeration of brick warehouses'. No 22 Shad Thames – The David Mellor Building – uses raw materials giving the building 'a finely honed industrial edge, which suggest a closer kinship with the craft-based approach of engineering than the packaged slickness of much contemporary architecture' (Slessor, 1990, p. 43) (Figure 7.14).

In addition, to these four white cube or concrete buildings, Horsleydown Square is a development that uses colour to juxtapose with the historic context. While making greater reference to the local context than the white cubes around the Design Museum, the architecture is visually lighter and contrasts sharply with the heavy monumentality of the Butler's Wharf warehouses. As Edwards states (1992, p. 98) 'they are not subservient structures trying to build unnoticed within a conservation

Figure 7.14

Saffron Wharf, 22 Shad Thames (The David Mellor Building) and – to the rear – the Clove Building on the part of Shad Thames parallel to St Saviour's Dock. These buildings establish a vibrant juxtaposition with the older brick warehouses; both enhancing and establishing a new character at Shad Thames.

area. This is assertive, confident, urban architecture which appeals more by bravado than cerebral considerations'. The use of public squares and courtyards enhances the public realm of the quarter, opening up and adding interest to the areas inland from the river and contrasting with the narrow passageway of Shad Thames (Figure 7.15). The courtyards create a series of well-used pedestrian routes, surrounded by a rich mix of shops, offices and apartments.

At Shad Thames, the historic character of the quarter is sufficiently strong that modern buildings can express themselves in this uncompromisingly contemporary manner. As Edwards (1992, p. 93) states: 'The dominating presence of yellow brick (yellow at least after cleaning) warehouses, and the industrial machinery

Figure 7.15

One of the new squares in the Horsleydown Square development opening onto Shad Thames and the
rear of the old Anchor Brewery. The building forms of this development are curvaceous and
streamlined, performing the traditional urban role of creating and enclosing spaces rather than being
objects in space.

often mounted on their façades, has provided a robust urban framework for new
buildings . . . It is an approach to urban infill which would not look right in Bath
or even Westminster, but here in tough and rugged historic Docklands the
resulting environment has great diversity and character.' What is significant is that
the juxtaposition is with the quarter's architectural character rather than with its
spatial character. The one building which breaks this rule is the one building that
marginally fails to work, the Design Museum (Figure 7.16). As Edwards (1992,
p. 96) describes: 'The Design Museum makes no reference to anything in sight: it
ignores the grain of historic Shad Thames, it refuses to be tall at the river edge
and it disdains pitched roofs.'

Figure 7.16

The Design Museum, Shad Thames. By refusing to be tall at the river edge, this is arguably one of the few buildings in Shad Thames that fails to respect the quarter's spatial character. Once the adjacent Spice Quay site – now a surface level temporary car park – has been developed, the Design Museum's effect might be less jarring.

It is important to reflect on the extent to which the aesthetic success of Shad Thames has been the result of the more 'relaxed' planning policies of the LDDC. No urban design framework had been considered necessary since the area was already well urbanized at the onset of the LDDC operations in 1981. Thus, the area was at the 'mercy' of private sector developers. Fortunately, the area benefited from 'enlightened developers' whose large landholdings in the area necessitated that they consider the composite value of their holding and ensure the quality of all developments in the area. Nevertheless, as there is a relatively large number of historic buildings in the quarter, the new buildings have been forced to fit into the remaining gaps. Thus, the scale of the new buildings has been kept quite small and there is a fine balance between old and new. However, this fine balance may not be maintained if further selective demolition of the older warehouses continues and the proportion of new build schemes increases. The challenge therefore in Shad Thames is to ensure that there is a continuity of visual character and that the vibrancy of controlled juxtaposition is maintained rather than sinking into visual chaos. The design of the key development site of Spice Quay – the vacant site between Butler's Wharf and the Design Museum – will be a major watershed for the quarter.

Contextual continuity

There is a polar view to the Modernist proposition of a radical break with the past, ushering in a new era. Rather than the dissimilarities, it stresses the continuity between time frames. This may be characterized as a postmodern view. Contemporary urban design is concerned with this historical continuity of city and of places. In the Modern period, architecture and construction became international and are no longer limited by indigenously available materials and construction methods. Modernism made a virtue of this internationalism – everything could be the same standard. Postmodernism permits and encourages a greater tolerance and respect for differences and localities. Paulo Portoghesi defines as postmodern 'any building that breaks the modern prohibition against historical reference, whether with ironic self-commentary or with vernacular earnestness' (Kolb, 1990, p. 89). In architectural terms, this has legitimized approaches to design which draw upon architectural precedent and tradition.

There has also been a popular reaction against the sterile monotony of much of the reductionist 'white box' Modernism of the International Style and visually shallow 'graph paper' façades resulting from standardized industrial production. Inspired in part by the conservation movement, there was a popular desire for the use of historical motifs and more decorative treatments – at least superficially – to make buildings more interesting. As Barnett (1982, p. 38) notes: 'Preservation as a form of hostility to Modernism has in turn promoted a re-examination of the basic concepts of Modern architecture ... architects have begun to explore the ornament and elaboration that had been rejected in the name of efficiency and machine production.' Thus, in reaction to Modernist dogma on the ornamentation of buildings, postmodernism has generally permitted a greater freedom with style and idiom, and with articulation, decoration and ornament.

Historical reference and allusion, however, is fraught with accusations of superficiality: 'Postmodernism and the heritage industry are linked, in that they both conspire to create a shallow screen that intervenes between our present lives, and our history. We have no understanding of history in depth, but instead we are offered a contemporary creation, more costume drama and re-enactment than critical discourse' (Hewison, 1987, p. 135). It can also be interpreted as mere repetition of what has gone before. Wilford (1984) for example argues that the contention that the typical or precedent (paradigm) is the starting point in a doctrine that can only lead to repetition and does not allow or encourage invention and originality. Nevertheless, Banerjee and Baer (1984) argue that environmental design is inherently a paradigmatic process: 'It tends to use preconceived models or patterns of a whole as its basis rather than drawing directly (and *de novo*) each time from theory or empirical findings. Thus, design consists largely of variations on an accepted stylistic theme rather than an entirely original conception devised from scratch for each design problem.'

However, the application of a precedential or paradigmatic approach, requires perpetual self-questioning and a continual testing of maintained validity, as inherently such a method runs the risk of applying an inappropriate and out-dated paradigm to a fresh problem. Richard Rogers (1988, pp. 879–880) warns: 'In all fields, not least in architecture, it is generally accepted that to learn from the past is the way forward and that history is a prime generator. But to imitate historical form without recognition of the content is to degrade its very importance'. Equally, both Venturi (1977, p. 13) and MacCormac (1983b) have poignantly cited T.S.Eliot: 'if the only form of tradition, of handing down, consisted in following the ways of the immediate generation before us in a blind or timid adherence to its successes, 'tradition' should be positively discouraged . . . the historical sense [of tradition] involves perception, not only of the pastness of the past, but of its presence'. It is this historical sense that, in Eliot's view, makes a writer – or architect: 'most acutely conscious of his place in time, of his own contemporaneity'. Venturi continues by rejecting the obsession of Modern architects who, to quote Aldo van Eyck, 'have been harping continually on what is different in our time to such an extent that they have lost touch with what is not different, with what is essentially the same' (from Venturi, 1977, p. 13).

Thus, provided there is an active involvement with the architectural tradition of the context, an approach informed by the context and history of the site need not inexorably result in pastiche; it becomes interpretation, not imitation. MacCormac (1983b, p. 751) states 'architecture should . . . satisfy several levels of understanding, including that of the past, so long as the past is transformed to become part of the present and not used literally'. Contextual continuity demands the evolution and transformation of the local tradition: 'History signifies a record of the past; tradition suggests a more active involvement in that process of transmitting the past' (Middleton, 1983, p. 730). This new or transformed tradition, as MacCormac (1983b, p. 748) – paraphrasing Karl Popper – notes, 'breaks out of an existing one . . . through this evolutionary rather than revolutionary process the art of architecture is advanced'.

The Merchant City quarter of Glasgow contains several examples of a contextual continuity approach to the design of infill development. In the Merchant City, the new developments are buildings of quality exhibiting a significant degree of responsiveness to the local context and tradition. The key development in the Merchant City is Ingram Square, which consists of a vibrant mixture of refurbishments, façadism and new build elements. Despite some flaws, as Johnson (1989, p. 37) states the building on the corner of Brunswick Street and Wilson Street: 'stands out as a skilful and serious attempt to create a new contextual urban language based on scale, proportion and massing rather than on playing stylistic games' (Figure 7.12). There are three new buildings in the Ingram Square development; their façades take their cues from the existing buildings on the site. The adjacent Nova Building, on Wilson Street and Candleriggs, previously converted for residential use, provides the pattern for the design particularly at street level. Two particular devices relate the smaller scale of the new residential uses to that of the historic warehouse buildings. Firstly, the scale of the ground floor element is raised by incorporating the lowest level of flats into the treatment of the ground floor element. Secondly, although required to build in brick for reasons of economy, the architects have disguised the brick scale and, by matching mortar and brick colours, have given the walls a flat homogeneous effect which harmonizes with the surrounding sandstone buildings. The corner building is also broken down into a series of blocks that read as separate buildings reflecting the piecemeal nature of Wilson Street.

Figure 7.17

The Circle, Shad Thames. The use of diagonals to organize the balconies and fenestration contrasts with local precedents, adding individuality and character. The diagonal creates movement in the façade and a liveliness that is absent from other new build developments that earnestly replicate a warehouse vernacular.

Much of the contextual success of these new buildings is that they follow the conventions of traditional urbanism, such as a progression of scale and detail from ground floor to skyline. The façades are clearly organized in three parts: the ground floor or lower floors which relate to the public realm; above this, the main part of the elevation; and the attic or roof top storey. Horizontal bands distinguish the different parts of the façade which are also handled differently. The designs also match the local rhythms of solid and void in the spacing of windows.

At Shad Thames, inland where the local cues and references are weaker, a new context and character has been established almost from scratch. The Circle in Queen Elizabeth Street is an extraordinary development of nearly 300 flats, occasional offices and shops grouped around a dramatic central circus (Figure 7.17). The circus space itself is cylindrical, its internal faces built of bright blue glazed bricks with a chunky dray horse statue at its centre. As Edwards (1992, p. 99) notes: 'After the confinement of Shad Thames and the busy squares of Horsleydown, The Circle has a theatrical unreality.' In terms of materials – apart from the blue bricks – and scale, the development blends in easily with the older, grimy warehouses. However, the use of diagonals to organize the balconies and fenestration and the circle on the site plan contrast with local precedents adding individuality and character. The use of the diagonal creates movement in the façade and a liveliness that is absent from other new build developments that earnestly replicate a warehouse vernacular. Through irony and humour, this development gets closer to contextual continuity; Edwards (1992, p. 100) observes: 'The warehouse vernacular is not slavishly copied, but reinterpreted and distorted.'

Conclusion

Perhaps the major and most damning criticism of contextual uniformity is that the historical evolution of the quarter is checked and ossified at a particular historic moment; the physical appearance of the quarter becomes frozen in time. The new contribution does not add value to the quarter; it merely further dilutes the historic character. Lynch (1972, p. 236) poignantly notes: 'The exposure of successive areas of history and the insertion of new material that enhanced the past by allusion and contrast would be encouraged, the aim being to produce a setting more and more densely packed with references to the stream of time rather than a setting that never changed.' The approaches of contextual juxtaposition and contextual continuity enable Lynch's visible references to the stream of time. Contextual uniformity should therefore only be used when the other approaches are precluded or inappropriate.

Without sufficient regard for the whole, however, contextual juxtaposition can create context-destroying monuments: new developments need a context with which to juxtapose. 'Contemporary urbanism cannot, however, treat every building as if competing in a commercial art gallery. The extent of more neutral buildings and the scale of restoration nearby mean [Shad Thames] is not suffocated by design pretension' (Edwards, 1992, p. 102). Further demolition of historic warehouses at Shad Thames, for example, will weaken the effect of the juxtaposition. However, extreme contextual juxtaposition can only be an occasional device since it achieves its effect by its contrast with a relatively homogeneous background. Too much diversity will destroy any sense of coherence in the local context. It is also important that the juxtaposition is with the quarter's architectural character rather than with its spatial character.

Contextual continuity is an approach that offers a middle way between the perils of an excess of juxtaposition that destroys the context's architectural coherence and a slavish uniformity that entombs and freezes the context at a particular historical moment. The three approaches are not mutually exclusive. In effect they exist along a continuum with uniformity and juxtaposition at each pole and continuity somewhere in the middle. Several developments in Shad Thames demonstrate an approach which straddles those of continuity and juxtaposition (Figure 7.9). These developments also display a greater fondness for playful postmodern irony than those of the Merchant City. What is witnessed is an engaging dialogue between new and old with various points of consensus and dispute.

ARCHITECTURAL DESIGN CONTROLS

To manage change in historic urban quarters requires controls. To operate effectively, architectural design guides and controls need to be designed and implemented with an understanding of the 'process' of design as well as the 'product' of design. Contextual uniformity, continuity and juxtaposition are classifications of the products of a design process. The emphasis should therefore be on principles rather than on detailed prescriptions. Design codes established and agreed before the design process are generally preferable to reviews of the final design product. Rather than being part of the external judgement of the design 'product', design codes become an explicit part of the design 'process', like the topography of the site or the building's functional requirements. Such design codes may be for the entire quarter or produced on a plot by plot or block by block basis. Some form of review, however, is still required to ensure that the resulting design is in accordance with the code.

Architecturally, design codes and guides tend to stress approaches that emphasize – to varying degrees – contextual uniformity or continuity. When used within control devices, the concepts of uniformity and continuity demand a close study and analysis of the existing context to act as a precedent; the architectural themes, patterns, rhythms and language which contribute to the architectural character and tradition of the locality. As the Italian architect, Giancarlo De Carlo (from MacCormac, 1991, p. 39) states: 'To design in an historic place one should read its architectural stratification and try to understand the significance of each layer before super-imposing a new one. This does not mean to indulge in imitation, as this would be a mean spirited approach, saying nothing about the present and spreading confusion about the past. What is called for is the invention of new architectural images to be authentic and at the same time reciprocal with existing images.'

By identifying what is preferred and therefore – by omission – what is not, design guides and codes inexorably narrow down the range of options and design possibilities. As a consequence, such guidance frequently keeps out the mediocre as well as the inspired. The limitations of a highly prescriptive approach, as in Bologna, have been identified. The Bologna 1969 plan was based on a long and thorough survey of the city's buildings and open spaces. Not only did this show the customary information such as use, structural condition and architectural importance, but the study also focused on identifying the local typologies. In effect, this was the local architectural syntax; the rules for organizing architectural form and language. As Cantacuzino and Brandt (1980, p. 9) argue: 'This analysis has been of undoubted benefit to Bologna's architects in so far as it has helped to prevent some of the aberrations committed, say, in Venice where no comparable study has taken place.

But it has also trapped the architects in their deep-rooted conservatism ... By elevating the typological exactitude to a matter of principle, by insisting on slavish imitation and reproduction, the Municipality of Bologna has denied architects the opportunity of creative experiment in housing, of responding both to tradition and to contemporary need' (Cantacuzino and Brandt, 1980, pp. 9–11).

CONCLUSION

The intention of this chapter has not been to dictate design approaches in historic urban quarters. Instead, in common with Brolin (1980, p. 17), it has sought to describe 'a way of looking at the whole of the architectural context which will encourage architects, planners and entrepreneurs to consider thoughtfully the visual effects of additions to their surroundings'. Whatever the design guidance and the process of design, the final effect will require an individual aesthetic judgement as to whether or not it is harmonious with its context; there is no mystic process by which following a due process inexorably creates a harmonious effect. Kolb (1990, p. 179) expresses the dilemma: 'We care how what we build relates to what is around, but we cannot rely on some secret essence or unified spirit of the locality.' The quality sought in design and development in historic urban contexts is respect for that context. As Pearce (1989, p. 166) states: 'All that is required for the rewarding addition of a new building in an old setting is the genius of the place to be complemented by the genius of the architect.' However, in all aspects of urban design, it is necessary to see through the formal appearance and consider the experience of the place; places have both aesthetic and functional dimensions, each of which must be in harmony. The functions themselves have physical, social and economic dimensions. The key design question in the various quarters is: 'What kind of place has been created?' The kind of place is both a physical and a functional/social construct. This is a key question that will be addressed in the final chapter.

8

TOWARDS THE SUCCESSFUL REVITALIZATION OF HISTORIC URBAN QUARTERS

INTRODUCTION

This book has discussed the revitalization of historic urban quarters. These quarters have a significant sense of place – a particular ambience – that derives from their history, architecture and townscape. Over the past two or three decades there has been an increasing awareness of the inherent qualities of such places. The change of attitudes described in Chapter Three, has made them a desirable, but scarce, commodity. Indeed some cities, such as Sacremento, have tried artificially to manufacture historic character to attract people and investment. To ward off the threat of large-scale clearance or gradual decay and demolition, informal, often middle-class, pressure groups have campaigned to raise public awarenesss and consciousness, and also to have these historic areas preserved. Thus, rather than being demolished and redeveloped as was often the case in the 1950s and 1960s, many historic urban quarters are now being revitalized to become lively, vital, animated parts of cities (Figure 8.1). This new lease of life may often be the result of having acquired new functions, such as housing, tourism and related facilities. The quarter once again becomes an attractive and desirable place in which to invest, live, work and play.

   The revitalization process starts when – and if – investments, driven by a multitude of motives and often attracted/supported by subsidies, are made in the historic urban quarter. Revitalization becomes necessary for all older parts of cities, not just those with greater historic character and qualities. However, the greater the authentic historical character and sense of place, the more likely it is that there will be efforts to *preserve* and revitalize them. It must be noted that the motives of those who invest and revitalize historic places are likely to be different from those initial preservation-ists who bring these areas into public consciousness. This can lead to conflicts

Figure 8.1

Quincy Market, Boston. Many revitalized historic places have become lively, vital, animated parts of cities.

between the demands of preservation which seeks to limit change and revitalization which seeks to accommodate necessary economic change.

The case studies in Chapters Four, Five and Six indicate that there is no standard formula for successful revitalization and that approaches to revitalization must be based on the local and the particular. Kotler *et al.* (1993, p. 20) note that: 'No two places are likely to sort out their strategies, use their resources, define their products, or implement their plans in the same way. Places differ in their histories, cultures, politics, leadership, and particular ways of managing public–private relationships.' As Freeman (1990) points out – 180 years after a Boston merchant had memorized the workings of mills in England and Scotland and replicated them in the USA – it is somewhat ironic that the rebirth of Lowell has been regularly cited as a precedent for the revitalization of many industrial quarters in the UK. However, while there are many useful ideas that can be adopted for the revitalization of UK and European urban quarters, there are also unique features of the US political and financial system. Falk (1986, p. 150), for example, identifies four key features that are peculiar to the USA: greater independence of local government; closer relations between the business community and local government; greater competition between financial institutions, and the existence of an extensive range of tax incentives. Furthermore, there is a danger that, without care and sensitivity, places will start to look the same and lose their individuality despite the apparent paradox that it is the historic urban quarter's sense of place that is the major attraction: 'Just as there is a standard high-rise office building vernacular . . . so there is also a standard preservation vernacular. I worry that more success will lead us to follow formulas more and more, rather than to think through each project anew' (Goldberger, 1976, p. 160). Thus, to achieve successful revitalization requires the recognition and exploitation of the assets and opportunities present within the quarter, its city, region and country.

ACHIEVING REVITALIZATION

The book has discussed historic urban quarters to understand the process of revitalizing them. The product is also of interest because the outcome in terms of the policies created, designed and implemented, and the continuing efforts to sustain what has been achieved can present general lessons for other quarters. The process of revitalization starts with recognizing and understanding the particular dimensions of obsolescence that each area suffers from; the quarter's resources and assets must be recognized together with its opportunities; finally the revitalization must be managed with careful and appropriate stewardship to ensure that the revitalization is sustained.

Addressing obsolescence

Cities experience growth, change and decay. The processes of such change are complex and have many different manifestations. In this book, a particular manifestation of change has been discussed: the obsolescence of nineteenth-century industrial, commercial and residential quarters. Obsolescence is a function of physical and economic change and the relative fixity of the buildings and places.

The changing pattern and balance of economic activities is part of the continuing evolution of cities and urban areas. In terms of the pattern of their economic activities, few cities are static: the fortunes of individual areas fluctuate over time. Many areas within cities have had a 'golden era' after which, for many, decline ensues. Many cities and parts of cities are now struggling to achieve a 'second golden era' and to reposition themselves within the global economy. Historic urban quarters are part of this strive for economic dynamism. Such quarters have also been affected by developments in the world economy and the emerging patterns of the post-industrial society. Many have become redundant as their original functions have moved to other countries, continents or relocated nationally as firms have moved from the rust belt to the sun belt, while residential quarters have declined principally due to the ecological processes identified by the Chicago School.

As discussed in Chapter Two, there are various dimensions of obsolescence: physical, functional, artificial, legal, image and locational. Many of these dimensions can be addressed directly: buildings can be repaired, their functional obsolescence addressed by rehabilitation; official obsolescence can be removed by rescinding the planning decisions that entailed demolition or clearance for road building schemes and the creation of conservation areas or historic districts; image obsolescence can be removed by physical improvements and by promotion of the area so that it is perceived differently, for example, as a tourism attraction rather than as a rundown industrial area. What is often the most intractable form of obsolescence is locational obsolescence. It is the relative locational obsolescence that often results in a low utilization and demand for the historic buildings because, for various reasons, other areas have a greater competitive advantage.

To remedy locational obsolescence and to restore the economic fortunes of an area requires the development of a competitive advantage for that area. The quarters in this book are trying to establish or maintain positions as centres of consumption and/ or production. This requires action to change the activities occurring within the area and its buildings. Where the existing uses are encouraged and enabled to operate more efficiently or profitably, this has been termed a functional regeneration. These efforts may involve exploitation of the quarter's historic character and buildings for tourism or residential uses, or its ambience for cultural activity. Additionally, historic urban quarters may become centres for post-industrial functions, for example, as a concentration of cultural production or media firms. Where new uses or activities displace existing functions or utilize previously vacant space, this has been termed a functional restructuring. A more limited restructuring that brings in new uses able to synchronize and support the quarter's existing economic base, has been termed a functional diversification. In both functional diversification and restructuring the historic attributes of the area might be exploited as assets.

The resource

The approach to revitalization must recognize and exploit the resources of the location. The sense of place and character found in historic urban quarters is a scarce resource but it needs protection and management both to preserve and exploit its positive attributes. This sense of place has both *physical* and *functional* dimensions.

Historic urban quarters have historic architectural settings and townscapes. Thus, due to its scarcity, the quarter's physical character has an economic value. However, controls are necessary to protect and maintain that physical character in order to sustain and reinforce the composite value of the quarter's property. The issues regarding urban design and architectural controls were discussed in Chapter Seven. To protect effectively, however, it is necessary to know what is being protected: 'It is axiomatic that to be able to pursue an active conservation policy, a planning authority must have full knowledge of what it is conserving . . . it must examine and classify the building stock in each area; identify the danger points and anticipate redundancy; prepare strict criteria for sympathetic redevelopment if the building is dispensable; or, alternatively, propose alternative new uses or other means of preservation; and document buildings by measuring, analysing and photographing them' (Cantacuzino, 1989, p. 9). Provided there is some investment or public subsidies, the physical conservation of historic urban quarters is relatively straightforward. The restrictions of preservation controls and conservation or historic district designation and their sensitive application mean that most development and investment in the area will result in the physical conservation of the historic building fabric.

The quarter's sense of place also has functional dimensions; the activities within the buildings contribute to its character and ambience. In the process of revitalization, the functional character is often threatened by gentrification. The functional character might derive from the traditional activities of the locality which are now in decline, as for example in the case of the Lace Market. Alternatively, as at Temple Bar, a desirable new functional character might arise from activities that have emerged due to the blighting of an area. Blighting disrupts the traditional pattern of property prices and land values. This permits – for a short period – other activities to occupy those spaces, which, in turn, might give a vibrant new character and vitality to the area. Thus, when revitalizing the area, it might be desirable to retain this character. However, those new activites are often threatened by the process of revitalization.

Arguably, gentrification is an inevitable outcome of the revitalization of historic urban quarters that have deteriorated and experienced obsolescence. Unless the existing buildings are vacant, there will usually be an element of displacement and gentrification, because as an area is revitalized it begins to experience higher property value uses and attracts users willing and able to pay higher rents. Gentrification is a term usually used pejoratively, what is important is the degree of gentrification and displacement. In SoHo, artists who took over unlet spaces were later displaced by middle-class occupiers who could pay more and increase the returns for the building owners. In the Marais quarter, there was an unsuccessful attempt to keep the artisans in the quarter, but few stayed as their expectations changed. To a lesser extent in Bologna the original residents moved and were replaced by students and single person households. LoDo, Pioneer Square and the Merchant City are examples of gestures to mitigate the impact of gentrification by attempts to diversify the quarter's residential population through the introduction of low-rent developments. In Shad Thames, the high cost of rehabilitation has meant that the premises can only be afforded by middle-class occupants. In the Jewellery Quarter, the solidarity of the traders has helped keep the original function and original traders in place. However, the cost has been the low level of physical improvements carried out by the owners of the premises. In the Lace Market, office developments replacing industrial units is another kind of gentrification – 'functional gentrification': the tertiary sector taking over premises from the secondary sector (industrial and manual to white collar). It is the city council's resistance to this change that arguably has resulted in the relative lack of revitalization in this quarter.

Problems associated with gentrification stem from the differing interests of those who prioritize the physical conservation of the quarter – the preservationists – and those who prioritize its functional character – usually those who live and work there. In the case of housing-led revitalization, as Ashworth and Tunbridge (1990, p. 115) note, there is an important distinction between those who live in historic premises and value the historic character, and those who, although resident in the same properties or areas, have a different set of motives and priorities, being relatively indifferent to the historic character and placing greater value on the area's centrality and low rents. Although, there will inevitably be a degree of overlap between the two groups, it is important to recognize that their interests may be in conflict. The significance of this distinction is that through gentrification, the second group are likely to be displaced by the first.

Several of the case study quarters have sought a functional as well as a physical conservation. Such conservations attempt to resist market forces and other forces of economic change, and, as a consequence, will ultimately be futile. For example, in the Lace Market, the resistance to the encroachment of office uses compromised the physical conservation of the area which those uses would have provided. Thus, it is often more important to protect the physical character rigorously but be more flexible with its functional character. Concern for functional character might frustrate attempts to generate the investment required to conserve and revitalize the quarter physically, leading to the deterioration and/or loss of the historic building stock. Further blight may result from the overzealous protection of the physical and/or functional character.

Recognizing opportunities

Recognizing the assets and resources of an area, the identification of an appropriate role for the quarter is the key requirement of successful revitalization. This demands an insight that identifies where potential demand lies and what uses are appropriate for a particular quarter in a particular city. The challenge is to build the capacity for such areas to compete. Like other areas, revitalized historic urban quarters need to create a diverse economic base and a balance between different needs and demands. This can be achieved by introducing or reintroducing mixed uses. Single function quarters are less likely to sustain their achievements as competition with other places is a continuing process. One problem at Lowell has been that its revitalization was also closely linked to the success of the Wang Corporation. Arguably, a quarter like Temple Bar which aims to achieve revitalization through a range of functions and different uses will be able to sustain its well-being longer as the impact of various economic changes will affect only some of its new functions at any given time. Efforts to base revitalization on a single major use can be very frustrating as exemplified by the Lace Market. Nottingham is belatedly accepting that they must pursue a mixed use strategy in order for this quarter to be revitalized.

Historic urban quarters are rarely autonomous functional zones and cannot be delimited in purely morphological terms. They are an integral part of the formal and functional complexity of the central area, often having a symbiotic relationship with the rest of the city and, in particular, its central area. Thus, rather than being considered in isolation, they must be considered within the context of the city as a whole as well as its region. Areas like Little Germany, the Jewellery Quarter, the Lace Market and Pioneer Square have suffered various degrees of dislocation as their linkages both to the city centre and the rest of the city have been affected – even severed – through road schemes in the 1950s and 1960s. As noted in Chapter Six, in Birmingham – a city where a major effort is being made to heal the environment of its central area – the Jewellery Quarter's linkage with the city centre is also being improved. There is a similar attempt in Nottingham where environmental improvements for a tourist trail and improvements to Weekday Cross are tying the Lace Market back into the city centre. Improving linkages to the Downtown and the sports area was a key element of the revitalization of Pioneer Square in Seattle. Many quarters such as the Merchant City, Temple Bar, SoHo, LoDo, Castlefield, the Marais quarter and central Bologna did not experience the same degree of severing of linkages. Thus, their revitalization efforts were not disadvantaged. Unfortunately, Bradford has not attempted to improve Little Germany's physical linkages to the central area of the city. Thus, consequently the quarter's potential contribution within the city is not being fully exploited.

Managing revitalization

The responsibility to revitalize obsolete areas of cities lies with the public agencies, major land owners, residents, businesses and local amenity groups that have a stake in their revitalization. Any of these players in the city or the quarter may take the lead. In Lowell, those politicians who took the lead not only brought vitality back to the town but propelled themselves onto the national political arena enabling them to bring further investment to the town. Individuals or agencies taking a key role in the revitalization of a quarter need to be resourceful, as well as committed. They need an ability to see problems as opportunities so that the vision can be turned into action (Falk, 1986, p. 151).

Although property development is a necessary but not sufficient condition of revitalization, the success or failure of revitalization projects is closely tied to the peaks and troughs of property markets. Where a restructuring or diversification approach is pursued, there are usually some initial key projects. These have to demonstrate that there is a viable market and demand for the new activity or function in order to encourage further investment. Where the projects are publicly subsidized, the degree of subsidy might taper out as the market becomes established and the projects become more commercially viable in their own right. With regard to private sector developments, in the early period of revitalization, planners need to have a flexible, *laisser faire* attitude. Investors and entrepreneurs with vision who pioneer developments in historic quarters are rewarded by larger proportional increases in the appreciated value of their property. However, once those initial projects are successful and the revitalization gathers momentum, planners have to control closely the supply of property and, thereby, manage the demand for it. In this respect, Shad Thames, at one time, had more than 400 converted – but empty – properties on the market for which there was no effective demand. The mismatch between supply and demand led to several bankruptcies and development companies going into receivership. Arguably, the buildings should have been developed much more slowly and in tune with market demand to avoid over supply. The property boom of the late 1980s was an opportune period for revitalizing historic urban quarters, but the early 1990s have been less opportune.

The process of revitalization that becomes visible through rehabilitated buildings, attractive spaces and increased utilization of those buildings also requires continuing stewardship. Successfully revitalized urban quarters have often benefited from partnerships between public agencies and the private sector and from having special agencies to manage them. In the case studies, good practice is seen in the USA in Lowell, Seattle and Denver. Having initiated the revitalization process, these cities all had civic leaders/politicians who ensured continued stewardship by creating dedicated agencies for the continued well-being of the quarters. In Britain there are also examples of this, in Bradford where the local authority and key players came together, albeit briefly, in Little Germany Action, and in Nottingham where the local authority has continued its support by establishing the Lace Market Development Company to provide stewardship. The Park Rangers at Lowell and Castlefield visually demonstrate the commitment to the stewardship of the revitalized quarters.

Active management, stewardship and custodianship of historic quarters should intend that each action within the quarter leaves it a little better than it was before. As Montgomery (1995b, p. 108) describes: 'Rather than comprehensive, rational planning, many urban areas require a bit more respect, a helping hand, an injection of new money and activity. This we call *urban stewardship*: helping a place to help itself. A sort of management by incremental change, coupled with selective strategic interventions and improvement' (Montgomery, 1995b, p. 108).

SUCCESSFUL REVITALIZATION

Although, it might instinctively be sensed when – and if – an historic urban quarter has been revitalized, revitalization can only be defined qualitatively; there are no magic thresholds above which it can be claimed empirically that revitalization has occurred. Revitalizing – bringing areas back into active use – is a dynamic process. Across the case study examples, the revitalization process has happened to varying degrees. Many of the quarters discussed still have a significant amount of buildings in poor repair, derelict or in need of rehabilitation, and temporary surface level car parks on vacant sites. Successful revitalization must manifest itself in physical, economic and social terms.

Physical revitalization

Physically, the successfully revitalized historic urban quarter is kept in good repair and is well maintained: layers of soot and grime are removed from old buildings, they are repaired and rehabilitated, streets are improved and the area attains a general

Figure 8.2

Covent Garden Piazza, London. Successfully revitalized historic urban quarters are kept in good repair and are well maintained: layers of soot and grime are removed from old buildings, they are repaired and rehabilitated, streets are improved and the area attains a general appearance of well-being.

appearance of well-being (Figure 8.2). This positive image makes a place attractive to investors, visitors and the residents.

In revitalizing historic urban quarters, highly visible, physical interventions are often the first stage. The first efforts in revitalizing an historic urban quarter usually entail physical improvements either to the stock of buildings or to the public realm or both. External environmental improvements are necessary to attract both new functions and people to the area. A number of studies show that people feel uncomfortable and fear places that are in disrepair and have visual signs of neglect (Oc and Trench, 1993, p. 164). Thus, physical revitalization is undertaken both as improvements to the public realm, usually funded by the public agencies, and/or to the stock of building by refurbishment for their existing use or by conversion for a new use, usually funded by the private sector assisted and encouraged by various kinds of public subsidies or tax incentives. In Britain, IIAs, CIAs and other schemes, such as 'Operation Clean-Up' were designed to ensure physical improvements. In Denver, the revolving fund encourages and enables the investors to undertake physical improvements of the buildings while the city carries out environmental improvements.

Economic revitalization

Nevertheless, property development and rehabilitation is a necessary – but not a sufficient condition – of revitalization. As well as property measures, concern and efforts have to be directed towards the quarter's economic infrastructure and development, the further stimulation of growth and greater utilization of the historic building stock. Thus, the revitalization of historic urban quarters involves both the renewal of the physical fabric and the active economic use – or utilization – of buildings and spaces. In the short term, physical revitalization can result in an attractive, well-maintained public realm that projects a positive image and encourages confidence in the location. In the longer term economic revitalization is required, as ultimately it is the productive utilization of the private realm that pays for the maintenance of the public realm. As Rypkema (1992, p. 208) states: 'a rehabilitated empty building does not particularly add to an economic revitalization strategy in those areas: that building filled with tenants does. People and economic activity, not paint and plumbing fixtures, ultimately add economic value'.

Social revitalization

Socially, the successfully revitalized historic urban quarter is a lively and vital place. A revitalized quarter has an attractive ambience and is a good place to be and to go: its streets are peopled and crime rates are reduced. Contemporary urban design is about creating a sense of place and place making. The presence of people turns *spaces* into *places* making them living, working, organic parts of the city. The emerging consensus is that, in all aspects of urban design, it is necessary to see through the formal appearance and consider the human experience of the place. Thus, good urban quarters are also good examples of urban design.

In this respect, it is important to appreciate that the public realm is both a physical *and* a social construct. Not only is a spatially defined physical public realm required, but that public realm needs to be animated by people; spaces become places through their use by people. The concern is for urban spaces to become animated by people:

Figure 8.3

Shad Thames, London. The challenge in creating a lively urban quarter is to ensure that the most interactive uses claim the appropriate street frontages.

such animation can be planned. MacCormac (1983a) discusses the osmotic properties of streets: the manner in which the activities within buildings are able to percolate through and infuse the street with life and activity. He notes that there are certain uses which have very little relation to people in the street, and others with which they are intimately involved: the sense of human presence and vitality within the urban spaces depends upon these relationships. MacCormac establishes a hierarchy of uses supportive of an animated public realm. This is not to suggest that some uses are unnecessary or have no place within an urban area, merely that they should have less claim to frontage onto the street and therefore onto the physical public realm. The extremes in MacCormac's hierarchy are car parking which has little or no significance to the passer-by and street markets which offer an intense series of transactions between the seller and the public, the stall and the street. Between these two lies a range of uses which can be classified in order of increasing relation to the street: car parks, warehousing, large-scale industry, large-scale offices, blocks of flats, supermarkets, small-scale offices and shops, housing, restaurants and bars, and, finally, street markets.

The challenge in creating a lively urban quarter is to ensure that the most interactive uses claim the appropriate street frontages (Figure 8.3). In Temple Bar, the *1992 Development Programme* introduced a detailed mixed-use plan that included the vertical zoning of land-uses. This policy concentrated on the social urban realm and encouraged active ground floor uses such as retail, bars, clubs, galleries and other cultural facilities to help animate the streets and provide a boost to the evening economy and, therefore, the safety of the quarter. The control over the upper floors was more relaxed and allows for a variety of more 'passive' uses such as residential and office accommodation. There is a similar policy in Denver's LoDo where a distribution of uses is encouraged that would create more pedestrian life and vitality in the quarter and, in addition, make it a safer place. Other factors which affect the pedestrian-friendly nature of the quarter are its *permeability* – the ease by which a pedestrian can move safely around the quarter – and its *legibility* – the ease by which a pedestrian can navigate around the quarter.

Montgomery (1995b, p. 104) notes that the animation of the public realm of historic urban quarters may also be stimulated through planned programmes of cultural animation. This involves programming events and spectacles to encourage people to visit, use and linger in urban places. As Montgomery (1995b, p. 104) describes: 'It usually involves contracting a cultural animateur to programme events and festivals across a range of venues, including public places, squares and parks. The idea is to provide a varied diet of events and activities – lunchtime concerts, art exhibitions, street theatre – so that people begin to visit an area just to see what's going on. And by having people on the streets, in the cafés and moving through the public realm, urban vitality is stimulated.' Nevertheless, the 'authenticity' of the quarter's animation is also important. Goldman, a developer in both New York's SoHo and Miami's Art Deco district is critical of what he sees as the 'contrived' street life in Covent Garden: 'That's not interesting to me. It's the Walt Disney route. It's got no smell, no authenticity. It's the colour of beige, and I don't like that colour. There needs to be grit' (Goldman, from Tredre, 1995, p. 26).

CONCLUSION

In all cities, including their historic urban quarters, the processes of change are on-going. In this book, the interest has been in revitalizing historic urban quarters; the conserving and bringing bring back to viable use – possibly with new functions – of quarters with significant historic character and sense of place. The process has to occur by taking advantage of social and economic changes, for example, over the last two decades, socio-demographic changes have led to the return of middle income groups to central areas of cities. Furthermore, due to their sense of place and attractive ambience, these areas have often attracted post-industrial economic activities. By virtue of their contribution to the re-imaging of cities, historic urban quarters also have cultural and economic importance to the wider city. Glasgow's Merchant City is an integral part of that city's ambition to re-image itself from the decaying capital of Red Clyde to the 'go-getting' city of the late twentieth century. Castlefield is an expression of Manchester's ambition to be a culturally, as well as economically, robust European city attracting post industrial functions like finance and tourism. Dublin's Temple Bar represents a major effort by the capital city of a country whose young people have traditionally migrated overseas. By supplementing economic factors, this new quarter is one of the factors ensuring that increasing numbers of young Irish stay in Dublin. An historic quarter becomes revitalized when people and activities return, making it a place people want to use and invest in and the quarters discussed in this book illustrate different ways by which this new vitality has or can be achieved.

BIBLIOGRAPHY

Alexander, C. (1965), 'A city is not a tree', *Architectural Forum*, April, reprinted in *Design*, No.6. February, 1966, pp. 46–55.

Alexander, C. *et al.* (1977), *A Pattern Language of Architecture*, Oxford University Press, Oxford.

Alexander, C. *et al.* (1979), *The Timeless Way of Building*, Oxford University Press, Oxford.

Alexander, C. *et al.*, (1987), *A New Theory of Urban Design*, Oxford University Press, Oxford.

Antoniou, J. (1991), 'Making sense of conservation', *Building Design*, 9 August, pp. 12–14.

Appleyard, D. (ed.) (1979), *The Conservation of European Cities*, MIT Press, Cambridge, MA.

Architecture Today (1995), 'Regeneration: Mixed media: Felim Dunne at Temple Bar', *Architecture Today*, 58, January, pp. 38–40.

Ashworth, G.J. and Tunbridge, J.E. (1990), *The Tourist–Historic City*, Belhaven Press, London.

Atkinson, R. and Moon, G. (1993) *Urban Policy in Britain*, Macmillan, London.

Balchin, P.N., Kieve, J.L. and Bull, G.H. (1988), *Urban Land Economics and Public Policy*, 4th edn, Macmillan, London.

Bandarin, F. (1979), 'The Bologna Experience: Planning and historic renovation in a communist city', in Appleyard, D. (ed.) *The Conservation of European Cities*, MIT Press, Cambridge, MA, pp. 178–202.

Banerjee, T. and Baer, W.C. (1984), *Beyond the Neighbourhood Unit: Residential Environments and Public Policy*, Plenum, New York.

Barlow, J. and Gann, D. (1993), *Offices into Flats*, Joseph Rowntree Foundation, York.

Barnett, J. (1982), *An Introduction to Urban Design*, Harper and Row, New York.

Barrett, H. (1993), 'Investigating townscape change and management in urban conservation areas: The importance of detailed monitoring of planned alterations', *Town Planning Review*, Vol.64 (4), pp. 435–456.

Bartlett, E. (1981), 'Miami Beach bets on art deco', *Historic Preservation*, Vol.33 (1), January/February, pp. 8–15.

Baumgarten, M. (1984), 'Building study: New Concordia Wharf, Pollard Thomas Edwards and Associates', *Architects Journal*, 4 July, pp. 47–62.

BEDU (Bradford Economic Development Unit) (1992), *Little Germany Factsheet No. 5*, BEDU, Bradford.

Bentley, I. *et al.* (1985), *Responsive Environments: A Manual for Designers*, Architectural Press, London.

Bianchini, F. and Parkinson, M. (1993), *Cultural Policy and Urban Regeneration: the Western European Experience*, Manchester University Press, Manchester.

Bianchini, F. and Schwengel, H. (1991), 'Re-imagining the city', in Corner, J. and Harvey, S. *Enterprise and Heritage: Crosscurrents of National Culture*, Routledge, London, pp. 212–234.

Bianchini, F., Dawson, J. and Evans, R. (1992), 'Flagship Projects in Urban Regeneration', in Healey, P. *et al.* (eds), *Rebuilding the City: Property-led Regeneration*, E. & F. N. Spon, London, pp. 245–255.

Binney, M. (1984), *Our Vanishing Heritage*, Arlington Books, London.

Birch, E.L. and Roby, D. (1984), 'The planner and the preservationist: An uneasy alliance', *Journal of the American Planning Association*, Spring, pp. 194–207.

Birmingham City Council (1984), *City of Birmingham Local Plan*, Birmingham City Council, Birmingham.

Black, A.F. (1976), 'Making historic preservation profitable – If you're willing to wait', in Latham, J.E. (ed.), *The Economic Benefits of Preserving Old Buildings*, The Preservation Press/National Trust for Historic Preservation, Washington DC, pp. 21–27.

Bradford City Council (1984), *Bradford City Centre Local Plan*, Bradford City Council, Bradford.

Bradford City Council (1993), *Bradford North Unitary Development Plan*, Bradford City Council, Bradford.

Bradford City Council (1994), *Bradford Unitary Development Plan*, Bradford City Council, Bradford.

Bradford Economic Development Unit (1991a), *Our Part in the Future of Bradford*, City of Bradford Metropolitan Council, Bradford.

Bradford Economic Development Unit (1991b), *Merchant's House, Peckover Street, Little Germany, Bradford*, City of Bradford Metropolitan Council, Bradford.

Bramwell, B. (1993), 'Planning for tourism in an industrial city', *Town and Country Planning*, January/February, pp. 17–19.

Brindley, T., Rydin, Y. and Stoker, G. (1989), *Remaking Planning: The Politics of Change in the Thatcher Years*, Unwin Hyman, London.

Brink, P.H. and Dehart, H.G. (1992), 'Findings and Recommendations', in Lee, A. J. (ed.), *Past Meets Future: Saving America's Historic Environments*, National Trust for Historic Preservation/The Preservation Press, Washington, DC, pp. 15–23.

Broadbent, G. (1990), *Emerging Concepts of Urban Space Design*, Van Nostrand Reinhold, London.

Brolin, B. C. (1980), *Architecture in Context: Fitting New Buildings with Old*, Van Nostrand Reinhold, New York.

Brown Morton III, W. (1992), 'Forging new values in uncommon times', in Lee, A.J. (ed.), *Past Meets Future: Saving America's Historic Environments*, National Trust for Historic Preservation/The Preservation Press, Washington, DC, pp. 37–41.

Bruttomesso, R. (ed.) (1991), *Waterfronts: A New Urban Frontier*, International Centre for Cities on Water, Venice.

Buchanan, P. (1988), 'What city? A plea for a place in the public realm', *Architectural Review*, November.

BUDS (Birmingham Urban Design Studies)/Tibbalds Colbourne Karski Williams Ltd (1990), *City of Birmingham: Urban Design Strategy: Stage 1*, Birmingham City Council/BUDS, Birmingham.

Burkart, R. and Medlik, P. (1981), *Tourism Past, Present and Future*, 2nd edn, London, Heinemann.

Burke, G. (1976), *Townscapes*, Penguin, Harmondsworth.

Burtenshaw, D., Bateman, M. and Ashworth, G.J. (1991), *The European City: A Western Perspective*, David Fulton Publishers, London.

Campbell, M. (ed.) (1990), *Local Economic Policy*, London, Cassell Educational.

Cantacuzino, S. (1975), *New Uses for Old Buildings*, The Architectural Press, London.

Cantacuzino, S. (1989), *Re/Architecture: Old Buildings/New Uses*, Abbeville Press, New York.

Cantacuzino, S. and Brandt, S. (1980), *Saving Old Buildings*, The Architectural Press, London.

Casson, Sir Hugh, (1984), Foreword to Royal Borough of Kensington and Chelsea, *Urban Conservation and Historic Buildings: A Guide to the Legislation*, Royal Borough of Kensington and Chelsea, London.

Castells, M. (1989), *The Informational City: Information Technology, Economic Restructuring and the Urban-Regional Process*, Basil Blackwell, Oxford.

Castells, M. and Hall, P. (1994), *Technopoles: The Making of Twenty-First-Century Industrial Complexes*, Routledge, London.

Castlefield Management Company (1993), *The Regeneration of Castlefield*, Castlefield Management Company, Manchester.

Castlefield Management Company (1994a), *Newsheet*, Castlefield Management Company, Manchester.

Castlefield Management Company (1994b), *Urban Regeneration Stimulating Tourism*, Castlefield Management Company, Manchester.

Central Manchester Development Corporation (1993), *Cityscope*, Central Manchester Development Corporation, Manchester.

Central Manchester Development Corporation (1994), *Castlefield Area Regeneration Framework*, Central Manchester Development Corporation, Manchester.

Chapman, B.K. (1976), 'The growing public stake in urban conservation', in Latham, J.E. (ed.), *The Economic Benefits of Preserving Old Buildings*, The Preservation Press/National Trust for Historic Preservation, Washington DC, pp. 9–13.

Children's Employment Commission (1862), *Third Report*, City of Birmingham, Birmingham.

City and County of Denver (1991), *Lower Downtown: Streetscape Design Guidelines*, City and County of Denver, Denver.

CGDC (City of Glasgow District Council Planning Department) (1992), *The Renewal of Glasgow's Merchant City*, City of Glasgow, Glasgow.

CGDC (City of Glasgow District Council Planning Department) (1995), *Results of the Merchant City Residents' Attitudes Survey*, City of Glasgow, Glasgow.

CGDC (City of Glasgow District Council Planning Department) (1994), *Merchant City: Policy and Development Framework*, City of Glasgow, Glasgow.

City of Seattle Department of Community Development (1990), *Mayor's Recommended Pioneer Square Plan Update*, City of Seattle, Seattle.

CMDC (Central Manchester Development Corporation) (1990), *Strategy for Central Manchester*, Central Manchester Development Corporation, Manchester.

Collins, R.C., Waters, E.B. and Dotson, A.B. (1991), *America's Downtowns: Growth, Politics and Preservation*, The Preservation Press, Washington, DC.

Colquhoun, I. (1995), *Urban Regeneration: An International Perspective*, B. T. Batsford Ltd, London.

Conran Roche, Coopers & Lybrand, Frank Innes, Edward Shipway and Partners, (1989), *Study of Lace Market Development Opportunities*, Nottingham City Council, Nottingham.

Conrads, U. (1964), *Programmes and Manifestoes of Twentieth Century Architecture*, Lund Humphries, London.

Cooke, P. (ed.) (1989), *Localities – The Changing Face of Urban Britain*, Unwin Hyman, London.

Corner, J. and Harvey, S. (1991), *Enterprise and Heritage: Crosscurrents of National Culture*, Routledge, London.

Coulson, A. (1990), 'Evaluating local economic policy', in Campbell, M. (ed.), *Local Economic Policy*, Cassell, London, pp. 174–194.

Crewe, L. and Forster, Z. (1993a), 'Markets, design, and local agglomeration: the role of the small independent retailer in the workings of the fashion system', *Environment and Planning D: Society and Space*, Vol.11 pp. 213–229.

Crewe, L. and Forster, Z. (1993b), 'A Canute policy fighting economics? Local economic policy in an industrial district: the case of Nottingham's Lace Market', *Policy and Politics*, Vol.21 (4), pp. 275–287.

Crewe, L. and Hall-Taylor, M. (1991), 'The restructuring of the Nottingham Lace Market: Industrial relic or new urban model?', *East Midlands Geographer*, Vol.14, pp. 14–30.

Cruickshank, D. (1990), 'Street Wise (Shad Thames)', *Architects Journal*, 16 May, pp. 26–29.

Cullen, G. (1961), *Townscape*, Architectural Press, London.

Cullen, G. (1971), *The Concise Townscape*, Architectural Press, London.

Cullinan, E.A. (1992), *Development Programme for Temple Bar*, Temple Bar Properties Ltd, Dublin.

Cullingworth, J.B. (1992), 'Historic preservation in the US: from landmarks to planning perspectives', *Planning Perspectives*, 7, pp. 65–79.

Culot, M. (1980), *In the Presence of the Past*, Venice Biennale, Venice.

Cunnington, P. (1988), *Change of Use: The Conversion of Old Buildings*, Alphabooks, A & C Black, London.

Datel, R.E. and Dingemans, D.J. (1980), 'Historic preservation and urban change', *Urban Geography*, Vol.1 (3), pp. 229–253.

Deakin, N. and Edwards, J. (1993), *The Enterprise Culture and the Inner City*, Routledge, London.

Dean, J. (1993), 'Why do we seek to conserve?', *The Planner*, April, pp. 13–14.

DOE (Department of the Environment) (1972), *Town and Country Planning (Amendment) Act*, HMSO, London.

DOE (Department of the Environment) (1977), *White Paper: Policy for the Inner Cities*, HMSO, London.

DOE (Department of the Environment) (1985), *The Urban Programme*, HMSO, London.

DOE (Department of the Environment) (1986), *Industrial Improvement Areas*, HMSO, London.

DOE (Department of the Environment) (1987a), *Re-Using Redundant Buildings*, HMSO, London.

DOE (Department of the Environment) (1987b), *Historic Buildings and Conservation Areas: Policy and Procedures*, HMSO, London.

DOE (Department of the Environment) (1988a), *Improving Urban Areas: Good Practice in Urban Regeneration*, HMSO, London.

DOE (Department of the Environment) (1988b), *Developing Businesses: Good Practice in Urban Regeneration*, HMSO, London.

DOE (Department of the Environment) (1988c), *Action for Cities: Building An Initiative*, HMSO, London.

DOE (Department of the Environment) (1990), *Tourism and the Inner City: An Evaluation of the Impact of Grant Assisted Tourism Projects*, HMSO, London.

DOE (Department of the Environment) (1992), *Planning Policy Guidance Note 21: Tourism*, HMSO, London.

DOE (Department of the Environment) (1993), *Evaluation of Urban Development Grant, Urban Regeneration Grant and City Grant*, HMSO, London.

DOE (Department of the Environment) (1994), *Planning Policy Guidance Note 15: Planning and the Historic Environment*, HMSO, London.

Dobby, A. (1978), *Conservation and Planning*, Hutchinson, London.

Doheny, D.A. (1993), 'Property rights and historic preservation', *Historic Preservation Forum*, Vol.7 (4), July/August, pp. 7–10.

Dublin Corporation (1990), *The Temple Bar Action Plan*, Dublin.

Duffy, F. and Henney, A. (1989), *The Changing City*, Bulstrode Press, London.

Dunlop, B. (1992), 'Coping with success', *Historic Preservation*, Vol.44 (4), July/August, pp. 56–63.

Dunne, F. (1993), 'Mixed media at Temple Bar', *Architecture Today*, No.38, May, pp. 38–40.

Economakis, R. (ed.) (1992), *Leon Krier: Architecture and Urban Design, 1967–1992*, Academy Editions, London.

Eddy, D.H. (1985), 'Authentic city', *RIBA Journal*, July, pp. 42–44.

Edwards, B. (1992), *London Docklands: Urban Design in an Age of Deregulation*, Butterworth Architecture, London.

Egan, D.J. (1983), 'Tourism and Employment', *The Planner*, July/August, p. 133.

Eisenman, P. (1982), 'Editor's introduction: The houses of memory: The texts of analogy', in Rossi, A. (English translation) *The Architecture of the City*, MIT Press, Cambridge, MA.

Elkin, T. and McLaren, D. with Hillman, M. (1991), *Reviving the City: Towards Sustainable Urban Development*, Friends of the Earth, London.

Ellis, C. (1990), 'Le Marais restaure', *Historic Preservation*, Vol.42 (2), March/April, pp. 22–29.

English Tourist Board (1978), *Planning for Tourism in England*, English Tourist Board, London.

English Tourist Board (1989), *Manchester, Salford and Trafford Strategic Development Initiative*, English Tourist Board, London.

English Tourist Board (1991), *Tourism and the Inner City: Planning Advisory Note 3*, English Tourist Board, London.

Falk, N. (1986), 'Baltimore and Lowell: Two American Approaches', *Built Environment*, Vol.12 (3), pp. 145–152.

Falk, N. (1987), 'From vision to results', *The Planner*, June, pp. 39–43.

Faulkner, P.A. (1978), 'A philosophy for the preservation of our historic heritage', *Journal of the Royal Society of the Arts*, Vol.126, pp. 452–80.

Firth, G. (1990), *Bradford and the Industrial Revolution: An Economic History 1760–1840*, Ryburn Publishing, Halifax.

Fishman, R. (1982), *Urban Utopias of Tomorrow: Ebenezer Howard, Frank Lloyd Wright and Le Corbusier*, MIT Press, Cambridge, MA.

Fitch, J. M. (1990), *Historic Preservation: Curatorial Management of the Built Environment*, University Press of Virginia, Charlottesville.

Fleming, R.L. (1981), 'Recapturing history: a plan for gritty cities', *Landscape*, Vol.25 (1), pp. 165–180.

Ford, L.R. (1994), *Cities and Buildings: Skyscrapers, Skid Rows, and Suburbs*, The John Hopkins University Press, London.

Freeman, A. (1990), 'Lessons from Lowell', *Historic Preservation*, Vol.42 (6), November/December, pp. 32–39, 68–69.

Freeman, R.W. (1976), 'Integrity in the Vieux Carre', in Latham, J.E. (ed.) *The Economic Benefits of Preserving Old Buildings*, The Preservation Press/National Trust for Historic Preservation, Washington, DC, pp. 111–115.

Gall, L. D. 'The Heritage Factor in Lowell's Revitalization', in Weible, R. (ed), (1991), *The Continuing Revolution: A History of Lowell, Massachusetts*, Lowell Historical Society, Lowell.

Gans, H. (1962), *The Urban Villages: Group and Class in the Life of Italian-Americans*, Free Press, New York.

Gans, H. (1968), *People and Plans: Essays on Urban Problems and Solutions*, Basic Books, New York.

Gay, P.H. (1992), 'The urgency of urban preservation', in Lee, A.J. (ed.) *Past Meets Future: Saving America's Historic Environments*, National Trust for Historic Preservation/The Preservation Press, Washington, DC, pp. 105–107.

Giedion, S. (1947), *Space Time and Architecture: The Growth of a New Tradition*, 7th edn, Oxford University Press, London.

Gleye, P.H. (1988), 'With heritage so fragile: A critique of the tax credit program for historic building rehabilitation', *Journal of the American Planning Association*, August, pp. 482–488.

Goldberger, P.J. (1976), 'The dangers of preservation success', in Latham, J.E. (ed.) *The Economic Benefits of Preserving Old Buildings*, The Preservation Press/National Trust for Historic Preservation, Washington, DC, pp. 159–161.

Goodall, B. (1987), 'Tourism policy and jobs in the UK', *Built Environment*, Vol.13 (2), pp. 109–123.

Gorst, T. (1994), 'Energy: Shades of green: Murray O'Laorie in Dublin', *Architecture Today*, 53, August, pp. 38–42.

Gosling, D. and Maitland, B. (1984), *Concepts of Urban Design*, Academy Editions/St. Martins Press, London.

Graeve, J. (1991), *Temple Bar Lives: Winning Architectural Framework Plan*, Temple Bar Properties Ltd., Dublin.

Granada Studios Tour (1995), *Press Information*, Granada Theme Parks and Hotels Ltd.

Gratz, R.B. (1989), *The Living City: How America's Cities are being Revitalized by Thinking Small in Big Ways*, Simon and Schuster, New York.

Gratz, R.B. and Freiberg, P. (1980), 'Has success spoiled SoHo?', *Historic Preservation*, Vol.32 (5), September/October, pp. 8–15.

Grieff, C.M. (1971), *Lost America: From the Atlantic to the Mississippi*, The Pyne Press, Princeton, New Jersey.

Griffiths, R. (1993), The politics of cultural policy in urban regeneration strategies, *Policy and Politics*, Vol.21 (1), pp. 39–46.

Gunn, C.A. (1994), *Tourism Planning: Basics, Concepts, Cases*, 3rd edn, Taylor and Francis, Washington.

Haas-Klau, C. (1986), 'Berlin: 'soft' urban renewal in Kreuzberg', *Built Environment*, Vol.12 (3), pp. 165–175.

Hall, P. (1991), 'Waterfronts: A new urban frontier', in Bruttomesso, R. (ed.) *Waterfronts: A New Urban Frontier*, International Centre for Cities on Water, Venice.

Hall, P. (1992), *Urban and Regional Planning*, 3rd edn, Routledge, London.

Hammer, Siler, George Associates (1990), *Lower Downtown: Economic Impact of Historic District Designation*, HSGA/City and County of Denver, Denver.

Hamshere, J.D. (1991), 'Regeneration catalysts or exclusion zones', *Town and Country Planning*, Vol.60 (8) pp. 247–248.

Hareven, T.K. and Langenbach, R. (1981), 'Living Places, Work Places and Historical Identity', in Lowenthal, D. and Binney, M. *Our Past Before Us – Why do we save it?*, Temple Smith, London, pp. 109–123.

Harvey, D. (1985), *The Urbanization of Capital*, Basil Blackwell, Oxford.

Harvey, J. (1987), *Urban Land Economics: The Economics of Real Property*, 2nd edn, Macmillan Educational, London.

Harvey, D. (1989a), *The Condition of Postmodernity: An Enquiry into the Origins of Cultural Change*, Basil Blackwell, Oxford.

Harvey, D. (1989b), *The Urban Experience*, Basil Blackwell, Oxford.

Haughton, G. and Hunter, C. (1994), *Sustainable Cities*, Jessica Kingsley Publishers, London.

Healey, P. (1991), 'Urban regeneration and the development industry', *Regional Studies*, Vol.25 (2) pp. 97–110.

Healey, P. and Nabarro, R. (eds) (1990), *Land and Property Development in a Changing Context*, Gower, Aldershot.

Healey, P., Davoudi, S., O'Toole, M., Tavsanoglu, S. and Usher, D. (eds) (1992), *Rebuilding the City: Property-led Urban Regeneration*, E. & F.N. Spon, London.

Hewison, R. (1987), *The Heritage Industry: Britain in a Climate of Decline*, Methuen, London.

Hoyle, B., Pinder, D., and Husain, M. (eds) (1988), *Revitalising the Waterfront*, Belhaven, London.

Hubbard, P. (1993), 'The value of conservation', *Town Planning Review*, Vol.64 (4), pp. 359–373.

Imrie, R. and Thomas, H. (1993), 'The limits of property-led regeneration', *Environment and Planning C: Government and Policy*, Vol.11 (1), pp. 87–102.

Jacobs, J. (1961), *The Death and Life of Great American Cities*, Random House, New York.

James, A. and Black, G. (1992), *The Lace Market, Nottingham: A Vision and a Strategy for Visitor Use*, Nottingham City Council, Nottingham.

Jencks, C. (1977), *The Language of Post Modern Architecture*, Academy Editions, London.

Jencks, C. (1986), *What is Post Modernism?*, Academy Editions, London.

Johnson, J. (1987), 'Bringing it all back home: Ingram Square, Glasgow', *Architects Journal*, 6 May, pp. 39–51.

Johnson, J. (1989), 'Merchant revival', *Architects Journal*, 3 May, pp. 36–51.

Johnson-Marshall, P. (1966), *Rebuilding Cities*, Constable Ltd, Edinburgh.

Karski, A. (1990), 'Urban tourism – A key to urban regeneration?', *The Planner*, 6 April, pp. 15–17.

Kearns, G. and Philo, C. (eds) (1993), *Selling Places: The past as cultural capital past and present*, Pergamon Press, Oxford.

Keister, K. (1990), 'Main Street makes good', *Historic Preservation*, Vol.42 (5), September/October, pp. 44–50, 83.

Keister, K. (1993a), 'The art of the deal', *Historic Preservation*, Vol.45 (5), September/ October, pp. 60–67, 100–101.

Keister, K. (1993b), 'Comeback on hold', *Historic Preservation*, Vol.45 (4), July/ August, pp. 50–57.

Kolb, D. (1990), *Postmodern Sophistications: Philosophy, Architecture, and Tradition*, University of Chicago Press, Chicago.

Kotler, P., Haider, D.H. and Rein, I. (1993), *Marketing Places: Attracting Investment, Industry and Tourism to Cities, Nations and States*, The Free Press, New York.

Krier, L. (1978a), 'The reconstruction of the city' in Deleroy, R.L. *Rational Architecture*, Archives d'Architecture Moderne, Brussels, pp. 38–44.

Krier, L. (1978b), 'Urban transformations', *Architectural Design* Vol.48 (4).

Krier, L. (1979), 'The cities within a city', *Architectural Design*, Vol.49 (1), pp. 19–32.

Krier, L. (1984), 'Houses, palaces, cities', *Architectural Design* Vol.54 (7/8).

Krier, R. (1979), *Urban Space*, Academy Editions, London.

LaBrecque, R. (1980), 'New industry for Mill City, USA', *Historic Preservation*, July/ August, Vol.32 (4), pp. 32–39.

Latham, J.E. (ed.) (1976), *The Economic Benefits of Preserving Old Buildings*, The Preservation Press/National Trust for Historic Preservation, Washington, DC.

Law, C.M. (1991), 'Tourism and urban revitalisation', *East Midlands Geographer*, Vol.14, pp. 49–60.

Law, C.M. (1992), 'Urban tourism and its contribution to economic regeneration', *Urban Studies*, Vol.29 (3/4), pp. 599–618.

Law, C.M. (1994), *Urban Tourism: Attracting Visitors to Large Cities*, Mansell, London.

Lawless, P. (1989), *Britain's Inner Cities*, Paul Chapman Publishing, London.

LDDC (London Docklands Development Corporation) (1987), *Docklands Heritage: Conservation and regeneration in London's Docklands*, LDDC, London.

Le Corbusier (1927/1946), *Towards a New Architecture*, Architectural Press, London.

Lee, A.J. (ed.) (1992), *Past Meets Future: Saving America's Historic Environments*, National Trust for Historic Preservation/The Preservation Press, Washington, DC.

Lichfield, N. (1988), *Economics in Urban Conservation*, Cambridge University Press, Cambridge.

Liddy, P. (1992), *Temple Bar, Dublin: An Illustrated History*, Temple Bar Properties Ltd., Dublin.

Lim, H. (1994), 'Urban tourism and the development of a tourism quarter – case studies of Temple Bar, Dublin, Ireland, and Sheffield, UK', unpublished conference paper given at the VIIIth AESOP conference, Istanbul.

Lottman, H.R. (1976), *How Cities Are Saved*, Universe Books, New York.

Lowenthal, D. (1981a), 'Introduction', in Lowenthal, D. and Binney, M. (1981), *Our Past Before Us – Why do we save it?*, Temple Smith, London, pp. 9–16.

Lowenthal, D. (1981b), 'Conclusion: Dilemmas of preservation', in Lowenthal, D. and Binney, M. *Our Past Before Us – Why do we save it?*, Temple Smith, London, pp. 213–237.

Lowenthal, D. (1985), *The Past is a Foreign Country*, Cambridge University Press, Cambridge.

Lowenthal, D. and Binney, M. (1981), *Our Past Before Us – Why do we save it?*, Temple Smith, London.

Lynch, K. (1960), *The Image of the City*, MIT Press, Cambridge, MA.

Lynch, K. (1972), *What Time is This Place?*, MIT Press, Cambridge, MA.

MacCormac, R. (1980), 'Architecture: The right mix', *Architects Journal*, 9 July, pp. 68–71.

MacCormac, R. (1983a), 'Urban reform: MacCormac's manifesto', *Architects Journal*, 15 June, pp. 59–72.

MacCormac, R. (1983b), 'The architect and tradition 2: Tradition and transformation', *Royal Society of Arts Journal*, November, pp. 740–753.

MacCormac, R. (1984), 'Actions and experience of design', *Architects Journal*, 4 and 11 January, pp. 43–47.

MacCormac, R. (1991), 'The pursuit of quality', *RIBA Journal*, September, pp. 33–41.

MacCormac, R. (1993), 'New buildings in historic contexts', *RIBA Journal*, Vol.100 (2), February, pp. 29–32.

Mageean, A. (1995), 'Sustaining the heart of the city: Bologna', *Report*, August, pp. 34–36.

Maitland, B. (1984), 'The use of history', in Gosling, D. and Maitland, B. *Concepts of Urban Design*, Academy Editions/St. Martins Press, London, pp. 4–7.

Manchester City Council (1974), *Manchester Structure Plan*, Manchester City Council, Manchester.

Manchester City Council (1982), *City of Manchester Local Plan*, Manchester City Council, Manchester.

Manchester City Council (1991), *City of Manchester Local Plan*, Manchester City Council, Manchester.

Manchester City Council (1992), *Report of the Officers Working Party*, Manchester City Council, Manchester.

Manchester Museum of Science and Industry (1995), *The History of the Museum and its Site*, Museum of Science and Technology, Manchester.

Markusen, A. (1981), 'City spatial structure, women's household work, and national urban policy', in Stimpson, C.R., Dixler, E., Nelson, M.J. and Yatrakis, K.B. (eds) *Women and the City*, University of Chicago Press, Chicago.

Mathieson, A. and Wall, G. (1982), *Tourism: economic, physical and social impacts*, Longman, New York.

McCue, G. (1981), *The Building Art of St. Louis: A guide to the architecture of the city and its metropolitan region*, Knight Publishing Company, St Louis.

Middleton, R. (1983), 'The architect and tradition: 1: The use and abuse of tradition in architecture', *Journal of the Royal Society of Arts*, November, pp. 729–739.

Mitchell, H.B. (1992), 'The States: 25 years in the middle', in Lee, A.J. (ed.), *Past Meets Future: Saving America's Historic Environments*, National Trust for Historic Preservation/The Preservation Press, Washington, DC, pp. 65–71.

Montgomery, J. (1995a), 'The story of Temple Bar: Creating Dublin's cultural quarter', *Planning Practice and Research*, Vol.10(2), pp. 135–172.

Montgomery, J. (1995b), 'Urban vitality and the culture of cities', *The Planner*, April, pp. 20–21.

Morton, D. (1993), 'Conservation Finance: Expectations and Resources', *The Planner*, April, pp. 20–21.

Moughtin, J.C. (1995), *Urban Design: Street and Square*, Butterworth-Heinemann, Oxford.

Moughtin, J.C., Oc, T. and Tiesdell, S. (1995), *Urban Design: Ornament and Decoration*, Butterworth-Heinemann, Oxford.

Mullin, J.R., Armsrong, J.H. and Kavanagh, J.S. (1986), 'From mill town to mill town: The transition of a New England town from a textile to a high-technology economy', *Journal of the American Planning Association*, Winter 1986, pp. 47–59.

Mumford, L. (1938), *The Culture of Cities*, Secker & Warburg, London.

Mumford, L. (1961), *The History of the City*, Harcourt Brace Johanovich, New York.

Murtagh, W.J. (1988), *Keeping Time: The History and Theory of Preservation in America*, The Main Street Press, Pittstown, NJ.

Murtagh, W.J. (1992), 'Janus never sleeps', in Lee, A.J. (ed.), *Past Meets Future: Saving America's Historic Environments*, National Trust for Historic Preservation/The Preservation Press, Washington, DC, pp. 51–57.

National Park Service (1992), *Official National Park Handbook 140: Lowell – The Story of an Industrial City*, National Park Service, Washington.

North West Tourist Board (1993), *Regional Tourism Facts: North West*, North West Tourist Board, Wigan.

Nottingham City Council (1989), *Lace Market Development Strategy*, Nottingham City Council, Nottingham.

Nottingham City Council (1992), *Nottingham's Economic Development Strategy 1992–93*, Nottingham City Council, Nottingham.

Nottingham City Council (1993a), *Lace Market Development Strategy Review*, Nottingham City Council, Nottingham.

Nottingham City Council (1993b), *Nottingham's Economic Development Strategy 1993–94*, Nottingham City Council, Nottingham.

Oc, T. and Tiesdell, S. (1991), 'The London Docklands Development Corporation (LDDC), 1981–1991: A perspective on the management of urban regeneration', *Town Planning Review*, Vol.62 (3) pp. 311–330.

Oc, T. and Trench, S. (eds) (1990), *Current Issues in Planning*, Gower, Aldershot.

Oc, T. and Trench, S. (1993), 'Planning and Shopper Security', in Bromley, R.D.F. and Thomas, C.J. *Retail Change*, UCL Press, London.

Oc, T. and Trench, S. (eds) (1995), *Current Issues in Planning (Vol. II)*, Gower-Avebury, London.

O'Laoire, M. (1994), 'Shades of green', *Architecture Today*, No.53, November, pp. 38–42.

O'Reilly, L. (1981), 'Dublin: Urban renewal in a rapidly expanding city region', *The Planner*, Vol.67 (6).

Owens, R. (1990), 'Blue circle', *Architects Journal*, 17 October, pp. 26–33.

Paddison, R. (1993), 'City marketing, image reconstruction and urban regeneration', *Urban Studies*, Vol.30 (2), pp. 339–350.

Page, I. (1986), 'Tourism promotion in Bradford', *The Planner*, TCPSS Proceedings, February, pp. 72–75.

Parkinson, M. (1989), 'The Thatcher Government's urban policy, 1979–1989: A Review', *Town Planning Review*, Vol.60 (4), pp. 421–440.

Parkinson, M., Foley, B. and Judd, D. (eds) (1988), *Regenerating the Cities: The UK Crisis and the US Experience*, Manchester University Press, Manchester.

Pearce, D. (1989), *Conservation Today*, Routledge, London.

Pearce, G. (1994), 'Conservation as a Component of Urban Regeneration', *Regional Studies*, Vol.28 (1), pp. 88–93.

Prentice, R. (1993), *Tourism and Heritage Attractions*, Routledge, London.

Ravetz, A. (1980), *Remaking Cities: Contradictions of the Recent Urban Environment*, Croom Helm, London.

Ravetz, A. (1985), *The Government of Space: Town Planning in Modern Society*, Faber and Faber, London.

Raymond, A. (1995), *From Past Historic to Future Imperfect?*, unpublished MA dissertation at the University of Nottingham.

Read, J. (1982), 'Looking backwards?', *Built Environment*, Vol.7 (2), pp. 68–81.

Richards, J. (1994), *Façadism*, Routledge, London.

Robins, K. (1991), 'Tradition and translation: National culture in its global context', in Corner, J. and Harvey, S. *Enterprise and Heritage: Crosscurrents of National Culture*, Routledge, London, pp. 21–44.

Robinson, J.M (1991), 'Civic offence', *Architects Journal*, 10 July, pp. 24–27.

Roelke, T.M. (1992), *Impact of Historic Designation, Lower Downtown, Denver, Colorado: Second Analysis 1990–1992*, City and County of Denver, Denver.

Rogers, R. (1988), 'Belief in the future is rooted in the memory of the past', *Royal Society of Arts Journal*, November, pp. 873–884.

Ross, M. (1991), *Planning and the Heritage*, E. and F.N. Spon, London.

Rossi, A. (1982) (English translation), *The Architecture of the City*, MIT Press, Cambridge, MA.

Rowe, C. and Koetter, K. (1975), 'Collage City', *Architectural Review*, August, pp. 203–212.

Rowe, C. and Koetter, K. (1978), *Collage City*, MIT Press, Cambridge, MA.

Ryan, L.A. 'The Remaking of Lowell and Its Histories', in Weible, R. (ed.), (1991), *The Continuing Revolution: A History of Lowell*, Massachusetts, Lowell Historical Society, Lowell.

Rypkema, D.D. (1992), 'Rethinking economic values', in Lee, A.J. (ed.), *Past Meets Future: Saving America's Historic Environments*, National Trust for Historic Preservation/The Preservation Press, Washington, DC.

Scruton, R. (1979), *The Aesthetics of Architecture*, Methuen, London.

Shacklock, V. (1993), 'Conservation in local authorities: An assessment', *The Planner*, April, pp. 14–16.

Sherlock, H. (1991), *Cities are Good For Us: The Case for Close-knit Communities, Local Shops and Public Transport*, Paladin, London.

Skipp, V. (1983), *The Making of Victorian Birmingham*, Studio Press, Birmingham.

Skolnik, A.M. (1976), 'A history of Pioneer Square', in Latham, J.E. (ed.), *The Economic Benefits of Preserving Old Buildings*, The Preservation Press/National Trust for Historic Preservation, Washington DC, pp. 15–19.

Slessor, C. (1990), 'Current account (Shad Thames)', *Architects Journal*, 16 May, pp. 38–53.

Smith, N. (1987), 'Of yuppies and housing: gentrification, social restructuring, and the urban dream', *Environment and Planning D: Society and Space*, Vol.5, pp. 151–172.

Smyth, H. (1994), *Marketing the City*, E. and F.N. Spon, London.

Solesbury, W. (1990), 'Property development and urban regeneration', in Healey, P. and Nabarro, R. (eds) *Land and Property Development in a Changing Context*, Gower, Aldershot, pp. 186–194.

Solesbury, W. (1993), 'Reframing urban policy', *Policy and Politics*, Vol.21 (1), pp. 31–38.

Stewart, M. (1987), 'Ten years of inner-city policy', *Town Planning Review*, Vol.58 (2), pp. 129–145.

Stewart, M. (1994), 'Between Whitehall and town hall: the realignment of urban regeneration policy in England', *Policy and Politics*, Vol.22 (2), pp. 133–145.

Strang, C. (1993), 'Conservation commandments: Ten things planners should do for conservation on their own patch', *The Planner*, April, pp. 17–19.

Strathclyde Regional Council (1995), *Glasgow City Centre Public Realm Strategy and Guidelines*, Strathclyde Regional Council, Glasgow.

Stungo, A. (1972), 'The Malraux Act 1962–72', *Journal of the Royal Town Planning Institute*, Vol.58 pp. 357–362.

Suddards, R.W. and Morton, D.M. (1991), 'The character of conservation area', *Journal of Planning and Environmental Law*, November, pp. 1011–1013.

Sudjic, D., Cook, P., and Meades, J. (1988), *English Extremists*, Fourth Estate Ltd/Blueprint, London.

Summerson, J. (1949), *Heavenly Mansions*, London.

Sweeney, T.W. (1990), 'Reclaiming Old Singapore', *Architects Journal*, 16 August, pp. 31–43.

Tabor, P. (1989), 'Boiler House to Bauhaus: The Design Museum', *Architects Journal*, 16 August, pp. 31–43.

Tarn, J.N. (1985), 'Urban regeneration: The conservation dimension', *Town Planning Review*, Vol.56 (2), pp. 245–268.

TBPL (Temple Bar Properties Ltd) (1991), *Temple Bar Lives! Winning Architectural Framework Plan*, Temple Bar Properties Ltd, Dublin.

TBPL (Temple Bar Properties Ltd) (1992), *Development Programme for Temple Bar*, Temple Bar Properties Ltd, Dublin.

Tibbalds Colbourne Karski Williams Ltd, (1990), *Birmingham City Centre Design Strategy*, Birmingham City Planning Department, Birmingham.

Tibbalds Colbourne Karski Williams Ltd, (1991), *National Heritage Area Study*, Nottingham City Council, Nottingham.

Tibbalds, F. (1992), *Making People-Friendly Towns: Improving the Public Environment in Towns and Cities*, Longman, London.

Tiesdell, S. (1995), 'Tensions between revitalization and conservation: Nottingham's Lace Market', *Cities*, Vol.12 (4), pp. 231–241.

Tredre, R. (1995), 'I'll take Manhattan', *Life: The Observer Magazine*, 12 March, p24–27.

Turok, I. (1992), 'Property-led urban regeneration: Panacea or placebo?', *Environmental Planning A*, Vol.1 (24), pp. 361–379.

Uhlman, W. (1976), 'Economics aside', in Latham, J.E. (ed.) *The Economic Benefits of Preserving Old Buildings*, The Preservation Press/National Trust for Historic Preservation, Washington, DC, pp. 5–7.

URBED with Segal Quince Wicksteed (1987), *The Jewellery Industry and Jewellery Quarter Development Study: Report for the City of Birmingham*, URBED/Birmingham City Council, Birmingham.

URBED (1992), *The Regeneration of Bradford's Historic Merchant Quarter*, URBED/Bradford City Council, Bradford.

US Conference of Mayors/National Trust for Historic Preservation (1966), *With Heritage So Rich*, National Trust for Historic Preservation, Washington, DC.

Venturi, R. (1977), *Complexity and Contradiction in Architecture*, 2nd edn, The Architectural Press, London.

Venuti, G.C. (1986), 'Bologna: From expansion to transformation', *Built Environment*, Vol.12 (3), pp. 138–145.

Vidler, A. (1978), 'The third typology', in Deleroy, R.L. *Rational Architecture*, Archives d'Architecture Moderne, pp. 28–32.

Watkin, D. (1977), *Morality and Architecture*, Clarendon Press, Oxford.

Webb, R.S. (1976), 'Overcoming preservation problems', in Latham, J.E. (ed.) *The Economic Benefits of Preserving Old Buildings*, The Preservation Press/National Trust for Historic Preservation, Washington, DC, pp. 117–120.

Weible, R. (ed.) (1991), *The Continuing Revolution: A History of Lowell, Massachusetts*, Lowell Historical Society, Lowell, MA.

Wilford, M. (1984), 'Off to the races or going to the dogs', *Architectural Design*, Vol.54 (1/2), pp. 8–15.

Wise, D. (1993), 'Rehabilitation and refurbishment: the contemporary dilemma', *Town Planning Review*, Vol.64 (3), pp. 229–232.

Yeomans, D. (1994), 'Rehabilitation and historic preservation: A comparison of British and American Approaches', *Town Planning Review*, Vol.65 (2), pp. 159–178.

Zukin, S. (1989), *Loft Living: Culture and Capital in Urban Change*, Rutgers University Press, New Brunswick, NJ.

INDEX